NEW THIRD STEPS
IN LATIN

NEW THIRD STEPS IN LATIN

Mary Van Dyke Konopka
Michael Klaassen
Mary Allen
Lee T. Pearcy
Michelle Domondon
William MacArdle
Thomas Kent

Department of Classical Languages
The Episcopal Academy

Focus Publishing
Newburyport, Massachusetts

PREFACE

New Third Steps in Latin is the final volume of the series which includes *New First Steps in Latin* (Focus Publishing, 2000) and *New Second Steps in Latin* (Focus Publishing, 2001). The series introduces Latin through the grammar-translation method, and this book continues the instructional practices of the first two: an austere presentation of material, with grammar and sentences for translation on facing pages. We have chosen this layout because it provides a clear sense to the student of what he or she must learn, and because it allows us a uniformity of presentation of the Latin: new material presented in a predictable and clear way creates a comfortable environment for all kinds of learners.

New Third Steps fills out the basic grammar of Latin, and begins the introduction of the "real" language. With the ability to run complex searches rapidly through electronic texts, we have been able to find many sentences from ancient authors, particularly Cicero, which use the vocabulary and syntax introduced in the lesson. When we quote the sentence directly, we give the appropriate citation, but many sentences are based, more or less loosely, on the works of Cicero, Vergil, Ovid, Livy and others, sometimes with only slight alterations.

The vocabulary of the whole series is based on Cicero, Vergil, Ovid and Pliny. *New Third Steps* adds around 350 words to the 380 words of the other two books. Many of the Latin words introduced here have multiple meanings, and many English words and syntactical structures have several possible translations into Latin, so the student will frequently have to decide which word is best in the context of the sentence.

Each of the first 20 lessons in *New Third Steps* includes passages from the Helvetian campaign in book 1 of Caesar's *De Bello Gallico*. The passages, which can be found following Lesson 30, have been altered only by omission of words. Notes and glosses are provided where they are necessary. After lesson 20, there are four passages from Vergil, Valerius Maximus, and Sallust.

We are pleased to be able to thank all those who have helped to make *New Third Steps* possible. The Episcopal Academy and its Class of 1944 have been generous in bringing our efforts to fruition. Of our colleagues and former colleagues in the department, Michelle Domondon and Bill MacArdle taught from the book and made many suggestions and corrections; Tim Kent and Liz Klaassen have contributed their intelligence, encouragement and valuable criticisms. The Episcopal Academy Class of 2007, the first class to use this book, offered their valuable perspective as learners. Ron Pullins and his staff at Focus Publishing have patiently and carefully produced the entire series. As ever, our most ardent supporters are our students at the Episcopal Academy, many of whom take Latin even though they are not required to do so. Their continued efforts and enthusiasm for our subject formed the impetus to begin this project, and it is with them in mind still that we have brought it to its completion.

Molly Konopka, Michael Klaassen,
Mary Allen, Lee T. Pearcy, Michelle Domondon,
William MacArdle, Tim Kent

It is assumed that students have a thorough knowledge of the contents of New First Steps as follows:

I. Vocabulary: All Words Listed in New First Steps
II. Forms:
    a) All Regular Declensions of Nouns
    b) All Regular Declensions of Adjectives
    c) All Regular Conjugations of Verbs in the Indicative, Active and Passive
    d) the Irregular Verb sum
III. Syntax:
    a) Agreement
        1. First Rule of Concord: Agreement of Subject and Verb
        2. Second Rule of Concord: Agreement of Adjective and Noun
        3. Agreement of Appositives
        4. Agreement of Predicate Noun, Predicate Adjective and Subject
    b) Uses of Cases
        1. Nominative:
            a) Subject
            b) Predicate Noun
            c) Predicate Adjective
        2. Genitive:
            a) Possession
            b) often translated by "of"
        3. Dative:
            a) Indirect Object
            b) with Certain Adjectives
            c) often translated by "to" or "for"
        4. Accusative:
            a) Direct Object
            b) Motion Towards or Place To Which (ad, in)
            c) Duration of Time or Time How Long
            d) with Certain Prepositions (ad, in)
        5. Ablative:
            a) Means or Instrument
            b) Personal Agent (with ā, ab)
            c) Accompaniment (with cum)
            d) Place Where or In Which (in, prō, sub)
            e) Motion Away From or Place From Which (ā, ab, dē, ē, ex)
            f) Time When
            g) with Certain Prepositions (ā, ab, cum, dē, ē, ex, in, prō, sine, sub)

CONTENTS
Lessons

Lesson I

SUBJUNCTIVE MOOD

The **SUBJUNCTIVE MOOD** is used mainly in subordinate clauses. It can express command, purpose, result, characteristic, indirect question, or circumstance. As a main verb, the subjunctive indicates possibility, probability, or wish. There are four tenses of the subjunctive: present, imperfect, perfect, and pluperfect.

Present Subjunctive

The present subjunctive of the first conjugation is formed by changing ā of the present stem to ē and adding the personal endings. In all other conjugations ā is inserted between the present stem and the personal endings.

		First	Second	Third	Third I-stem	Fourth
Singular	1st person	amem	moneam	dūcam	capiam	audiam
	2nd person	amēs	moneās	dūcās	capiās	audiās
	3rd person	amet	moneat	dūcat	capiat	audiat
Plural	1st person	amēmus	moneāmus	dūcāmus	capiāmus	audiāmus
	2nd person	amētis	moneātis	dūcātis	capiātis	audiātis
	3rd person	ament	moneant	dūcant	capiant	audiant
Singular	1st person	amer	monear	dūcar	capiar	
	2nd person	amēris	moneāris	dūcāris	capiāris	audiāris
	3rd person	ametur	moneatur	dūcatur	capiatur	audiatur
Plural	1st person	amēmur	moneāmur	dūcāmur	capiāmur	audiāmur
	2nd person	amēminī	moneāminī	dūcāminī	capiāminī	audiāminī
	3rd person	amentur	moneantur	dūcantur	capiantur	audiantur

There is no standard translation of the subjunctive verb; the translation of a subjunctive verb is determined by its context.

Present Subjunctive of Sum and Possum

The present subjunctives of **sum** and **possum** are irregular and must be memorized.

		sum	possum
Singular	1st person	sim	possim
	2nd person	sīs	possīs
	3rd person	sit	possit
Plural	1st person	sīmus	possīmus
	2nd person	sītis	possītis
	3rd person	sint	possint

Hortatory/ Jussive Subjunctive

The present subjunctive used as the main verb indicates the ideas of encouragement, wish, or command.

A verb used in this way in the first person is called **HORTATORY** and in the third person **JUSSIVE**.

The hortatory/ jussive subjunctive is translated into English with "let" or "may."

    Vīvat rēgīna!   *May the queen live!*   **Moneāmus rēgem.** *Let us <u>warn</u> the king.*

The negative adverb for this construction is **nē**.

    Nē capiāmus urbem.   *Let us not capture the city.*   **Nē urbs capiātur.**   *May the city not be captured.*

2

Vocabulary I

Fourth Declension Masculine Nouns		First Conjugation Verbs	
adventus,-ūs, *m.*	*approach, arrival*	appellō, (1)	*accost, address, name*
conspectus,-ūs, *m.*	*sight*	confirmō (1)	*encourage, strengthen*
cursus,-ūs, *m.*	*course*	temptō (1)	*test, try*
impetus,-ūs, *m.*	*attack*	**Conjunction**	
magistrātus,-ūs, *m.*	*magistracy, magistrate*		
metus,-ūs, *m.*	*fear*	nē (+ subj.)	*not*
Third Declension Adjectives		**Adverbs**	
dīligens,-ntis	*careful*	clam	*secretly*
potens,-ntis	*capable, powerful*	confestim	*immediately*
prūdens,-ntis	*prudent, sensible*	haud	*not at all*

Exercise I

A.

1. Hīc impetum hostium maneāmus.
2. Nē fidem potentium amīcōrum temptēmus.
3. Prūdens in neutram partem metū moveātur.
4. Tōtōs nōs reī pūblicae sine metū dēmus.
5. Sit ille prīmus consul, quī maximē idōneus est.
6. Pater metum fīliae moritūrae in oculīs vidēre potuit.
7. Conspectus magistratūs potentis invidiam servōrum confestim confirmāvit.
8. Hīc diūtius maneāmus, ventī enim haud facilēs sunt.
9. Dux Gallōrum adventum Caesaris in Belgicam haud bene tulit.
10. Parvās puellās, quae sē inter umbrās ab impetibus Gallōrum tegere poterunt, in silvās mittāmus.
11. Dīligentēs prūdentēsque semper nōbīs adsint.
12. Senātum neque adventū neque conspectū suō movēre poterat.

B.

1. May he not call us!
2. Let us remain here.
3. Fear of the arrival of the god drove the maidens into flight.
4. Let the sailors hold the course of the ships, for Britain is in our sight.
5. The devoted boy announced the arrival of Caesar to the powerful queen.
6. Let us not fear death.
7. Let us approach; let us accost the king.
8. Let us depart at night and journey secretly to our city.
9. Let the deeds of these Roman soldiers strengthen immediately the minds of the powerful magistrates.
10. Let all prudent (people) stop here immediately and depart from the city secretly.
11. He said that his course toward the city was not at all swift.
12. Let us all sit and let us think about these matters diligently.

Lesson II

IRREGULAR SUBJUNCTIVES

The present subjunctives of the verbs **volō**, **nōlō**, **mālō** and **eō** are irregular and must be memorized.

	volō	nōlō	mālō	eō
Singular				
1st person	velim	nōlim	mālim	eam
2nd person	velīs	nōlīs	mālīs	eās
3rd person	velit	nōlit	mālit	eat
Plural				
1st person	velīmus	nōlīmus	mālīmus	eāmus
2nd person	velītis	nōlītis	mālītis	eātis
3rd person	velint	nōlint	mālint	eant

Purpose Clauses

A **PURPOSE CLAUSE** is a subordinate clause which gives the reason behind an action. It answers the question "why?" or "for what purpose?" In Latin a purpose clause has a verb in the subjunctive. Most often a positive purpose clause begins with the conjunction **ut** and a negative purpose clause begins with the conjunction **nē**.

Veniō <u>ut audiam</u>.	*I come <u>to hear</u> (in order that I may hear, in order to hear, so that I may hear, so as to hear).*
Fugiunt <u>nē sē videātis.</u>	*They flee <u>lest you see them</u> (in order for you not to see them, lest you see them, in order that you may not see them, so that you may not see them).*
Lēgātus vēnit ut pācem petat.	*The envoy has come to seek peace.*

There are many ways to express purpose in English, but, unlike English, Latin rarely uses the infinitive to show purpose.

Relative Clause of Purpose

A **RELATIVE CLAUSE OF PURPOSE** uses the relative pronoun in place of **ut**.

Lēgātus mittitur quī pācem petat. (= **Lēgātus mittitur ut pācem petat.**)	*An envoy is sent to seek peace (in order to seek peace, so as to seek peace, in order that he may seek peace, so that he may seek peace).*
Epistulās scrībit quibus tē laudet. (= **Epistulās scrībit ut tē laudet.**)	*He writes letters with which to praise you.* *He writes letters by which he may praise you.* *He writes letters to praise you.*

4

Vocabulary II

Third Declension Feminine Nouns		Verbs	
aetās,-tātis, f.	age	contineō, -ēre, continuī, contentum	contain, hold together, sustain
auctōritās,-tātis, f.	authority, influence	obtineō, -ēre, obtinuī, obtentum	hold, obtain
calamitās, -tatis, f.	calamity	pertineō, -ēre, pertinuī, pertentum	extend, pertain
cīvitās,-tātis, f.	citizenship, state	retineō, -ēre, retinuī, retentum	hold back, restrain, keep (from)
cupiditās,-tātis, f.	desire, greed (+ gen.)	sustineō, -ēre, sustinuī, sustentum	hold (up), sustain
difficultās,-tātis, f.	difficulty	differō, differre, distulī, dilātum	defer, differ, scatter
lībertās,-tātis, f.	freedom, liberty	perferō, perferre, pertulī, perlātum	endure, report
pax, pacis, f.	peace		
potestās,-tātis, f.	power		
Adverbs		Conjunction	
ferē	almost, nearly	ut (+ subj.)	in order that, so that, with the result that
paenē	almost	nē (+ subj.)	lest, so that…not

Exercise II

A.

1. Cum hostibus contendunt nē vincantur.
2. Multās difficultātēs perferet ut lībertātem obtineat.
3. Ferē omnēs hae rēs nōbīs pertinent.
4. Obtinēre aut retinēre amīcōs haud poteram.
5. Ad urbem venit quī illa iūra obtineat quae cīvitās dederat.
6. Scrībō epistulās quibus mea verba dē eius maximā cupiditāte ad tē perferantur.
7. Sē sustinet nē dē cursū inceptō lābātur.
8. Semper dīcēbat magistrātūs nōn potestātibus, sed auctōritāte differre.
9. Vestrae aetātēs aut nihil aut nōn multum inter sē differunt.
10. Magnopere contendunt ut nunc aut magistrātum gerant aut in suā potestāte habeant eōs quī sunt in magistrātū.
11. Sōlās cupiditātēs sequuntur quibus suās vītās meliōrēs faciant.
12. Postquam amīcīs gratiās ēgimus, invidiam sequī nōlīmus.

B.

1. They will defend the walls in order to save the citizens.
2. We carry lights in order that we not wander from the way.
3. They endure angry masters in order to obtain their freedom.
4. Let us restrain them through fear lest they wage war against us.
5. Let us be willing to make the journey with them lest they have any difficulties.
6. A few (men) run suddenly to the gates in order to keep the enemy from the camp.
7. Let him prefer to have authority rather than power.
8. They will destroy liberty with the sword in order to preserve their power.
9. Let us prefer to hold back our anger rather than to wage war.
10. You will uphold the laws of the republic in order that you may have the liberty which you have sought.

5

Lesson III

IMPERFECT SUBJUNCTIVE

The Imperfect Subjunctive is formed by adding the active or passive personal endings to the present active infinitive.

		First	Second	Third	Third I-stem	Fourth
Singular	1st person	amārem	monērem	dūcerem	caperem	audīrem
	2nd person	amārēs	monērēs	dūcerēs	caperēs	audīrēs
	3rd person	amāret	monēret	dūceret	caperet	audīret
Plural	1st person	amārēmus	monērēmus	dūcerēmus	caperēmus	audīrēmus
	2nd person	amārētis	monērētis	dūcerētis	caperētis	audīrētis
	3rd person	amārent	monērent	dūcerent	caperent	audīrent

Deponent verbs add -re- (or –ere- for the third and third I-stem conjugations) to the present stem before the passive personal endings.

		First	Second	Third	Third I-stem	Fourth
Singular	1st person	conārer	verērer	sequerer	paterer	mentīrer
	2nd person	conārēris	verērēris	sequerēris	paterēris	mentīrēris
	3rd person	conārētur	verērētur	sequerētur	paterētur	mentīrētur
Plural	1st person	conārēmur	verērēmur	sequerēmur	paterēmur	mentīrēmur
	2nd person	conārēminī	verērēminī	sequerēminī	paterēminī	mentīrēminī
	3rd person	conārentur	verērentur	sequerentur	paterentur	mentīrentur

Sequence of Tenses

Tenses in Latin are divided into two sequences: **PRIMARY** and **SECONDARY/HISTORICAL**. The tense of the main verb determines the tense of the subjunctive verb in certain subordinate clauses. If the main verb is present, future, present perfect (with "have" or "has"), or future perfect, the sequence is primary and the present or perfect subjunctive is used in the subordinate clause. If the main verb is imperfect, aorist, or pluperfect, the sequence is secondary and the imperfect or pluperfect subjunctive is used in the subordinate clause.

Sequence	Main Verb	Subjunctive Verb in Subordinate Clause
Primary/ Present	Present Future Present Perfect (has/have) Future Perfect	Present (action at the same time or after the main verb) Perfect (action prior to main verb)
Secondary/ Historical	Imperfect Aorist Pluperfect	Imperfect (action at the same time or after the main verb) Pluperfect (action prior to main verb)

Purpose Clauses in Secondary Sequence

A purpose clause has a present subjunctive if the main verb is in primary sequence and an imperfect subjunctive if the main verb is in secondary sequence.

Veniēbam <u>ut audīrem</u>.	*I was coming <u>to hear</u> (in order that I might hear, so that I might hear, in order to hear, so as to hear).*
Fūgeram <u>nē vidērer</u>.	*I had fled <u>lest I be seen</u> (in order that I might not be seen, so that I might not be seen, in order not to be seen, so as to not be seen).*
Īvit <u>ut pācem peteret</u>.	*He went <u>to seek peace</u>.*

6

Vocabulary III

First Declension Feminine Nouns		Third Conjugation Verbs	
amīcitia,-ae, *f.*	*friendship*	āmittō, -ere, āmīsī, āmissum	*lose*
insula,-ae, *f.*	*island*	animadvertō, -ere, animadvertī, animadversum	*notice, pay attention to*
littera,-ae, *f.*	*letter (of the alphabet),* pl. *letter, literature*	dēligō, -ere, dēlēgī, dēlectum	*choose*
pecūnia,-ae, *f.*	*money*	incendō, -ere, incendī, incensum	*burn, outrage, set fire to*
prōvincia,-ae, *f.*	*province*	intellegō, -ere, intellēgī, intellectum	*understand*
sententia,-ae, *f.*	*opinion*		
First Conjugation Verbs		Adverbs	
comparō (1)	*achieve, gather, prepare*	undique	*everywhere, from all sides, on all sides*
spērō (1)	*hope*		

Exercise III

A.

1. In illō locō manēbat ut in urbem clam incēderet.
2. Litterās mīsī nē ex prōvinciā excēderēs.
3. Īrā incendor quod mē nōn dēfendēbās.
4. Pecūniam comparāvit quī potestātem suam sustinēret.
5. Gallī in insulā duās noctēs constitērunt ut urbem prīmā lūce capere comparārent.
6. Spērāvit sē causās bellī intellegere posse quibus pācem comparāret.
7. Pater fīliam dīcere vetuit ut iussa mātris animadverteret.
8. Mīlitēs difficultātēs fugae veritī ex castrīs excessērunt ut aquam equōsque ab hostibus caperent.
9. Litterae rēgum sententiās dē cīvitāte quās legere sed nōn perferre possum continuērunt.
10. Animadvertī enim et doctus sum ex tuīs litterīs tē omnibus in rēbus habuisse bonam causam.
11. Ducēs in prōvinciīs pācem cīvitātis et amīcitiam proximārum gentium sustinuērunt ut potestātem suam confirmārent.

B.

1. He gathered his friends in order to sustain his magistracy.
2. The king hoped that our friendship would preserve the peace on all sides.
3. I have come to the city in order to prepare the boys before their father dies.
4. The Romans decided to burn the city lest the people test the power of their authority.
5. He hoped that he would lose the desire of money so that he might not also lose his friends.
6. I understand that a prudent man has been chosen to speak to the magistrates on behalf of the citizenry.
7. The girls hoped that the day would be beautiful so that they could lead their friends almost to the sea.
8. The pirates held the sailors in secret for many days so that money would be given for their lives.
9. He hoped that he would receive the best province so that he could bring back as much money as possible.
10. His opinions show that he understands nothing about literature.

Lesson IV

PERFECT SUBJUNCTIVE

The perfect subjunctive active is formed by adding –erī plus the active personal endings to the perfect active stem of the verb.

		First	Second	Third	Third I-stem	Fourth
Singular	1st person	amāverim	monuerim	dūxerim	cēperim	audīverim
	2nd person	amāverīs	monuerīs	dūxerīs	cēperīs	audīverīs
	3rd person	amāverit	monuerit	dūxerit	cēperit	audīverit
Plural	1st person	amāverīmus	monuerīmus	dūxerīmus	cēperīmus	audīverīmus
	2nd person	amāverītis	monuerītis	dūxerītis	cēperītis	audīverītis
	3rd person	amāverint	monuerint	dūxerint	cēperint	audīverint

The perfect subjunctive passive is formed with the perfect passive participle, declined to agree with the subject, followed by the appropriate form of the present subjunctive of **sum**.

	First	Second	Third	Third I-stem	Fourth
Singular	amātus,-a sim	monitus,-a sim	ductus,-a sim	captus,-a sim	audītus,-a sim
	amātus,-a sīs	monitus,-a sīs	ductus,-a sīs	captus,-a sīs	audītus, -a sīs
	amātus,-a,-um sit	monitus,-a,-um sit	ductus,-a,-um sit	captus,-a,-um sit	audītus,-a,-um sit
Plural	amātī,-ae sīmus	monitī,-ae sīmus	ductī,-ae sīmus	captī,-ae sīmus	audītī,-ae sīmus
	amātī,-ae sītis	monitī,-ae sītis	ductī,-ae sītis	captī,-ae sītis	audītī,-ae sītis
	amātī,-ae,-a sint	monitī,-ae,-a sint	ductī,-ae,-a sint	captī,-ae,-a sint	audītī,-ae,-a sint

Result Clauses

A **RESULT CLAUSE** is a subordinate clause which explains the outcome of an action or situation. It is introduced by the subordinating conjunction **ut** and has its verb in the subjunctive. A negative result is introduced by **ut** and a negative adverb, pronoun or adjective (**nōn, nēmō, nihil, numquam**, etc.). The sentence which introduces a result clause often contains one of the following adjectives or adverbs, which anticipates and points to the result clause.

Adjectives

tantus, -a, -um	*so large, so much, so great* (showing quantity)
tālis, -e	*such, of such a sort* (showing quality)
tot (indeclinable)	*so many*

Adverbs

adeō	*so, to such an extent*
ita	*so*
sīc	*so, in such a way* (modifies verbs only)
tam	*so, such* (modifies adj. and other adv. only)

Rēx tam īrātus est ut fīlius eum timeat.   *The king is so angry that (his) son fears him.*

Rēx ita dīcēbat ut rēgīna prope eum nōn steterit.   *The king was speaking in such a way that the queen did not stand near him.*

Result clauses do not follow the sequence of tenses. The perfect subjunctive is commonly used after a main verb in secondary/historical sequence.

Rōmānus exercitus tantus erat ut nēmō eum vīcerit.   *The Roman army was so large that no one defeated it.*

Vocabulary IV

Adverbs		Third Conjugation -io Verbs	
adeō	*so, to such an extent*	excipiō, -ere, excēpī, exceptum	*greet, receive*
ita	*so, thus*	praecipiō, -ere, praecēpī,	*advise, direct, order* (with
item	*likewise*	praeceptum	dat. of person commanded)
sīc	*so, thus* (only modifies verbs)	recipiō, -ere, recēpī, receptum	*accept, receive*
tam	*so* (only modifies adjectives	sē recipere	*retreat*
	and adverbs)	suscipiō, -ere, suscēpī,	*support, take up, undertake*
		susceptum	

Adjectives		Second Declension Masculine Nouns	
firmus,-a,-um	*firm, resolute, strong*	numerus,-ī, *m.*	*number*
tantus,-a,-um	*so great*	populus,-ī, *m.*	*people*
tālis,-e	*such*	vīcus,-ī, *m.*	*village*
tot	*so many* (indeclinable)		

Exercise IV

A.

1. Vīcus ita parvus erat ut ibi cōnsistere nōluerint.
2. Tantā īrā incensus est ut sē nōn retinēre potuerit.
3. Tanta erat potestās in eius magistrātū, ut cīvēs eum rētinēre nōluerint.
4. Verbīs īrātīs nihil facilius mittitur, nihil celerius excipitur.
5. Iter mihi per tuam prōvinciam tāle erat, ut illum vīcum ante tertium diem nōn vīderim.
6. Amīcōs tam male dēlēgistī ut in tantō numerō tuōrum neque audiās virum bonum neque ūnum videās.
7. Sallustius scrīpsit Catilīnam tam ardentem in cupiditāte esse ut rem pūblicam dēlēre temptāverit.
8. Ego semper docuī, monuī, bene praecēpī omnia quae possum.
9. Praecepta deōrum adeō secutus est, ut nocte ad Italiam cum sociīs nāvibusque fūgerit.
10. Tot sunt fructūs labōrum eius ut fēlīcissimus ab omnibus habeātur.

B.

1. There were so many ships in the sea that they could not see the water.
2. He was a man of such a sort that he undertook any task.
3. He stood so firmly on the wall that he could not be moved.
4. The consul is so firm in his opinions that no one is able to move him.
5. So great was the authority in that man that very many (people) wished to follow him.
6. Then night so dark received us that the stars in the sky were scarcely able to be seen.
7. He received so many very bad men into his friendship that we all heard about his evil deeds.
8. Your letter reported so many bad (things) to me that I withdrew immediately from my province.
9. The population is likewise so wretched that no one wishes to get hold of the city.
10. He will make the journey in such a way that he comes before night.
11. The rage of the goddess was so great that she wished to destroy the man, his weapons and all his ships.

9

Lesson V

PLUPERFECT SUBJUNCTIVE

The pluperfect subjunctive active is formed by adding –issē- plus the active personal endings to the perfect active stem of a verb.

		First	Second	Third	Third I-stem	Fourth
Singular	1st person	amāvissem	monuissem	dūxissem	cēpissem	audīvissem
	2nd person	amāvissēs	monuissēs	dūxissēs	cēpissēs	audīvissēs
	3rd person	amāvisset	monuisset	dūxisset	cēpisset	audīvisset
Plural	1st person	amāvissēmus	monuissēmus	dūxissēmus	cēpissēmus	audīvissēmus
	2nd person	amāvissētis	monuissētis	dūxissētis	cēpissētis	audīvissētis
	3rd person	amāvissent	monuissent	dūxissent	cēpissent	audīvissent

The pluperfect subjunctive passive is formed with the perfect passive participle, declined to agree with the subject, followed by the appropriate form of **sum.**

	First	Second	Third	Third I-stem	Fourth
Singular	amātus,-a **essem**	monitus,-a **essem**	ductus,-a **essem**	captus,-a **essem**	audītus,-a **essem**
	amātus,-a **essēs**	monitus,-a **essēs**	ductus,-a **essēs**	captus,-a **essēs**	audītus,-a **essēs**
	amātus,-a, -um essett	monitus,-a,-um esset	ductus,-a,-um esset	captus,-a,-um esset	audītus,-a,-um esset
Plural	amātī,-ae **essēmus**	monitī,-ae **essēmus**	ductī,-ae **essēmus**	captī,-ae **essēmus**	audītī,-ae **essēmus**
	amātī,-ae **essētis**	monitī,-ae **essētis**	ductī,-ae **essētis**	captī,-ae **essētis**	audītī,-ae **essētis**
	amātī,-ae,-a **essent**	monitī,-ae,-a **essent**	ductī,-ae,-a **essent**	captī,-ae,-a **essent**	audītī,-ae,-a **essent**

Cum Clauses

Cum, in addition to being a preposition meaning *with,* can also be a subordinating conjunction meaning *when, after, since,* or *although.*

In a **TEMPORAL CLAUSE,** (where **cum** means *when* or *after,*) the verb is indicative if the main verb is in primary sequence and subjunctive if the main verb is in secondary sequence.

Cum librum habeō, legō.	*When(ever) I have a book, I read.*
Cum haec dīxisset, signum dedit.	*When he had said this, he gave the signal.*

In a **CAUSAL CLAUSE,** (where **cum** means *since,*) the verb must be subjunctive and follows the sequence of tenses.

Cum hostīs videāmus, currimus.	*Since we see the enemy, we run.*
Cum hostīs vīdissēmus, cucurrimus.	*Since we had seen enemy, we ran.*

In a **CONCESSIVE CLAUSE,** (where **cum** means *although,*) the verb is subjunctive and follows the sequence of tenses. **Tamen,** *nevertheless,* is often found in the main clause of such a sentence.

Cum hostīs nōn videāmus, tamen currimus.	*Although we do not see the enemy, nevertheless we are running.*
Cum hostīs nōn vīdissēmus, tamen currēbāmus.	*Although we had not seen the enemy, nevertheless we were running.*

Vocabulary V

First and Second Declension Adjectives		Second Declension Neuter Nouns	
angustus,-a,-um	*narrow*	forum,-ī, *n.*	*marketplace*
dignus,-a,-um	*worthy* (+ ablative)	impedīmentum,-ī, *n.*	*hindrance*, pl. *baggage*
propinquus,-a,-um	*near, neighboring*	perīculum,-ī, *n.*	*danger, peril*
reliquus,-a,-um	*remaining, rest*	praesidium,-ī, *n.*	*assistance, defense, protection*
		proelium, proeliī, *n.*	*battle*
Third Declension Nouns		signum,-ī, *n.*	*sign, signal, standard*
honor, honōris, *m.*	*esteem, office*	vinculum,-ī, *n.*	*chain, fetter*
mōs, mōris, *m.*	*custom, habit,*	**3rd Conjugation -io Verbs**	
mōrēs, mōrum	pl. *behavior, character*	ēripiō, -ere, ēripuī, ēreptum	*rescue, snatch*
mōs maiōrum	*tradition*	sē ēripere	*escape*
First Conjugation Verb		aggredior, aggredī, aggressus sum	*approach, attack*
incitō (1)	*arouse, urge on*	ēgredior, ēgredī, ēgressus sum	*go out, leave*

Exercise V

A.

1. Cum hoc signum vidēre velimus, puellās quae id accipiant mittimus.
2. Cum adessem, tamen verbum dīcere territus sum.
3. Nihil dē proximā nocte dīcam, cum semper amīcus mihi fuerīs.
4. Cum mōs māiōrum mīlitēs dignōs donō agrōrum esse habeat, tamen consul nōn dat.
5. Cum pecūnia dē manibus ērepta esset, dominus equōs per propinquās viās incitāvit ut malōs agricolās caperet.
6. Cum clarissimum sīdus trēs virōs in vīcum dūxisset, paucōs diēs mansērunt ut fīnīs vidērent.
7. Cum hostis tēlum dē eius manū ēriperet, ille cum celeritāte saxum propinquum cēpit ut sē dēfenderet.
8. Cum haec virīs dīcta essent et clam ē castrīs excessissent, ad campum ēgredī parāvimus.
9. Cum nēmō aut auxilium aut praesidium populō ferret, angustum per iter excessērunt ut impetum in hostīs facerent.
10. Cum mōrēs huius gentis tam similēs illius sint, duae haud inter sē differunt.

B.

1. When the enemy will be in our camp for a long time, we order them to be held in chains.
2. Since the leader had chosen the narrow way through the mountains, he ordered the army to march through it.
3. Since part of the camp had been destroyed by the storm, the remaining part was moved to guard the baggage.
4. Although the allies were gravely wounded in the battle, yet the remaining soldiers fought bravely to night.
5. Since the little boy had approached the messenger to lead him to the forum, he was held in the highest honor by his friends.
6. Although the task was undertaken by very many people, nevertheless the senate was unwilling to ask for money from the consuls.
7. Since the dangers of the city frighten mothers, they cannot bear their daughters to go out of their own houses or into the forum.
8. Although the Roman people undertook great works in their city, those works have nevertheless collapsed due to age.

Lesson VI

REVIEW: LESSONS I – V

Overview of the Subjunctive Mood

	Active		Passive	
	Formula	Examples	Formula	Examples
Present	Present stem + vowel + active personal endings	**amem** **moneam** **dūcam** **capiam** **audiam**	Present stem + vowel + passive personal endings	**amer** **monear** **dūcar** **capiar** **audiar**
Imperfect	Present active infinitive + personal endings	amārem monērem dūcerem caperem audīrem	Present active infinitive + passive personal endings	amārer monērer dūcerer caperer audīrer
Perfect	Perfect stem + -eri- + personal endings	**amāverim** **monuērim** **dūxerim** **cēperim** **audīverim**	Perfect passive participle (-us, -a,-um) + present subjunctive of **sum**	amātus,-a sim monitus,-a sim ductus,-a sim captus,-a sim audītus,-a sim
Pluperfect	Perfect stem + -isse- + personal endings OR Perfect active infinitive + personal endings	**amāvissem** **monuissem** **dūxissem** **cēpissem** **audīvissem**	Perfect passive participle (-us, -a, -um) + imperfect subjunctive of **sum**	amātus,-a essem monitus,-a essem ductus,-a essem captus,-a essem audītus, -a essem

Remember that **sum, possum, volō, nōlō,** and **mālō** have irregular forms and must be memorized.

Uses of the Subjunctive

Independent Use	Hortatory / Jussive -main verb is present subjunctive	**Moneam regem.** *Let me warn the king.* **Moneant regem.** *May they warn the king.*
Subordinate Uses	Purpose Clause **-ut/nē** + subjunctive verb	**Veniō ut audiam.** *I come to listen.*
	Relative Clause of Purpose - relative pronoun + subjunctive verb	**Virum mīsī quī pācem peteret.** *I sent a man to ask for peace.*
	Result Clause - **ut** or **ut ... nōn** + subjunctive verb -main clause often contains **tantus,-a, -um, talis,-e, tot, adeō, ita, sīc, tam**	**Sīc virum vocāvī ut constīterit.** *I called the man in such a way that he stopped.*
	Cum Clauses -Temporal: *when; after* (primary sequence uses indicative, secondary sequence uses subjunctive) -Causal: *since* (subjunctive) -Concessive: *although* (subjunctive)	**Cum librum habet, legit.** *When he has a book, he reads.* **Cum hostīs vīderit, currit.** *Since he has seen the enemy, he is running.* **Cum amīcum videret, tamen fūgit.** *Although he saw a friend, (nevertheless) he ran away.*

Exercise VI

A.

1. Celeriter eāmus ut amīcōs nostrōs ē vinculīs ēripiāmus.
2. Nōs tam amīcē excipiēbat ut perīculum nōn animadverterēmus.
3. Hanc urbem dēlēre nōlint!
4. Plūrimōs labōrēs passa est ut obtinēret id quod habuit.
5. Intellegāmus potentissimōs prūdentissimōsque inter sē differre.
6. Sīc omnia clam parāvistī ut mihi nihil aut ā tē ipsō aut ab ullō aliō dē tuō adventū scrīptum sit.
7. In conspectū paenē tōtius urbis domus est mea, ut nēmō mē vocāre nōn possit.
8. Cum reliquī mīlitēs perīculum excipere malint quam ē proeliō ēripī, nōs signum magnā cum virtūte suscipiēmus.
9. Magistrātus prūdens nullās difficultātēs habēbit cum sententiās populī intellegat et iūra cīvium sustineat.
10. Animī servōrum inter spem et metum sīc captī sunt, ut auctōritāte consulis modo dīxerint.
11. Spēs lībertātis servōs adeō ēgit ut magnā cum dīligentiā labōrārent.
12. Sensit sē in tantō perīculō esse ut nullā viā ēripī posset.

B.

1. We will hold back our anger in order to be your friends.
2. He loved her to such an extent that he did not leave her alone.
3. Since we had left the forum, we were unable to undertake the remaining tasks.
4. May you be careful and sensible in all your deeds.
5. I am unable to punish him in such a way that he wishes always to be away from the city.
6. It is the custom of that man always to seek peace and friendship so that he may avoid fear and envy.
7. He carried himself so bravely that he strengthened their slipping spirits for all things.
8. In the sight of all, this wicked (man) so stirred up the people that they were not able to restrain themselves.
9. Let us secretly select a worthy man who should direct our sons in the customs of our ancestors.
10. Such great hatred followed him that he was killed in the sight of gods and men in (his) most sacred magistracy.
11. Let another, more worthy of these chains, stand before you so that I may sit among you, free.
12. When I had read your first letter, I thought about all the disasters which you and I have suffered.

13

Lesson VII

CORRELATIVES

CORRELATIVES are paired words which express or imply a comparison. Commonly used correlatives include the following:

Adverbs (indeclinable)			**Adjectives**	
tam...quam	*as...as*		**talis...qualis**	*such...as*
tantum...quantum	*as much...as*		**alius...alius**	*one...another*
tantō...quantō	*the...the*		**aliī...aliī**	*some...others*
	(by how much...by so much)		**alter...alter**	*the one...the other*
totiens...quotiens	*as often...as*		**tantus...quantus**	*as great...as*
			tot...quot (indeclinable)	*as many...as*

Nihil est **tam** turpe **quam** hoc scelus.	*Nothing is as disgraceful as this crime.*
Quantō avidius loquitur, **tantō** minus animadvertō.	*The more eagerly he speaks, the less I pay attention.*
Tale est tuum carmen nōbīs **qualis** somnus fessīs.	*Such is your song to us as sleep (is) to the weary.*

Names of Towns, Small Islands, domus, and rūs

For the names of towns, small islands, **domus**, and **rūs**, no preposition is used to express place where, place to which, and place from which.

Place where is expressed by the **LOCATIVE CASE**. The locative case is the same as the genitive for singular nouns of the first and second declensions. For all other declensions and all plural nouns, the locative case is the same as the ablative.

1st declension singular	Genitive form	**Romae**	*at* or *in Rome*
2nd declension singular	Genitive form	**Corinthī**	*at* or *in Corinth*
		domī	*at* or *in the home*
3rd declension and plurals	Ablative form	**Athenīs**	*at* or *in Athens*
		rūrī	*at* or *in the country*

A noun in apposition with a locative must be in the ablative case, with or without a preposition.

Romae, pulcherrimā urbe, manēre vult.   *He wants to stay in Rome, a very beautiful city.*

Place to which is expressed by the accusative case.

Romam eāmus.	*Let us go to Rome.*	**Domum ībimus.**	*We will go home.*

Place from which is expressed by the ablative case.

Exercitus Romā Brundisium contendit.   *The army marched from Rome to Brundisium.*

Irregular Noun: vīs, vīs, f.

Vīs, vīs, f. is an irregular noun and declines in the following way. The genitive singular and dative singular are rare.

	Singular: *force; violence*	Plural: *strength*
Nominative	vīs	vīrēs
Genitive	(vīs)	vīrium
Dative	(vī)	vīribus
Accusative	vim	vīrīs (-ēs)
Ablative	vī	vīribus

Do not confuse **vīs** with **vir, virī**, m., *man*, a noun of the second declension.

14

Vocabulary VII

First and Second Declension Adjectives		Third Conjugation Deponent Verbs	
avidus,-a,-um	*eager, greedy*	colloquor, colloquī, collocūtus sum	*converse*
certus,-a,-um	*certain, set*	loquor, loquī, locūtus sum	*speak, talk*
inimīcus,-a,-um	*hostile, unfriendly*	nanciscor, nanciscī, nactus sum	*get, obtain*
invītus,-a,-um	*unwilling*	nascor, nascī, nātus sum	*be born*
vīvus,-a,-um	*alive*	proficiscor, proficiscī, profectus sum	*set out*
Adverb		Third Declension Nouns	
umquam	*ever*	rūs, rūris, *n.*	*country, countryside*
		vīs, vīs, *f.* (*pl.* vīrēs, vīrium)	*force, violence,* (pl.) *strength*

Exercise VII

A.

1. Semper tālis cīvis sit, quālis hodiē est.
2. Quot hominēs, tot sententiae sunt.
3. Nēmō tam avidē in forō loquitur quam ille.
4. Quantō liber longior est, tantō etiam peior est.
5. Tempus habēs tāle quāle nēmō habuit umquam. (Cic. *Philippics* 7.27)
6. Mōs eōrum erat esse tam laetī cum propinquīs Rōmae, quam rūrī cum familiā.
7. Cum nōbīscum rūs profectus esset, tamen semper Rōmae esse volēbat.
8. Ego mē tantum numerum inimīcōrum nactum esse videō, quantus est hominum in urbe.
9. Dīxit, "Tālis tum fortuna huius urbis erit, quālis vīs Rōmānī imperiī fuerat."
10. Invidiam eōrum adeō aegrē tulit, ut sē rūs clam moverit et ibi multōs annōs manēret.

B.

1. He is such a man as his father was.
2. There are as many enemies as friends among you.
3. Setting out for home from Rome, he spoke with his friend about all that had been done in the senate.
4. I have acquired these things so that you love me as much as I wish (to be loved).
5. He gave as great thanks to the dead man as he has ever given to a living one.
6. He acquired his magistracy as much by friendship as by hatred.
7. By how much more avidly you will have sought peace, by so much will war be more difficult.
8. Although you were conversing avidly and happily, they thought that you were speaking with them unwillingly.
9. She has acquired so many enemies in the city that she prefers to live her life in the country rather than in Rome.
10. The senate and the Roman people not only allow but even want the authority of Cicero to be as great as one man's authority can be in a free state.

Lesson VIII

DIRECT QUESTIONS

A **DIRECT QUESTION** is an interrogative sentence that gives the exact words of the speaker. A direct question may begin with an **INTERROGATIVE PRONOUN, ADJECTIVE,** or **ADVERB.**

The interrogative pronoun **quis, quid,** is used to introduce many questions. Note that the plural of this word is the same as the plural of the relative pronoun.

	Singular		Plural		
	Masc./Fem.	Neuter	Masculine	Feminine	Neuter
Nominative	quis	quid	quī	quae	quae
Genitive	cuius	cuius	quōrum	quārum	quōrum
Dative	cui	cui	quibus	quibus	quibus
Accusative	quem	quid	quōs	quās	quae
Ablative	quō	quō	quibus	quibus	quibus

Quis haec dīxit?	*Who said this?*
Cuius liber est ille?	*Whose book is that?*
Quōs vocāvistī?	*Whom did you invite?*

The following interrogative adjectives can also introduce a question.

quī, quae, quod	*which? what?*	**quot** (Indeclinable)	*how many?*
quālis, quāle	*what kind of?*	**uter, utra, utrum**	*which (of two)?*
quantus, quanta, quantum	*how great?*		

Quem librum lēgisti?　*Which book did you read?*

The following interrogative adverbs can also introduce a question.

ubi	*where?*	**quō**	*where to?*	**quamdiū**	*how long?*
unde	*where from?*	**cūr**	*why?*	**quōmodo**	*how?*
quandō	*when?*	**quotiēns**	*how often?*		

When a question is not introduced by any of these interrogative words, an **INTERROGATIVE PARTICLE**, which is expressed but not necessarily translated, is used in Latin.

A question that can expect either a yes or no answer begins with a word to which the enclitic **–ne** is attached (which is often the verb).

Curruntne equī?　　*Are the horses running?*

Nōnne (nōn+ne) beginning the sentence indicates that the expected answer is yes.

Nōnne omnēs adsunt?　*Aren't they all here? They are all here, aren't they? Surely they are all here?*

Num beginning the sentence indicates that the expected answer is no.

Num id verēris?　　*You aren't afraid of that, are you? Surely you are not afraid of that?*

Some questions offer a choice of alternatives. These begin with the word **utrum** and use **an** or **annōn** in the second part.

Utrum opus facere potes, annōn?　*Can you do the work, or not?*
Utrum māter tua ea dīxit an pater?　*Did your mother say that or your father?*

16

Vocabulary VIII

Interrogative Pronoun		Third Conjugation Verb	
quis, quid	*who?, what?*	incolō, -ere, incoluī, —	*inhabit*
Adjectives		**Adverbs**	
fīnitimus,-a,-um	*neighboring*	cūr	*why?*
quantus,-a,-um	*how great?, how much?*	omnīnō	*altogether*
fidēlis,-e	*faithful, loyal*	quamdiū	*how long?*
nōbilis,-e	*noble*	quandō	*when?*
quālis,-e	*what kind of?, what sort of?*	quō	*to where?, whither?*
quot	*how many?* (indeclinable)	quōmodo	*how?*
Second Declension Nouns		quotiēns	*how often?*
cibus,-ī, *m.*	*food*	unde	*from where, whence*
lēgātus,-ī, *m.*	*envoy, legate*	utrum...annōn	*(whether)...or not*
tribūnus,-ī, *m.*	*tribune*	utrum...an	*(whether)...or*
		-ne	*(introduces a yes or no question)*
		nōnne	*surely* (expects a "yes" answer)
		num	*surely...not* (expects a "no" answer)

Exercise VIII

A.

1. Quis cibum mīlitibus mīsit?
2. Quam partem terrae incolunt illī Gallī, quibuscum bellum gerere saepē volēbāmus?
3. Tuīne fīliī fīliaeque litterās rēgis legunt?
4. Quamdiū tribūnus mīlitum iussa consulis verēbātur?
5. Nōnne fidēlis servus auxilium rēgīnae nōbilī feret?
6. Utrum Caesarem ipsum diē illō dīcentem audīvistī, annōn?
7. Num iam nocte ex urbe ēgrederis ?
8. Unde nuntius fidēlis epistulam tulit quae mortem patris nuntiāvit?
9. Utrum ipse rem pūblicam servābit, an aliōs dēlēre patiētur?
10. Uter consul in urbe aderit et uter in provinciīs aberit?
11. Cum servus esset omnīnō invītus impedimenta dominī portāre, confestim aliōs vocāvit quī onera ferrent.

B.

1. What tribes inhabit this land?
2. Where will the queen wish to go to, when we undertake (fut. perf) the war?
3. How many men will be sent to seek food in the night?
4. With what sort of books will you teach literature?
5. What gifts does fortune give to the faithful, and when?
6. Where did the envoys set out to and when will they return?
7. How often has the envoy been sent into Gaul to seek peace?
8. How great a fire did the soldiers make when they destroyed the farmer's fields?
9. Why do the students not listen to every word of the teacher, who has terrified them?
10. As often as the nobles snatched them from danger, so often did the citizenry give thanks to the gods.

17

Lesson IX

THE IMPERATIVE MOOD

The **IMPERATIVE MOOD** is commonly used to express commands or entreaties.

The present imperative active singular is the same as the present stem (+ -e for the 3rd conjugation).

The present imperative active plural is formed by adding –te to the present stem (+-ite for the 3rd conjugation).

Imperative Active

	First	Second	Third	Third I-stem	Fourth
Singular	amā	monē	tege	cape	audī
Plural	amāte	monēte	tegite	capite	audīte
	Love!	*Warn!*	*Cover!*	*Take!*	*Hear!*

Imperative Passive

The present imperative passive singular is formed by adding –re to the present stem of the verb (-ere for the 3rd conjugation). The present imperative passive plural is formed by adding -minī (-iminī for the 3rd conjugation).

Passive forms are most commonly used with deponent verbs.

	First	Second	Third	Third I-stem	Fourth
Singular	conāre	verēre	sequere	patere	mentīre
Plural	conāminī	verēminī	sequiminī	patiminī	mentīminī
	Try!	*Be afraid!*	*Follow!*	*Endure!*	*Lie!*

Irregular Imperatives

The four verbs, **dīcō, dūcō, faciō**, and **ferō**, have irregular singular forms in the present imperative active: **dīc, dūc, fac, fer. Ferō** has an irregular plural present imperative active: **ferte.**

Negative Commands

Latin does not use the word **nōn** to express a negative command. A negative command may be expressed two ways:

Nōlī (singular) and **nōlīte** (plural) with the present infinitive:

Nōlī mē pūnīre!	*Don't punish me!*
Nōlīte mē punīre!	*Don't punish me!*

Nē with the 2nd person perfect subjunctive:

Nē eum cēperītis!	*Don't seize him!*

The Vocative Case

The **VOCATIVE CASE** is used for direct address and is often offset by commas in English. It has the same form as the nominative except in the second declension, where nouns and adjectives ending in -us have the vocative singular ending -e. Nouns and adjectives ending in -ius and the adjective **meus** in the masculine singular have the vocative ending -ī. The plural vocatives of nouns and adjectives are generally the same as the nominative.

dominus - domine	**Marcus - Marce**	**Lūcīlius - Lūcīlī**
filius - fīlī	**meus - mī**	**nūntius - nūntī**

Venī domum, mī fīlī!	*Come home, my son!*
O rēgīna, audī mea carmina!	*O queen, listen to my songs!*

Vocabulary IX

Third Declension Nouns		Third Conjugation Verbs	
factiō, factiōnis, *f.*	*faction*	accēdō, -ere, accessī, accessum	*go towards*
multitūdō, multitūdinis, *f.*	*crowd, multitude*	admittō, -ere, admīsī, admissum	*admit, allow*
ōrātiō, ōrātiōnis, *f.*	*speech*	āmittō, -ere, āmīsī, āmissum	*lose, send away*
ōrātiōnem habēre	*give a speech*	cēdō, -ere, cessī, cessum	*go, yield*
ratiō, ratiōnis, *f.*	*reason, theory*	committō, -ere, commīsī, commissum	*engage, entrust*
servitūs, servitūtis, *f.*	*slavery*	concēdō, -ere, concessī, concessum	*grant, yield*
sollicitūdō, sollicitūdinis, *f.*	*care, worry*	dīmittō, -ere, dīmīsī, dīmissum	*dismiss, send away*
virtūs, virtūtis, *f.*	*excellence, strength, virtue*	remittō, -ere, remīsī, remissum	*send back*
clāmor, clāmōris, *m.*	*noise, shout*		

Exercise IX

A.

1. Audīte clāmōrēs mīlitum!
2. Nōlī, mī Marce, id facere quod ego fēcī.
3. Factiōnem parāvī, Antōnī, ut mihi magistrātum concēdās.
4. Nē clāmōrī multitūdinis cesserīs; patere istum virum dīcere.
5. Quantō metū senātus ā tē incitātus est, quantā sollicitūdine cīvitās!
6. Consul vim multitūdinis timens et īrā mōtus, ōrātiōnem ūtilissimam reī pūblicae habuit.
7. Dīcite quod vultis dīcere; nolīte facere quod facere nōn vultis. Omnia ista vōbīs concēdam et remittam.
8. Lēgātus nuntiāvit metum exercitūs tantum esse ut mīlitēs angustam viam animadvertere nōn possent.
9. Āmīsit vītam, sed fāmam nactus est; dedit vītam, patriam accēpit.
10. Populus erat tam incēnsus ut multī in urbem tot factiōnibus incitātam admittī nōn possent.
11. Māter post id factum neque domum ad sē venīre fīlium passa est neque in conspectum.

B.

1. Send away your worry!
2. Lead them into slavery!
3. Say nothing about this matter to my enemies!
4. Approach, my son, stop and look upon the wretched body of your father!
5. Do not, my Brutus, send your Cicero away from you, but lead him with you.
6. The wisest say that virtue alone makes a life happy. Let us concede this to them.
7. I am sending back this gift for the same reason for which I sent back those others.
8. Although he was almost dead, still he did not wish to be sent back into slavery.
9. Let us concede that virtue without reason is not able to be in a human being.
10. Do not entrust yourself to the loyalty of those men.
11. Worry is slavery for the mind; let reason admit courage into the heart.
12. Do not say that this man did the same thing which his friend did.

Lesson X

IRREGULAR VERB: FĪŌ

fīō, fierī, factus sum *be made, be done, become, happen*

Fīō is used as the passive of the verb **faciō**. **Fīō** and **faciō** have no passive endings in the present, imperfect, and future.

Indicative

	Active	Passive	
Present	faciō	**fīō**	*I am made, become*
	facis	**fīs**	*you are made, become*
	facit	**fit**	*he is made, becomes (it is done)*
	facimus	**fīmus**	*we are made, become*
	facitis	**fītis**	*you are made, become*
	faciunt	**fīunt**	*they are made, become, are done*
Imperfect	faciēbam	fīēbam	*I was being made, was becoming*
Future	faciam	fīam	*I will be made, will become*
Perfect	fēcī	factus,-a sum	*I have been made, have become*
Pluperfect	fēceram	factus,-a eram	*I had been made, had become*
Future Perfect	fēcerō	factus,-a erō	*I will have been made, will have become*

Subjunctive

	Active	Passive
Present	faciam	fīam
Imperfect	facerem	fīerem
Perfect	fēcerim	factus,-a sim
Pluperfect	fēcissem	factus,-a essem

Participles

				Infinitives		
Present	faciens, facientis	--------		Present	facere	fierī
Perfect	--------	factus,-a,-um		Perfect	fēcisse	factus,-a,-um esse
Future	factūrus, -a,-um	--------		Future	factūrus,-a,-um esse	factum īrī

Imperatives

Singular	**fac**	**fī**
Plural	**facite**	**fīte**

certiōrem facere, *to inform;* **certior fierī**, *to be informed*

Certior modifies the direct object of **faciō** or the subject of **fīō**.

Tē certiōrem faciam.	*I will inform you. (I will make you more certain)*
Eōs certiōrēs fēcit.	*He informed them. (He made them more certain)*

Fīō is used to express the passive, *to be informed*.

Rēx certior dē cōnsiliō fit.	*The king is being informed about the plan.*

Vocabulary X

	Verbs		Adverbs
fīō, fīerī, factus sum	*be made, become, happen*	itaque	*and so*
creō (1)	*create, elect*	spontē	*of one's own accord, voluntarily*
impetrō (1)	*obtain (by asking)*		Nouns
augeō, -ēre, auxī, auctum	*increase*	celeritās, celeritātis, *f.*	*speed, swiftness*
addūcō, -ere, addūxī,	*influence, lead to*	facultās, facultātis *f.*	*ability, opportunity, skill*
adductum			Preposition
dēdūcō, -ere, dēdūxī,	*draw (a weapon),*	apud (+acc.)	*among, at the house of,*
dēductum	*lead away, remove*		*in the presence of*

Exercise X

A.

1. Māter dē fīliā certior fit.
2. Scrība fīēs, ego magister.
3. Nōlō umquam inimīcus fierī.
4. Spontē suā Camilla in bellō in Trōiānōs pugnāvit.
5. Cum discipulī dē operibus Cicerōnis certiōrēs fīerent, maximā cum cūrā audīvērunt.
6. Quotiēns ab perīculīs clāmōribusque forī tē pācem mentis petentem ēripuistī?
7. Servī intellēxērunt esse facultātem lībertātis; itaque consilium āvidē temptāre comparāvērunt.
8. Cum legātus exercitum dē celeritāte hostium certiōrem vōce auctā fēcerit, ducem ex castrīs sequī contendunt.
9. Cum neque cibum neque pecuniam itinerī habērem, apud Crassum constitī, ubi impetrāvī.
10. Postquam opera P. Ovidiī Nāsōnis lēgerant, discipulī pūtābant sē omnia dē amantibus intellegere.
11. Mōre maiōrum vir in vinculīs positus est, cum mīlitēs in urbem dūxisset.
12. Quibus malīs adeō Poēnī perterritī (sunt), ut etiam auxilia ab Rōmānīs petīverint eaque impetrāverint. (Cornelius Nepos, *Hamilcar* 2.3)

B.

1. Your slave will become free tomorrow.
2. A way can be made by force.
3. They became most careful in all matters.
4. He informs the pirates about the arrival of the ships and their leader.
5. Contend with your enemies with great virtue and defeat them!
6. Elect Cicero consul, so that he may be able to preserve the city in bad times.
7. Do not abandon the city of your own accord! Wait in order to be informed by your leaders.
8. Don't draw your weapons in the sight of your mother!
9. Since the water was led to the village, the leaders obtained power over the resources of the people.
10. Become greater than your father was since you have had greater opportunity.
11. The maiden will be made queen when her father, the king, dies.
12. The leader was informed that the enemy had obtained food from their neighbors.

21

Lesson XI

REVIEW: LESSONS VI – X

CORRELATIVES: paired words that show or imply comparison.

LOCATIVE CASE: With the names of cities, small islands, towns, and **domus** and **rūs**, the locative case is used to express place where.

1st declension singular	genitive form	**Romae**	*at* or *in Rome*
2nd declension singular	genitive form	**Corinthī**	*at* or *in Corinth*
		domī	*at* or *in the home*
3rd declension and plurals	ablative form	**Athenīs**	*at* or *in Athens*
		rūrī	*at* or *in the country*

Note that these same nouns are used in the ablative to show motion away from and the accusative to show motion towards without any preposition.

DIRECT QUESTIONS: Questions can be introduced by an interrogative pronoun, adjective or adverb. A question expecting a yes or no answer is introduced by an interrogative particle.

open question	**-ne** is attached to first word	**Statne puer?**	*Is the boy standing?*
expecting a yes	**nōnne** introduces the question	**Nōnne puer stat?**	*Surely the boy is standing?*
expecting a no answer	**num** introduces the question	**Num puer stat?**	*The boy isn't standing, is he?*

IMPERATIVE MOOD: The formation of the imperative mood of a verb is as follows:

Present imperative	active singular	= present stem;	third conjugation = present stem +	-e
	active plural	= present stem + -te;	third conjugation = present stem +	-ite
	passive singular	= present stem + -re;	third conjugation = present stem +	-cre
	passive plural	= present stem +-minī;	third conjugation = present stem +	-iminī

Four verbs have irregular forms in the present imperative active:

> **dīc, dūc, fac, fer/ ferte** (plural)

Negative imperatives are formed in two ways: (1) **nōlī** or **nōlīte** + present infinitive
                                                 (2) **nē** + 2nd person perfect subjunctive

VOCATIVE: The vocative case is used for direct address. It has the same form as the nominative except in the following:

2nd declension masculine nouns ending in **–us**	-e	**Marce**	*Marcus!*
		domine	*master!*
words ending in **–ius**	-ī	**nuntī**	*messenger!*
		Vergilī	*Vergil!*
meus	-ī	**mī fīlī**	*my son!*

Fīō is used as the passive form of **faciō** and has only passive meanings.

The idiom **certiōrem facere** means *to inform:*

> **Nuntius eum certiōrem faciet.**   *The messenger will inform him.*

The passive uses the nominative case with **fīō:**

> **Magister dē discipulō certior fit.**   *The teacher is being informed about the student.*

Exercise XI

A.

1. Librōs quantum sine īrā tantum sine invidiā scrīpsit.
2. Perīcula bellī praesidiō pācis concēdant.
3. Fac ut prōvinciam retineās in potestāte reī pūblicae.
4. Arma, virī, ferte arma; vocat lūx ultima (*final*) victōs. (Vergil, *Aeneid* 2.668)
5. Hī duo ad cōnsulem aggrēdī cōnātī ut eum interficerent, eius domō celeriter āmissī sunt.
6. Cum confestim Brundisium profectus esset, suam prōvinciam diūtius obtinēre nōn poterat.
7. Decem nāvēs, nōn pīrātārum adventū, nōn vī tempestātis, sed scelere sociōrum āmissae sunt.
8. Dī maris et terrae tempestātumque potentēs, ferte viam ventō facilem. (Vergil, *Aeneid* 3.528)
9. Maluit domī adesse quam longē ab urbe.
10. Utrum mēcum domī manēbis, an in senātum ībis ut cum aliīs sententiam dēs?
11. Amīcitiā omnium optimōrum adeō sustentus eram ut undique dēfenderer.

B.

1. Stay at home!
2. Do not send them back into slavery!
3. Set out for Rome at once!
4. By whom was the course of your honors held back?
5. The law forbids him to give a speech in front of the people.
6. A shout is made through the house.
7. He prudently remained in secret at Rome for many days before he undertook his magistracy.
8. Because of his greed he undertook such great crimes that he sent all virtue from himself.
9. Although he often speaks with his enemies, they receive him into their camp unwillingly.
10. These two men, having approached the consul in order to speak with him, were admitted immediately into his house.
11. Although he set out from Rome at once, surely he wished to stay longer among us?
12. Hasn't Caesar been informed that the Helvetians want to make a journey through the province?
13. We will approach danger on behalf of the state so that our virtue may increase.

Lesson XII

INDIRECT QUESTIONS

An **INDIRECT QUESTION** (or **REPORTED QUESTION**) is a statement, which reports a direct question.

Direct Question	Indirect Question
Who are you?	*I know who you are.*

An indirect question depends on a main verb of asking, saying, thinking, knowing, telling, perceiving, or showing. It is a subordinate clause introduced by an interrogative word and containing a subjunctive verb. The tense of the subordinate verb follows what it would be in English. The following interrogative words are frequently used to introduce the subordinate clause in indirect questions.

quis, quid	*who? what? which?*	unde	*whence? from where?*	num	*whether?*
quī, quae, quod	*which? what?*	quō	*whither? to where?*	quem ad modum	*how?*
qualis, quale	*what kind?*	quārē	*why?*	quotiens	*how often?*
quantus, -a, -um	*how great?*	quandō	*when?*	ubi	*where?*

Sciō <u>quis sīs</u>.	*I know <u>who you are</u>.*
Rogāvistī <u>quid faceret</u>.	*You asked <u>what he was doing</u>.*
Mihi dīxit <u>quandō excedere voluerit</u>.	*He told me <u>when he wanted to leave</u>.*
Nescīvī <u>quārē illud scrīpsisset</u>.	*I didn't know <u>why he had written that</u>.*

When the subordinate clause in the indirect question is in the future, use the future active participle + the present subjunctive of **sum** for primary sequence or the imperfect subjunctive of **sum** for the historical sequence.

Dīc mihi <u>quid pater dictūrus sit</u>.	*Tell me <u>what the father will say</u>.*
Scīvit <u>quid puellae cantātūrae essent</u>.	*He knew <u>what the girls were going to sing</u>.*

Indirect yes-or-no questions are formed the same way that direct ones are, except that **num** does not imply a negative and is used instead of **–ne**, and **nōnne** is only used after the verb **quaerō**.

Rogāvī <u>num illud vīdissēs</u>.	*I asked <u>whether you had seen that</u>.*

Both direct and indirect questions use **utrum**, but **annōn** is usually replaced by **necne**.

Nesciō <u>utrum adsit an absit</u>.	*I don't know <u>whether he is present or absent</u>.*
Nesciō <u>utrum adsit necne</u>.	*I don't know <u>whether he is present or not</u>.*

Vocabulary XII

Verbs		Nouns	
narrō (1)	*relate, tell*	arbor, arbōris, *f.*	*tree*
indūcō, -ere, indūxī, inductum	*influence, lead in*	amor, amōris, *m.*	*love*
trādūcō, -ere, trāduxī, trāductum	*lead across*	rūmor, rūmōris, *m.*	*rumor*
conveniō, īre, convēnī, conventum	*come together, convene, meet*	Adjective	
inveniō, -īre, invēnī, inventum	*come upon, find*	vērus,-a,-um	*true*
nesciō, -īre, nescīvī/nesciī, nescītum	*not know*	Preposition	
perveniō, -īre, pervēnī, perventum	*arrive, come to*	praeter (+acc.)	*along, by, in front of, past*

Exercise XII

A.

1. Sciō quandō pervēnerīs, sed nēsciō quamdiū mansūrus sīs.
2. Nesciēbam quis ea verba dīxisset.
3. Rogāvit quem ad modum cōnsul creārētur.
4. Pater nescīvit quālēs arborēs essent in agrō.
5. Scīsne quō nāvis nāvigāverit, quae Brundisium herī pervēnerat?
6. Nēsciō quārē consul mīlitēs trans campōs ad castra hostium trādūxerit.
7. Consul invenīre voluit quārē Caesar Galliam relīquisset, cum perīculum copiīs auctum esset.
8. Mea puella amōrem suum esse maiōrem quam meum nūntiāvit.
9. Rēx Priamus et filiī convēnērunt ut consilium celeriter caperent.
10. Dīc mihi unde iter fēcerīs.
11. Nesciō utrum pater perīcula bellī nōbīs prōhibuerit necne.
12. Domum pervēnit invēnitque mātrem, patrem, et equōs trans flūmen trāductōs esse.
13. Quotiens invēnimus rūmōrēs dē nōbīs ab nostrīs inimīcīs inceptōs esse?

B.

1. I understand why you are present; I understood why they were away.
2. I know who met with you yesterday; I knew what reason you had given.
3. He showed me which kinds of trees he had placed around his house.
4. The father did not know whether his son was present.
5. The mother asked whether the gossip about her daughter was true.
6. The master asked where the horses had been led during the night.
7. By the sight of the trees, the farmer knows when a storm will arrive in the fields.
8. He said that he was unable to report whether our men had defeated the enemy or not.
9. The people went out of the city so that they might see the punishment of the pirates, who had destroyed the bridges.
10. Having been asked how great the winds would be after they went out from the sheltered water, the sailor said that he did not know.

Lesson XIII

THE ABLATIVE CASE

Ablative with Special Verbs

The following verbs and their compounds take an ablative rather than an accusative.

fungor	*perform*
fruor	*enjoy*
potior	*gain possession of*
ūtor	*use*
vēscor	*eat, live on*

<u>Pāce</u> fruāmur.	*Let us enjoy <u>peace</u>.*	<u>Captīs</u> potītur.	*He gains possession of <u>the captured</u>.*
<u>Officiīs</u> fungitur.	*He performs his <u>duties</u>.*	<u>Consiliō</u> eius ūtēbātur.	*He made use of his <u>advice</u>.*

Ablative of Separation

The **ABLATIVE OF SEPARATION** is used with verbs of *preventing, depriving, removing, freeing, lacking,* etc. Sometimes a preposition, **ā/ab** or **ē/ex**, is used. Note that the Ablative of Place From Which, in contrast, must have a verb of motion.

cīvīs <u>cibō</u> interclūdere	*to cut off the citizens <u>from food</u>*
Caesar hostīs <u>ā nostrīs fīnibus</u> prohibet.	*Caesar keeps the enemy <u>from our borders</u>*
Rēx cīvīs <u>perīculō</u> līberāvērunt.	*The king freed the citizens <u>from danger</u>.*

Ablative of Specification

The **ABLATIVE OF SPECIFICATION** is commonly found with nōmine, *by name,* and certain adjectives, such as dīgnus.

Rēx, Rōmulus <u>nōmine</u>, Rōmam condidit.	*The king, Romulus <u>by name</u>, founded Rome.*
Puer similis patrī <u>fīde</u> est.	*The boy is like his father <u>in loyalty</u>.*
<u>Corpore</u> senex est, <u>animō</u> numquam.	*He is an old man <u>in body</u>, (but) never <u>in spirit</u>.*

Ablative of Description

The **ABLATIVE OF DESCRIPTION** must be modified by an adjective.

Vir <u>magnā virtūte</u> est.	*He is a man <u>of great courage</u>.*
Virgō <u>haud crēdibilī pulchritūdine</u> est.	*She is a maiden <u>of unbelievable beauty</u>.*
Fac ut <u>bonō</u> sīs <u>animō</u>.	*Be <u>of good cheer</u>.*

Ablative Uses in *New First Steps* and *New Second Steps*

Accompaniment	<u>Cum</u> exercitū vēnit.	*He came <u>with an army</u>.*
Cause	<u>Factīs</u> laudātus est.	*He was praised <u>for his deeds</u>.*
Comparison	Epistula brevior <u>librō</u> est.	*A letter is shorter <u>than a book</u>.*
Degree of Difference	Flūmen altius <u>quinque pedibus</u> est.	*The river is <u>five feet</u> deeper.*
Manner	<u>Magnā cum virtūte</u> rēxit.	*He ruled <u>with great courage</u>.*
Means or Instrument	<u>Tēlō</u> vulnerātus est.	*He was wounded <u>with a weapon</u>.*
Place From Which	Animalia <u>ex umbrīs</u> vēnērunt.	*Animals came <u>out of the shadows</u>.*
Personal Agent	Fīlius <u>ā mātre</u> amātus est.	*The son was loved <u>by his mother</u>.*
Place Where or In Which	Formīcae <u>sub terrā</u> vivunt.	*Ants live <u>under the ground</u>.*
Time When	<u>Primā lūce</u> somnō excitāta est.	*<u>At dawn</u> she was awakened from sleep.*

Vocabulary XIII

Deponent Verbs with the Ablative		Verbs	
potior, -īrī, potītus sum (+abl.)	*gain possession of*	līberō (1)	*free, liberate*
fruor, fruī, frūctus sum (+abl.)	*enjoy, profit from*	superō (1)	*surpass*
fungor, fungī, functus sum (+abl.)	*perform*	prohibeō, -ēre, prohibuī, prohibitum	*keep off, prevent*
ūtor, ūtī, ūsus sum (+abl.)	*enjoy; experience; use*	condō, -ere, condidī, conditum	*bury; found (a city)*
vescor, vescī, ---- (+abl.)	*eat, feed on*	conscrībō, -ere, conscrīpsī, conscrīptum	*enlist, enroll*
Third Declension Nouns		expōnō, -ere, exposuī, expositum	*explain, expose*
aes, aeris, *n.*	*bronze*	interclūdō, -ere, interclūsī, interclūsum	*block, shut off*
aes aliēnum	*debt*	Second Declension Neuter Nouns	
arx, arcis, *f.*	*citadel*	negōtium,-ī n.	*business*
ops, opis, *f.*	*power, (pl.) resources*	officium,-ī n.	*duty, office*
sōl, sōlis, *m.*	*sun*		

Exercise XIII

A.

1. Bene libertāte suā usus est.
2. Hostēs mox omnī hāc terrā potientur.
3. Multae cīvitātēs omnī aere aliēnō liberātae sunt.
4. Nāve et opibus, quās affert, interclūdēminī.
5. Mīlitēs ab domibus cīvium prohibēbantur.
6. Rōmānī opibus prōvinciārum ūsī sunt ut potestātem in illā regiōne confirmārent.
7. Cum hostēs castrīs potītī sint, ibi nocte manēre nōn possumus; itaque iter ad proximam urbem faciēmus.
8. Arx templa Jūnōnis Monetae, Jovis Statōris et Concordiae continuit.
9. Discipulus paucīs cum magistrō hōrīs et librīs, quōs iussit mē legere, frūctus est.
10. Ascanius nōvam urbem, Albam Longam, condidit ut suōs cīvīs ā perīculīs līberāret.
11. Hic populus omnēs fide, virtūte, et numerō hominum superat.
12. Consul, quem creāvistī, negōtiīs reī pūblicae magnā cum virtūte fungētur.

B.

1. We will soon be freed from our debt.
2. You have profited from his friendship.
3. The soldiers, who have been fighting with Caesar's troops, eat all the food which they can find in the forest.
4. The farmers were enrolled in the army in order to fortify the bridges and gates of the city.
5. Gaius Julius is said to have performed well the duties of the Pontifex Maximus.
6. You have explained well the fortunes of that small city founded by the son of Aeneas (*Aenēae*).
7. The works of the two consuls, men of the greatest resources, freed the people of Rome from the very serious dangers of wars.
8. Among those tribes, he surpassed all in skill and resources.
9. At Rome, the consuls explained the new business of the senate to the legates of the Gauls.
10. Hearing about the Gorgons with (their) hands (out) of bronze, I used to have great fear which kept me from sleep.

Lesson XIV

ABLATIVE ABSOLUTE

The **ABLATIVE ABSOLUTE** is a Latin phrase describing circumstances surrounding the action of the main clause. It consists of at least two words in the ablative case, usually a noun and a participle. The noun in the ablative absolute cannot be the same as the subject or direct object of the main clause.

Participle modifying subject	**Dux vulnerātus fūgit.**
	The leader, having been wounded, fled.
Ablative Absolute	**Duce vulnerātō, mīlitēs fūgērunt.**
	The leader having been wounded, the soldiers fled.

It is preferable to use a temporal, causal, or concessive clause as a translation for the ablative absolute. Appropriate translations may include *when, since, although, after, if,* and similar words.

The "absolute translation" (e.g. "*the leader having been wounded*") should be a last resort in translating.

    Duce vulnerātō, mīlitēs fūgērunt.   *Since the leader was wounded, the soldiers fled.*

Both the noun and the participle in an ablative absolute can be modified.

    Duce graviter vulnerātō, mīlitēs fūgērunt.   *Since the leader was badly wounded, the soldiers fled.*
    Duce nostrō vulnerātō, mīlitēs fūgērunt.   *Since our leader was wounded, the soldiers fled.*

Most perfect participles are passive in meaning; only deponent verbs can express a perfect active participle.

    Duce locūtō, impetum fēcērunt.   *After the leader had spoken* (lit. *the leader having spoken*),
        they made an attack.

A present participle is sometimes used.

    Nōbīs audientibus, haec dīxit.   *With us listening, he said these things.*
    Deō volente, hostīs vincēmus.   *If God is willing, we will conquer the enemy.*

Since **esse** has no present participle, two nouns, a noun and a pronoun, or a noun and an adjective may form an ablative absolute.

Caesare duce	*Caesar being leader* (or *with Caesar as a leader*)
Caesare et Lentulō consulibus	*in the consulship of Lentulus and Caesar*
hōc locō castrīs idōneō	*this place being suitable for camp*

Vocabulary XIV

Adjectives		Third Conjugation Verbs	
commūnis,-e	*common, general, shared*	cogō, -ere, coēgī, coactum	*collect, force, gather*
incolumis,-e	*safe, unharmed*	ērumpō, -ere, ērūpī, ēruptum	*break out, burst out*
insignis,-e	*distinguished, prominent*	exigō, -ere, exēgī, exactum	*collect, demand, drive out,*
satis (indeclinable)	*enough*		*finish (a life)*
turpis,-e	*disgraceful, shameful*	revertō, -ere, revertī, _____	*return, turn back*
quisque, quaeque,	*each*		*(deponent in present)*
quidque		solvō, -ere, solvī, solūtum	*loosen, untie*
Adverb		sūmō, -ere, sūmpsī, sumptum	*take up*
interim	*meanwhile*	**Third Declension Nouns**	
praesertim	*especially*	eques, equitis, *m.*	*horseman, (pl.) cavalry*
ūnā	*together*		

Exercise XIV

A.

1. Vītā eius miserē exactā, corpus in terrā conditum est.
2. Aere aliēnō solūtō, sollicitūdine omnī līberātus est.
3. Capī Rōma mē consule potuit? (Livy, *Ab Urbe Conditā*, 3.67.3)
4. Coactīs in unum locum omnibus mīlitibus ducibusque, magnam pecuniam eīs dedit.
5. Regēs tandem ā populō exactī revertere ad urbem voluērunt.
6. Spērābam onus meum futūrum esse commune vōbīscum.
7. Vinculīs solūtīs, Perseus Andromedam patrī dare poterat.
8. Ōrātiōne graviter habitā, animus cuiusque acriter incitātus est.
9. Hostibus celeriter superātīs, quisque dux in Italiam cum equitibus contendit.
10. Hīs gentibus victīs, Caesar iterum in Germāniam ēgressus est, nullīsque hostibus ibi inventīs incolumis revertit.
11. Vestrā auctōritāte satis confirmātā, facilius et reliquam pecuniam exigere et exactam servāre poterimus.
12. Nōminibus hōrum equitum tot atque tantōrum expositīs, sē illōrum praecepta sequī dīxērunt.
13. Marcum Catōnem insignem habēmus, quī Marciō et Manilio consulibus mortuus est, annō LXXXVI ipsō *(exactly)* ante Cicerōnem consulem.

B.

1. While those men were consuls, Rome did not fear.
2. After the city was founded, the strength of the citizens increased.
3. When the camp also had been lost, he fled most disgracefully, alone and conquered.
4. After these things were said, Caesar led his men across the mountains to subdue the Gauls.
5. The Romans, driving the kings from the city, said that they could not accept peace with slavery.
6. Since those people have been informed about these things, I scarcely know what you want me to write.
7. I do not know what each person said in the senate of their own state or in the common plans of their people.
8. Let us loosen those chains so that our anger, for a long time restrained, may be able to break out against our common enemy.
9. After all who have taken up arms against us have been gathered in one place, let us set out towards the city.
10. Although the republic was saved from these dangers by my courage, nevertheless I was punished for my deeds.

Lesson XV

THE DATIVE CASE
Dative of Interest with Special Verbs

crēdō	*believe, entrust*
faveō	*support, favor*
ignoscō	*forgive*
noceō	*harm*
parcō	*spare*
pareō	*obey*
placeō	*please*
studeō	*be eager, be devoted*

Fīliī <u>matribus</u> paruērunt.   *The sons obeyed (their) <u>mothers</u>.*

Dative of Possession

The **DATIVE OF POSSESSION** uses the verb **sum** to show possession and **dēsum** to show lack. The possessor is in the dative; the possession is in the nominative.

<u>Vōbīs</u> sunt librī.   <u>*You*</u> *have the books.*   (lit: *The books are to you.*)

Librī <u>mihi</u> dēsunt.   <u>*I*</u> *have no books.*   (lit. *Books are lacking to me.*)

Dative of Purpose

The **DATIVE OF PURPOSE** is used to express *why* or *for what purpose* something is done.

Locum <u>castrīs</u> invēnit.   *He found a place for camp.*

Dative of Reference

The **DATIVE OF REFERENCE** shows the person affected by the action or service rendered.

Hoc <u>mihi</u> fēcit.   *He did this <u>for me</u>.*

Double Dative

The **DOUBLE DATIVE** pairs the Dative of Purpose and the Dative of Reference in the same clause.

Hoc <u>auxiliō</u> <u>mihi</u> fēcit.   *He did this <u>as a help</u> <u>to me</u>.*

Cupiditātēs <u>impedimentō</u> <u>tibi</u> fuērunt.   *Their desires were <u>a hindrance to you</u>.*

Dative Uses in *New First Steps* and *New Second Steps*

Indirect Object: **Puerō librum dedī.**   *I gave <u>the boy</u> a book.*

With Certain Adjectives: **Puella <u>mātrī</u> similis est.**   *The girl is like <u>(her) mother</u>.*

30

Vocabulary XV

Third Conjugation Verbs		Second Conjugation Verbs	
crēdō, -ere, crēdidī, crēditum (+dat.)	*believe, entrust something (acc.) to someone (dat.)*	faveō, -ēre, fāvī, fautum (+dat.)	*favor, support*
		noceō, -ēre, nocuī, nocitum (+dat.)	*harm*
ignoscō, -ere, ignōvī, ignōtum (+dat.)	*forgive*	pāreō, -ēre, pāruī, pāritum (+dat)	*obey*
		placeō, -ēre, placuī, placitum (+dat.)	*be pleasing*
ostendō, -ere, ostendī, ostentum	*display, show*	studeō, -ēre, studuī, (+dat.)	*be eager for, desire*
		More Verbs	
parcō, -ere, pepercī,---- (+dat.)	*spare*	appropinquō, (1)	*approach*
		dēsum, dēesse, dēfuī, dēfutūrus (+dat.)	*be lacking, fail*
First and Second Declension Adjectives		**First Declension Noun**	
perītus,-a,-um	*experienced, skilled*	nātūra,-ae, *f.*	*character, nature*
summus,-a,-um	*highest, top of*		

Exercise XV

A.

1. Ignosce timōrī nostrō. (Cicero, *Epistulae Ad Familiārēs* 6.7.1)
2. Rōmānī Gallīs suam salūtem crēdidērunt.
3. Quōmodo pater suīs filiābus nocēre potest?
4. Cum pater puerum manibus tenuerit, filium esse sibi magnō gaudiō sēnsit.
5. Consul dūcibus exercitūs ignōvit, postquam ad urbem redīerant.
6. Dominus dicēbat opera discipulōrum sibi placēre, sed posse meliōra esse.
7. Rēx aurum et aes et ferrum impetrāta cīvibus ostendit ut scīrent quantae opēs essent Gallīs.
8. Dē minōribus autem erat C. Sulpicius Gallus, quī maximē omnium nobilium Graecīs litterīs studuit. (Cicero, *Brutus* 78)
9. In rē publicā quid agātur, crēdō tē ex eōrum litterīs cognoscere. (Cicero, *Epistulae ad Familiārēs* 12.28.3)
10. Vōbīs populī Rōmānī praesidia nōn dēsunt; vōs populō Rōmānō nē dēsitis.

B.

1. Your life is a great concern to me.
2. In those days my reputation was a glory to me.
3. The gods do not favor the works of men, nor men (the works) of the gods.
4. You will lack neither good fortune nor money; all these things will be as a gift for you.
5. The king spared the life of the enemy, who had approached with a weapon so that he might kill him.
6. The teacher asked which poet, expert in the use of words, was devoted to the works of Ovid.
7. The pirate injured the shoulder of the captured sailor so seriously that his life could not be preserved.
8. Since we have spoken about all the dead, tell me the reason for which you particularly wish to speak nothing about the living.
9. A man of highest virtue will spare his enemies, but not always favor his friends.
10. He was so eager for the worst factions in the state that no one trusted him.

Lesson XVI

REVIEW: LESSONS XII – XV

INDIRECT QUESTIONS: Main verb + interrogative /**num**/**utrum** + subjunctive

ABLATIVE USES: Verbs with Ablative of Instrument: **fungor, fruor, potior, ūtor, vēscor**

Description(Quality)	with adjective	**vir magnā virtūte**	*a man of great courage*
Separation	verb of separation	**perīculō liberāre**	*to free from danger*
	or **ā/ab** or **ē/ex**	**ā fīnibus prohibērī**	*to be kept from the territory*
Specification	w/ noun or adjective	**puer, Marcus nomine**	*a boy, by the name of Marcus*

ABLATIVE ABSOLUTE: An ablative absolute describes the circumstances of the main clause but is not connected grammatically to the main clause.

    (1) noun + participle – both in the ablative case.

    (2) noun + participle with modifiers or direct object – noun and participle in ablative, modifiers and direct object in appropriate cases

    (3) noun + noun or adjective (with a present participle of **sum** understood) – both words in the ablative case

The ablative absolute should be translated using *when, since, although, after, if, etc.*

DATIVE CASE: The following verbs take the dative case:

crēdō	*trust, believe*
dēsum	*be lacking; fail*
faveō	*show favor to*
ignoscō	*forgive*
noceō	*harm*
parcō	*spare*
pareō	*obey*
placeō	*please*
praecipiō	*instruct*
studeō	*desire; be eager for*

DATIVE USES:

Possession	**sum** or **dēsum**	**Fīlius mihi est.**	*I have a son.*
Purpose		**Hoc auxiliō fēcit.**	*He did this as a help.*
Reference		**Hoc mihi fēcit.**	*He did this for me.*
Double Dative	purpose and reference	**Subsidiō tibi erō.**	*I will be a support for you.*

Exercise XVI

A.

1. Sunt nōbīs tot amīcī ut nullus metus mihi sit.
2. Equitēs equīs suīs vescēbantur, cum cibus sibi dēesset.
3. Mīlitēs rogāvērunt num rūmor dē hostibus vērus esset.
4. Num scelera hostium tam turpia erant? Nōnne nostrīs fīliīs fīliābusque pepercērunt?
5. Natūrā locī cōpiīs expositā, dux rogāvit quī arma sumptūrī essent et iter ūnā factūrī essent.
6. Fīliī patribus diū parent ut, patribus mortuīs, opibus potiantur.
7. Est vir summā virtūte, magnō reī publicae amōre, multāque auctoritāte apud mīlitēs.
8. Praesidiīs hostium superātīs, tamen certam pācem facere aut populum sollicitūdine liberāre nōn poterāmus.
9. Nēsciō quārē mihi aut peperceris aut ignoveris.
10. Nōbīs exposuit quot bonī studuissent illī hominī pessimō.

B.

1. Those who are most experienced in the course of the stars have shown that the sun cannot be moved.
2. In those places huge trees keep off the light of the sun from the inhabitants.
3. Surely the truest and most noble man will be elected consul?
4. The crowd used their weapons as aid for the brave men.
5. Since they had been enrolled before the war, the Romans fought bravely and with great courage against the Germans.
6. He asked how I had performed my duties so well.
7. We enjoyed both his virtue and his friendship for many years.
8. Let us loosen the chains from the captives and return as quickly as possible to the city.
9. Each skilled (person) is able to tell how he acquired his ability.
10. We thought that he would be a hindrance to us.

Lesson XVII

CONDITIONS

A **CONDITIONAL SENTENCE** has at least two clauses: the **PROTASIS** is a subordinate clause stating the condition; the **APODOSIS** is the main clause stating the conclusion. The protasis is generally introduced by **sī** (*if*) or one of its compounds such as **etsī** (*even if*), **nisi** (*if...not, unless*). Most conditional sentences fall into one of three categories: simple or general conditions, future conditions, or contrary-to-fact conditions.

Simple Conditions

SIMPLE CONDITIONS use an indicative verb in both the protasis and the apodosis. They can be either present or past.

Simple Present

    Sī cantat, laetus est.   *If (whenever) he sings, he is happy.*

Simple past

    Sī cantābat, laetus erat.   *If (whenever) he was singing, he was happy.*

    Sī cantāvit, laetus fuit.   *If (whenever) he sang, he was happy.*

Future Conditions

There are two kinds of **FUTURE CONDITIONS**:

FUTURE MORE VIVID CONDITIONS use the future or future perfect indicative in the protasis and the future indicative in the apodosis.

    Sī cantābit, laetus erit.   *If he sings, he will be happy.*

The future perfect in the protasis emphasizes completion of the condition before the conclusion takes effect.

    Sī hostēs victī erunt, imperātor laudābitur.   *If the enemy is (will be, will have been) conquered, the general will be praised.*

FUTURE LESS VIVID CONDITIONS use the present subjunctive in both the protasis and the apodosis. To translate, follow the pattern of the example.

    Sī cantet, laetus sit.   *If he should sing, he would be happy.* (or *Should he sing, he would be happy.*)

Contrary-to-fact Conditions

CONTRARY-TO-FACT CONDITIONS may be present or past. Contrary-to-fact conditions are hypothetical.

Present contrary-to-fact conditions use the imperfect subjunctive in both the protasis and the apodosis. To translate, follow the pattern of the example.

    Sī cantāret, laetus esset.   *If he were singing, he would be happy.*

Past contrary-to-fact conditions use the pluperfect subjunctive in both the protasis and the apodosis. To translate, follow the pattern of the example.

    Sī cantāvisset, laetus fuisset.   *If he had sung, he would have been happy.*

Vocabulary XVII

First Declension Nouns		Third Declension Nouns	
cōpia, cōpiae, f.	abundance, supply, (pl.) provisions, troops	decus, decoris, n.	dignity, glory, honor
familia, familiae, f.	family, household slaves	laus, laudis, f.	praise
forma, formae, f.	form	ordō, ordinis, m.	order, rank
glōria, glōriae, f.	fame, glory	plebs, plebis, f.	common people, plebs
inopia, inopiae, f.	lack	princeps, principis, m.	chief, leader
memoria, memoriae, f.	memory		
Third Conjugation Verbs		**Preposition**	
discēdō, -ere, discessī, discessum	withdraw	contrā (+acc.)	opposite, toward
cōnsequor, cōnsequī, cōnsecūtus sum	follow, gain, pursue	**Indefinite Pronoun**	
confīdō, -ere, confīsus sum, (semi-deponent)	trust	aliquis, aliquid	anyone, anything

Exercise XVII

A.

1. Eī nōn pepercissem, nisi eius virtūtī confīsus essem.
2. Sī cōpia cibī nōbīs esset, statim reverterēmus.
3. Nisi illī studeāmus, nōn eum consequāmur.
4. Aliquid insigne et dignum memoriā laudeque facere voluit.
5. Nisi sibi magnopere confīsa esset, nōn tantam auctoritātem consecūta esset.
6. Sī illa hostibus nūntientur, ab hīs locīs discēdant; parcāmus vītīs aliōrum et nostrōrum.
7. Et facere et patī fortia Romanum est. Nec ūnus in tē ego hōs animōs gessī; longus post mē ordō est idem petentium decus. (Livy 2.12.10, Mucius to Porsenna)
8. Sī istīs nullum corpus cīvitātis, nec senātum, nec plēbem, nec magistrātūs esse patiāmur, aliquis spēs pācis populō Rōmānō sit.
9. Mē nēminem formā pulchriōrem vīdisse aut vōce dulciōrem audīvisse quam tē putō.
10. Illī autem, quibus haec ā natūrā minōra data sunt, tamen eīs ita utī possunt, ut laudemque decusque cōnsequantur.
11. Nisi Pompeius, quī princeps in rē publicā erat, hanc potestātem et glōriam maximīs rēbus gestīs consecūtus esset, nōn in eius partem eō tempore accessissem.

B.

1. If you were wise, you would yield to his authority.
2. If you should trust them, you would spare (them).
3. If you had a larger supply of words, you would be able to make a better speech.
4. If our order (use *ordō*) had not been so hard on the Roman plebs, they would have yielded to us.
5. If we wished to be the best, we would seek nothing more than dignity, glory and praise.
6. Through anxiety and lack of money the whole family was brought to destruction.
7. Zopyrus said that he was able to understand anyone's nature from (*ex*) the form of his body, eyes and other things.
8. If he were not so trusting in himself, he would not be able to deal with that very serious matter.
9. I bore the death of your daughter heavily and as a shared calamity. If I had been present, I would not have been lacking to you.

Lesson XVIII

GERUNDS

The **GERUND** is a verbal noun. The English translation always ends in *-ing*. The Latin gerund is formed by adding -nd- (or -end- in third and fourth conjugation verbs) to the present stem with the second declension neuter singular endings of only the oblique cases (i.e. genitive, dative, accusative, and ablative).

The gerund of **eō** is irregular.

	First	Second	Third	Third I-stem	Fourth	eō
Nominative	—	—	—	—	—	—
Genitive	amandī	monendī	ducendī	capiendī	audiendī	eundī
Dative	amandō	monendō	ducendō	capiendō	audiendō	eundō
Accusative	amandum	monendum	ducendum	capiendum	audiendum	eundum
Ablative	amandō	monendō	ducendō	capiendō	audiendō	eundō

Other irregular verbs and deponents form their gerunds regularly.

The verbs **sum** and **fīō** do not have gerunds.

The gerund functions like a noun in its respective cases. As a verb it can have an object and can be modified by an adverb or prepositional phrase. The object of a gerund will be in the accusative case unless the verb normally takes another case; e.g. **ūtor** takes the ablative.

The genitive of a gerund can depend on either a noun or an adjective. It can also precede the words **causā** or **gratiā** to show purpose.

Cupidus <u>bellum gerendī</u> est.	*He is desirous <u>of waging</u> war.*
Spem <u>hostīs vincendī</u> dēposuit.	*He has put aside hope <u>of defeating</u> the enemy.*
<u>Legendī causā</u> venit.	*He comes for the sake <u>of reading</u>.*

The dative of a gerund is used infrequently.

The accusative of a gerund is used with **ad** with certain adjectives, such as **parātus, idōneus, aptus,** and **ūtilis,** or to show purpose.

<u>Ad</u> librōs <u>legendum</u> venit.	*He comes <u>to read</u> books.*
Equus fortis est aptus <u>ad fugiendum</u>.	*A strong horse is useful <u>for escaping</u>.*

The ablative of a gerund is often used to express means or cause. It also follows the prepositions **ā/ab, dē, ē/ex,** or **in**.

<u>Legendō</u> discimus.	*We learn <u>by reading</u>.*
<u>Legendō</u> laetī sumus.	*We are happy <u>because of reading</u>.*
De <u>pugnandō</u> loquuntur.	*They talk <u>about fighting</u>.*

When a gerund is needed as the subject, predicate nominative, or direct object, Latin uses the infinitive.

Nominative:	**Legere est difficile.**	<u>*To read*</u> (or *reading*) *is difficult.*
Accusative:	**Legere amat.**	*He loves <u>to read</u>.*

Vocabulary XVIII

Verbs	
conspiciō, -ere, conspexī, conspectum	*catch sight of, observe, spot*
dēlīberō (1)	*consider, deliberate*
discō, -ere, didicī,- ---	*learn*
despiciō, -ere, despexī, despectum	*look down on*
perspiciō, -ere, perspexī, perspectum	*examine, observe*
tollō, tollere, sustulī, sublātum	*lift, raise*

Nouns		First and Second Declension Adjectives	
vespera,-ae, *f.*	*evening*	bellus,-a,-um	*fine, handsome, nice, pretty*
vesper, vesperis, *m.*	*evening*	cupidus,-a,-um	*eager, greedy, longing*
iuvenis,-is, *m.*	*young man, youth*	īmus,-a,-um	*at the bottom of, deepest, lowest*
hiems, hiemis, *f.*	*winter*	integer, integra, integrum	*untouched, whole*
ratiō, ratiōnis, *f.*	*reason, theory*	studiōsus,-a,-um	*devoted, eager, zealous*
		tardus,-a,-um	*late, slow*
		tūtus,-a,-um	*safe*

Exercise XVIII

A.

1. Parāte vōs ad discendum!
2. In hāc terrā novōs mōrēs et aliās viās etiam pugnandī invēnimus.
3. Iuvenēs sunt cupidī pugnandī; itaque signum tollātur et aciēs consistat!
4. Studiōsī ūnā colloquendī, vesperā sedēbāmus cibumque sumēbāmus.
5. Num impedimenta fūgiendī grātiā relinquimus?
6. Eōrum mōs erat ibi cōnsistere loquendī causā.
7. Cicerō dīxit patriam fortiter pugnandō servārī posse.
8. Plūrima dē rērum natūrā avidissimē legendō discēmus.
9. Aliī fortiter vincendī grātiā pugnant, aliī propter amōrem pugnandī.
10. Iōvī maria, terrās, lītora, regna, populōs de caelō despicientī omnia sunt cūrae.

B.

1. He is a handsome man, and eager for learning.
2. Since winter had come we were eager for departing.
3. They often held the hope of conquering.
4. He lifted fear from all by sparing many.
5. The soldiers were so desirous of fighting that they were contained with great difficulty.
6. The girls were so slow to depart that they did not arrive in the city before evening.
7. The beautiful maidens have come to the forum this evening to find the youths.
8. We shall surpass the enemy in thinking, not in talking.
9. If anyone has gained glory by harming others, I do not know his name.
10. We convened at the foot of the untouched mountain in order to begin to climb to the top together.

Lesson XIX

GERUNDIVES

The **GERUNDIVE** is a verbal adjective belonging to the 1st/2nd declension. It is always passive in meaning. It is formed like the gerund but has all the endings of an adjective. The gerundive agrees with the noun it modifies in case, number and gender.

	Singular			Plural		
	Masculine	Feminine	Neuter	Masculine	Feminine	Neuter
Nominative	amandus	amanda	amandum	amandī	amandae	amanda
Genitive	amandī	amandae	amandī	amandōrum	amandārum	amandōrum
Dative	amandō	amandae	amandō	amandīs	amandīs	amandīs
Accusative	amandum	amandam	amandum	amandōs	amandās	amanda
Ablative	amandō	amandā	amandō	amandīs	amandīs	amandīs

It is very common to use a noun modified by a gerundive instead of a gerund with an object. Both expressions can be translated the same way.

GERUND + OBJECT

librōs legendō   by reading books

NOUN + GERUNDIVE

librīs legendīs   *by reading books* (lit. *by books being read*)

The uses of the gerundive are very similar to those of the gerund.

Genitive:

Cupidus <u>bellī gerendī</u> est.   *He is desirous <u>of waging war</u>* (lit. *<u>of war being waged</u>*).

<u>Librī legendī</u> causā venit.   *He comes for the sake <u>of reading the book</u>* (lit.*<u>of the book being read</u>*).

Accusative:

Ad <u>librōs legendōs</u> venit.   *He comes <u>to read books</u>* (lit. *<u>for books being read</u>*).

Equus fortis est ad <u>hostīs fugiendōs</u> aptus.   *A strong horse is useful for <u>fleeing the enemy</u>.*

Ablative:

<u>Librīs legendīs</u> discimus.   *We learn <u>by reading books</u>* (lit. *<u>by books being read</u>*).

<u>Librō legendō</u> fēlīcēs sumus.   *We are happy <u>because of reading the book.</u>*

De <u>bellō gerendō</u> loquuntur.   *They talk about <u>waging the war</u>* (lit. *<u>about the war being waged</u>*).

Vocabulary XIX

Nouns		Verbs	
ēloquentia,-ae, *f.*	*eloquence*	reperiō, -īre, repperī, repertum	*discover, find (by looking)*
ingenium,-ī, *n.*	*character, talent*	iuvō, -āre, iūvī, iūtum	*help*
senex, senis, *m.*	*old man*	conficiō, -ere, confēcī, confectum	*accomplish, finish, make ready*
Pronoun		referō, referre, rettulī, relātum	*bring back, carry back, relate*
quīdam, quaedam, quoddam	*certain*		

Exercise XIX

A.

1. mōrēs optimōs amandō; mōribus optimīs amandīs; mōrēs optimōs amandī gratiā; mōrum optimōrum amandōrum grātiā; ad natūram mōrēsque perspiciendum; ad natūram mōrēsque perspiciendōs.
2. comparandō amīcitiam; comparandā amīcitiā; comparandī amīcitiam causā; comparandae amīcitiae causā; ad amīcitiam comparandum; ad amīcitiam comparandam.
3. Iam ad certās rēs conficiendās quōsdam hominēs dēlectōs habēbat.
4. Omnibus illīs rēbus iam confectīs, consulēs ad senātum referunt num sociī iuvandī sint.
5. Illī dīxērunt sē nōn ex aciē discessūrōs esse nisi tēlī reperiendī aut sumendī causā, aut cīvis servandī.
6. Ipsum consulem Rōmae manēre ad conscrībendōs omnēs quī arma ferre possent optimum vīsum est. (Livy 3.4.10)
7. Nisi tam breve tempus eī ad ingenium monstrandum et ēloquentiam augendam fuisset, num rogārēmus quanta vīs loquendī eī ā natūrā data esset?
8. Intellegite aliās quāsdam viās ad consequendam ēloquentiam esse meliōrēs.
9. Sciunt eadem cōnsilia bellīs dēmittendīs sumendīsque nōn esse omnibus.

B.

1. by helping the old men; for the sake of helping the old men; in order to help the old men (translate two ways)
2. by examining his true character; for the sake of examining his true character; in order to examine his true character
3. The old man was able to help his own (people) by examining the talents and customs of men, and their reasons.
4. Since everyone is asking for these things from me, I have been led to write to you for the sake of explaining the reason for war with this letter.
5. If anyone should kill a man, let there be for the Roman people the power of exacting punishment.
6. He was so influenced by certain friends that he undertook everything for accomplishing so great a crime.
7. The Romans, led farther from their camp in order to help the cities of their allies, were able to be captured.
8. I will not become tired by relating the deeds of that man again.
9. They knew that they wished to remain only for acquiring glory.
10. Led on by the desire of finishing the war quickly, he became a danger to himself and to others.

Lesson XX

PASSIVE PERIPHRASTIC

The **PASSIVE PERIPHRASTIC** expresses necessity or obligation.

Passive Periphrastics

The passive periphrastic is formed by the gerundive plus an appropriate form of **sum**. This form shows necessity or obligation. The gerundive portion of the verb agrees with its subject in case, number and gender. This is always passive form.

pres.	**dūcendus sum**	*I must be led.*
impf.	**dūcendus eram**	*I had to be led.*
fut.	**dūcendus erō**	*I will have to be led.*
perf.	**dūcendus fuī**	*I had to be led.*
plup.	**dūcendus fueram**	*I had had to be led.*
f. per.	**dūcendus fuerō**	*I shall have had to be led.*

The subjunctive forms are the gerundive plus the forms of **sim**, **essem**, **fuerim**, and **fuissem**. The infinitives are the gerundive plus **esse** and **fuisse**.

There are many possible translations for the different tenses:

Hoc faciendum est. {
This must be done.
This should be done.
This has to be done.
This ought to be done.
This is to be done.

Hoc faciendum erat. {
This had to be done.
This was to be done.

Hoc faciendum erit. {
This will have to be done

The person by whom the action must be done in these constructions is expressed by the dative case without a preposition. This is called the **DATIVE OF AGENT**. With this agent in the sentence, the construction would be translated as an active necessity or obligation.

Tibi dūcendus sum.	<u>You</u> must lead me. (lit. *I must be led <u>by you</u>.*)
Pāx nōbīs petenda erat.	<u>We</u> had to seek peace. (lit. *Peace had to be sought <u>by us</u>.*)

With intransitive verbs, which take no direct object, or with transitive verbs without an object, the subject of the passive construction is the impersonal "it." In these constructions, the gerundive is in the neuter nominative singular form. Since the literal passive English translations are not acceptable, the constructions must be translated actively.

Tibi eundum est.	*You must go* (lit. *It must be gone by you*).
Nāvibus nāvigandum erat.	*The ships had to sail* (lit. *It had to be sailed by the ships*).

Vocabulary XX

Verbs	
abeō, abīre, abiī (-īvī), abītum	*go away*
adeō, adīre, adiī (-īvī), adītum	*go to*
exeō, -īre, exīvī/exiī, exītum	*go out, withdraw*
ineō, -īre, inīvī/iniī, initum	*adopt (plan), enter*
praetereō, -īre, praeterivī/-iī, praeteritum	*go past, skip*

First and Second Declension Adjectives		Adverbs	
aequus, -a, -um	*even, fair, flat, level*	frustrā	*in vain*
aliēnus,-a,-um	*foreign, unrelated*	hīc	*here*
aptus,-a,-um	*appropriate*	hinc	*from here, from this place*
inīquus,-a,-um	*uneven, unfair*	hūc	*to this place*

Exercise XX

A.

1. Mihi huic reī apta sententia reperienda est.
2. Exercitus saepe magnā pecuniā nōbīs confirmandus erat.
3. Haec celeriter nōbīs facienda sunt; hoc tibi nunc suscipiendum erit.
4. Catilīna multōs amīcōs aere aliēnō eōrum semper suscipiendō nactus est.
5. Caesar intellēxit pontem delendum esse nē Helvetiī in prōvinciam incēderent.
6. Rūmōrēs inīquī dē meā puellā omnibus praetereundī sunt.
7. Sī senātus prō mē grātiās agendās esse putet, grātiās mihi ipsī esse referendās nōn putem?
8. Praetereō illa quae nōn praetereunda sunt; dīcam hunc esse hominem magnō ingeniō, insignī eloquentiā, summā fidē.
9. Plinius dīxit Sīlium Italicum carmina maiōre cūrā quam ingeniō scrīpsisse.
10. Quis est tam patiēns huius malae urbis ut putet īram suam tenendam esse?

B.

1. I must do these things; you had to follow your desires; we ought to find them.
2. He must be considered unrelated to our family.
3. A camp most appropriate for waging war must be found here by us.
4. They asked whether they had to come to Rome in order to keep the state from calamity.
5. They have a town in an appropriate place, to which (= where to) people often must go with ships.
6. Sallust says that virtue is always foreign to kings.
7. We must preserve a level mind in difficult and good times.
8. Some must go out into battle; others must protect the camp.
9. I pass over many things which in those times had to be found or completed by us.
10. If they did not trust you, you should not have been spared.

Lesson XXI

REVIEW: LESSONS XVII – XX

CONDITIONS:

Type of condition	Latin	English
Simple Present	present indicative in both clauses	present in both clauses
	Sī cantat, laetus est.	*If (whenever) he sings, he is happy.*
Simple Past	past indicative (imperfect or perfect) in both clauses	past in both clauses
	Sī cantābat, laetus erat.	*If (whenever) he was singing, he was happy.*
	Sī cantāvit, laetus fuit.	*If (whenever) he sang, he was happy.*
Future More Vivid	future indicative in both clauses or future perfect in the protasis	present in the protasis, future in the apodosis
	Sī cantābit, laetus erit.	*If he sings, he will be happy.*
	Sī vīcerit, laetus erit.	*If he conquers (will have conquered), he will be happy.*
Future Less Vivid	present subjunctive in both clauses	should…, would…
	Sī cantet, laetus sit.	*If he should sing, he would be happy. (Should he sing, he would be happy.)*
Present Contrary-to-Fact	imperfect subjunctive in both clauses	was -----ing, would …
	Sī cantāret, laetus esset.	*If he were singing (but he is not), he would be happy.*
Past Contrary-to-Fact	pluperfect subjunctive in both clauses	had …, would have …
	Sī cantāvisset, laetus fuisset.	*If he had sung (but he has not), he would have been happy.*

GERUNDS AND GERUNDIVES: Gerunds and gerundives have a very similar formation. Gerunds have only the genitive, dative, accusative, and ablative singular neuter forms. Gerundives have all the forms of 1st/2nd declension adjectives.

Gerund formula: Present Stem + -nd- (-end- for 3rd and 4th conjugations) + -ī, -ō, -um, and -ō

Gerundive formula: Present Stem + -nd- (-end- for 3rd and 4th conjugations) + -us, -a, -um , etc.

The noun modified by a gerundive is more frequently used than the gerund with an object. Gerunds are generally used without an object. Both constructions can be translated the same way.

PASSIVE PERIPHRASTIC: The passive periphrastic is used to show obligation or necessity (gerundive + form of **sum**):

    Laudanda est.   *She should be praised.*

The passive periphrastic takes a dative of agent.

    Pāx nōbīs petenda est.   *We must seek peace. (Peace must be sought by us).*

Intransitive verbs or transitive verbs without a direct object use the impersonal construction.

    Mīlitibus proficiscendum erit.   *The soldiers will have to set out.*

42

Exercise XXI

A.

1. Sī quis umquam rōget ubi incolam, narrā eī mē Rōmae nunc diū esse.
2. Hiemē urbs Rōma est saepe ātra inimīcaque. Nē nōbīs eundum sit!
3. Hoc ipsum est, quod maximē discendum est quodque ab hīs, quī docent, minimē dīcitur.
   (Aulus Gellius 1.3.16)
4. Nisi mē dē nātūrā bellī docuisset, cum Graecīs pugnans mortuus essem.
5. Sī prīncēps vīrēs suārum copiārum perspiciet, quōsdam dēlectōs ad īmum montem ponet quī urbem servent.
6. Sī rēgīna consilia rēgis moritūrī ineat, laudem magnam accipiat.
7. Ineundō cōnsilium principis, iuvenēs tūtī dōmum revertere poterant.
8. Studiōsus iuvenis ad summum montem vesperā adīvit sīderum conspiciendōrum et nōminum eōrum discendōrum causā.
9. Principī ad provinciās adeundum erat ut pācem regiōnī referret.
10. Haec sī fēcerit, erit integra potestās nōbīs deliberandī. (Cicero, *Philippicae* 7.26)
11. Contrā patriam arma prō amīcō sumenda nōn sunt. (Aulus Gellius, *Noctēs Atticae* 1.3.18)

B.

1. The old man spoke with such eloquence that the youths became desirous of learning all things.
2. The people do not easily trust a foreign leader, but he can gain their faith by ruling them fairly and by bringing glory to the state.
3. They must go to the city Rome before evening.
4. If he has a need for food, he is very unhappy.
5. If the youth, eager for learning, should have a mind keen and suited to reading, the old man would be able to teach him very many things well.
6. The pirates worked into the evening for the sake of finishing the ship well.
7. The soldiers must pursue the Gauls lest they influence the inhabitants of the province with their eloquence.
8. If those who have been gathered here were pleasing to you, you would not be harming them in this way.
9. If these matters had been announced to us, we would have departed from here before they could find us.

Lesson XXII

INDIRECT COMMANDS

An **INDIRECT COMMAND** (or reported command) is a sentence that reports a direct command as a subordinate clause or an infinitive construction.

Direct Command	Indirect Command
Remain!	*He asks us to remain.*

Latin uses two different constructions to express this kind of construction. The choice of which construction should be used is dependent on what main verb introduces the indirect command. Some verbs are followed by a subject accusative + infinitive construction; others, by a subordinate subjunctive clause.

Indirect Commands with Accusative and Infinitive Construction

The following verbs are followed by the subject accusative + infinitive construction (much like the indirect statement).

iubeō	*order*	**prohibeō**	*prevent*	**patior**	*allow, suffer*
vetō	*forbid*	**cōgō**	*compel*	**cupiō**	*desire*
volō	*wish*	**nōlō**	*wish not*		

Mīlitēs manēre iubet.   *He orders <u>the soldiers to remain</u>.*

Iubeō is never followed by a negative construction; instead **vetō** is used.

Mīlitēs manēre <u>vetat</u>.   *He <u>forbids</u> the soldiers to remain. (or He <u>orders</u> the soldiers <u>not</u> to remain.)*

Indirect Commands with Accusative and UT Clause

When other main verbs are used with an indirect command, they used **ut** or **ne** to introduce a subjunctive clause. The subordinate verb is a present subjunctive in primary sequence and imperfect subjunctive in historical sequence. The following verbs take an accusative of the person or thing commanded, + **ut/nē** + a subjunctive command clause.

rogō	*ask*	**moneō**	*advise, warn*
ōrō	*beseech, beg*	**obsecrō**	*beseech, beg*
hortor	*urge, encourage*		

Caesar <u>patrem</u> rogat <u>ut puerōs doceat</u>.   *Caesar asked <u>the father to teach the boys</u>.*

Indirect Commands with a Dative and UT Clause

The following verbs take a dative of person or thing commanded, + **ut/nē** + a subjunctive command clause.

imperō	*command, order*	**praecipiō**	*charge*	**persuadeō**	*persuade*

Caesar <u>mīlitibus</u> persuadet <u>ut fortiter pugnent</u>.   *Caesar persuades <u>the soldiers to fight bravely</u>.*

Indirect Command with ā/ab + Ablative of Person Commanded

The following verbs use **a/ab** and an ablative of person or thing commanded, + **ut/nē** + a subjunctive command clause.

petō	*beg, ask*	**postulō**	*demand*

Caesar postulavit <u>ā mīlitibus</u> ut <u>castra oppugnent</u>.   *Caesar has demanded <u>that the soldiers attack the camp</u>.*

Vocabulary XXII

Verbs		Adverb	
imperō (1)	*demand, order*	modo	*merely, only*
obsecrō (1)	*beg, beseech*	Nouns	
ōrō (1)	*beg, beseech*	auxilium,-ī, *n.*	*aid, help*
postulō (1)	*demand*	salus, salūtis, *f.*	*safety (personal), well-being*
hortor, hortārī, hortātus sum	*encourage, urge*		
persuadeō, -ēre, persuāsī, persuasum	*persuade*		

Exercise XXII

A.

1. Rogāvit mē ut sēcum abīrem.
2. Persuāsit eīs nē iter facerent.
3. Petō ā tē nē diūtius quam duōs diēs Rōmae maneās.
4. Eī imperandum est nē contrā inimīcōs consilium capiat.
5. Obsecrō tē nē ēgrediāris nunc, nam haec terra est aliēna mihi et sciō nēminem.
6. Nōs hortātus est ut omnia quae perspicī ā nōbīs possunt dīcāmus.
7. Hīs atque aliīs huius modī saepe dīctīs, populō persuādēbat, ut lēgātī ad rēgem mitterentur.
8. Postulāvit ut dīcerēmus vēra nunc et semper.
9. Lēgātīs relīquīs praecēpit ut exīrent cum castra mūnīta essent.
10. Vōs, tribūnī, ōrāmus ut prīmum omnium intellegātis potestātem istam ad populum iuvandum, nōn ad omnia dēlenda comparātam esse.
11. Eīs praecēpit ut celeriter Rōmam contenderent et salūtem populī defenderent.
12. Faciam, sī mihi fidem quam postulō dederis.

B.

1. They asked us to bring help.
2. You advise me to trust no one.
3. He ordered me to approach.
4. He begged me to take up his cause while you were present.
5. And so I asked the rest that they defer the whole matter for another day.
6. I ask of you only that you write diligently to me, as your nature and our friendship demand.
7. We hoped that he would either persuade them or would allow them to persuade him.
8. I urged him to say the things which he knew without fear.
9. Catiline kept on urging his allies not ever to be without a weapon.
10. They demanded that either the matter be referred to the senate, or that the consul be a help to the citizens.
11. By your fortunes and by your children, I beseech and beg you not to do anything more serious concerning your safety.
12. I warn you not to adopt a plan foreign to your customs and nature.

Lesson XXIII

SUBJUNCTIVE RELATIVE CLAUSES
Relative Clause of Characteristic

The **RELATIVE CLAUSE OF CHARACTERISTIC** describes a quality or characteristic of the antecedent. It begins with a relative pronoun and has a verb in the subjunctive. It describes the antecedent as a member of a group, "the kind of person who…"

Is est quī fortiter pugnet.   *He is one who fights bravely. /He is the kind of man who fights bravely.*

Contrast with the indicative:

Is est quī fortiter pugnat.   *He is the man (or the one) who is fighting bravely.*

The following clauses often introduce a relative clause of characteristic:

nēmō est quī	*there is no one who*
nihil est quod	*there is nothing that*
quis est quī	*who is there who*
quid est quod	*what is there that*
multī sunt quī	*there are many who*
paucī sunt quī	*there are a few who*

Relative Clause of Purpose

The **RELATIVE CLAUSE OF PURPOSE** begins with a relative pronoun instead of **ut**. (Lesson II)

Missī sumus quī tuōs caperēmus.   *We were sent to seize your men.*

If the antecedent is indefinite (*men, people, someone*), it is not expressed in Latin.

Caesar mīsit quī urbem caperent.   *Caesar sent (men) to capture the city.*

Relative Clause of Result

The **RELATIVE CLAUSE OF RESULT** is a dependent clause beginning with a relative pronoun, which expresses the result of the main clause. These results are not actual, but rather imagined or anticipated. Often the main clause will contain an adjective or adverb which anticipates and points to the result of the main clause: **tam, tālis, tantus, ita, sīc, ādeō,** etc.

Nēmō tam stultus est quī eum interficere temptet.   *No one is so foolish as to try to kill him.*

Vocabulary XXIII

Verbs			Nouns		
aperiō, īre, aperuī, apertum		*open, reveal, uncover*	beneficium,-ī, *n.*	*favor, kindness, support*	
finiō, -īre, finīvī/finiī, finitum		*define, limit*	gaudium,-ī, *n.*	*joy*	
convocō (1)		*call together*	praemium,-ī, *n.*	*prize, reward*	
existimō (1)		*consider, regard, think*	spatium,-ī, *n.*	*room, space*	
expugnō (1)		*storm*	Adverbs		
importō (1)		*bring in, carry in*	aliquandō	*anytime, sometime*	
doleō, -ēre, doluī, dolitum		*grieve*	cottīdiē	*daily*	
exerceō, -ēre, exercuī, exercitum		*train*	forte	*by chance*	
fleō, flēre, flēvī, flētum		*weep*			
respondeō, respondēre, respondī, responsum		*answer, respond*			
cupiō, -ere, cupīvī, cupītum		*desire, long for, wish*			

Exercise XXIII

A.

1. Suōs convocāvit quī ā sē cōnsilium castrōrum hostium expugnandōrum audīrent.
2. Nēmō est tam credens quī existimet beneficium ab hostibus vērum esse.
3. Nullum bellum ita pugnātur quō omnēs mīlitēs incolumēs domum redeant.
4. Portae eīs aperiuntur quī castra Dōrica (Greek), locaque vacua, lītora relicta vidēre velint.
5. Ille lēgātōs mīsit quī hostēs sequantur et praemia capiant.
6. Athēniēnsēs mē mīsērunt quī cum Rōmānīs dē bellō contrā pīrātās dēlīberārem.
7. Quid est quod tē, Catilīna, terreat magis quam hī virī in hōc locō sacrō nobilēs insignēsque?
8. Nāvēs ad Galliam equitēs importāvērunt quī imperium illārum gentium finīrent.
9. Multī sunt quī sē bellō cottīdiē exerceant sed paucī quī fortiter pugnent.
10. Summa in eam cīvitātem studia et beneficia contulit quibus dignissimus memoriā vidērētur.

B.

1. Almost no one is so evil that he always commits crimes.
2. The space in the forum is so small that the slaves were sent away.
3. No kindness is so great that it may change the heart of the evil man.
4. Caesar responded that the troops had been sent to seize the city and to carry back their own reward.
5. There is no one who weeps more about the dangers of war than the mother of a soldier.
6. Who is there who would train daily that the city may be saved from the anger of the gods?
7. (There) are few who grieve the death of a son as you have grieved.
8. What leader is so bold as to send his men onto a plain against the Gauls without weapons?
9. If they had been able to sustain the attack of the cavalry, they would not have fled into the woods.
10. Should she not have faith in herself, she would not be able to do those things.
11. Let all the trees of the forest sing for joy for the lord has come.

Lesson XXIV

SUPINES AND REVIEW OF PURPOSE CONSTRUCTIONS
Supine

The **SUPINE** is a verbal noun of the fourth declension and is usually formed from the fourth principal part of the verb. It is always neuter singular, but it is used only in the accusative and ablative cases.

	First	Second	Third	Third I-stem	Fourth
Accusative	amātum	monitum	ductum	captum	audītum
Ablative	amātū	monitū	ductū	captū	audītū
Translation	*to love*	*to warn*	*to lead*	*to capture*	*to hear*

The accusative supine is used after verbs of motion to show purpose. It may have a direct object.

Pugnātum vēnī.	*I have come <u>to fight</u>.*
Urbem captum proficiscitur.	*He sets out <u>to capture the city</u>.*

The ablative supine is used after certain adjectives as an ablative of specification.

mīrābile <u>dictū</u>	*amazing <u>to say</u>*
facile <u>factū</u>	*easy <u>to do</u>*
Turpe <u>vīsū</u> est.	*It is disgraceful <u>to see</u>.*

Review of Purpose Constructions

The following chart shows five ways to express purpose in Latin which are nearly interchangeable.

The English translation may be the same for all.

Remember that Latin never uses the infinitive to express purpose.

Construction	Formula	Examples
purpose clause	main clause + **ut /nē** + subjunctive verb	**Veniunt <u>ut urbem videant</u>.** *They come <u>to see the city</u>.*
relative clause of purpose	main clause + relative pronoun + subjunctive verb	**Veniunt <u>quī urbem videant</u>.** *They come <u>to see the city</u>.*
gerund and gerundive constructions	genitive of gerund/gerundive + **causā/gratiā**	**Urbis videndae causā veniunt.** *They come <u>to see the city</u>.* **Videndī causā veniunt.** *They come <u>for the purpose of seeing</u>.*
	ad + accusative of gerund/gerundive	**Ad urbem videndum veniunt.** *They come <u>to see the city</u>.* **Ad videndum veniunt.** *They come <u>for the sake of seeing</u>.*
supine in the accusative	verb of motion + accusative of the supine	**Urbem vīsum veniunt.** *They come <u>to see the city</u>.*

48

Vocabulary XXIV

Adjectives		Verbs	
falsus,-a,-um	*mistaken, untrue*	memorō (1)	*bring up, mention*
ūmidus,-a,-um	*damp, moist*	fingō, -ere, finxī, fictum	*compose, fashion,*
mīrābilis,-e	*amazing, remarkable, wonderful*		*imagine, make, make up*
vetus, veteris	*old*		
Adverb		**Noun**	
velut/velutī	*even as, just as*	nefās (indecl.), *n.*	*evil, wrong*

Exercise XXIV

A.

1. Numquam illa pulchrior visū fuit.
2. Quaerunt quid optimum factū sit.
3. Dīxit sē rēgem interfectūrum esse et id facile factū futūrum esse.
4. Nox et sequentis diēī pars carminum fingendōrum causā datae sunt.
5. Nē scrīpserīs ad mē etiam docendum dē maximīs rēbus in rē pūblicā gestīs, nisi ad mē ipsum pertinēbunt.
6. Illī, ut melius intellegantur, nova verba fingunt magis quam veteribus ūtuntur.
7. Caesarem conditum, nōn laudātum vēnī.
8. Tua epistula dē morte amīcī nostrī ā mē accepta statim lacrimīs meīs ūmida facta est et, nefās dictū, invītīs oculīs lecta est.
9. Epistulam tibi mittam quā sciās quam invītē hīc sōlus maneam.
10. Victus tuīs beneficiīs, vēnī tibi gratiās actum.

B.

1. I have pursued those things eagerly from which true glory may be born.
2. The words, with which I may persuade you, do not fail me.
3. They decided that this was the best to do.
4. He informed us about his arrival so that we would not trust false rumors.
5. When you tell about great virtue and glory of good men, many think these things are easy to accomplish.
6. They said that the city would be captured.
7. They said that they would come to capture the city.
8. We have come to warn you, not to praise you.
9. They have come to advise you, not to order you.
10. Catiline ordered his friends, gathered together in one place, to go out in order to kill the best people.
11. They announce that he is already present in order to cut off flight.

Lesson XXV

SUBORDINATE CLAUSES IN INDIRECT DISCOURSE

A subordinate clause depending upon **INDIRECT DISCOURSE** is called a **SUBOBLIQUE CLAUSE**. If the subordinate clause was part of the original direct statement, its verb is subjunctive in indirect discourse. The tense of the subjunctive follows the sequence of tenses based on the tense of the main verb of *saying, thinking, reporting, asking*, etc.

DIRECT STATEMENT

Mihi librum dat quem mīsērunt.   *He is giving me the book which they sent.*

The relative clause **quem mīsērunt** is a subordinate clause of the original direct statement.

INDIRECT STATEMENT

Māter dīcit eum mihi librum dare quem mīserint.   *The mother says that he is giving me the book which they sent.*

Māter dīxit eum mihi librum dare quem mīsissent.   *The mother said that he was giving me the book which they had sent.*

DIRECT QUESTION

Quī urbem dēfendunt quam Rōmānī habent?   *Who are defending the city that the Romans hold?*

INDIRECT QUESTION

Rogat quī urbem dēfendant quam Rōmānī habeant.   *He asks who are defending the city that the Romans are holding.*

Rogāvit quī urbem dēfenderent quam Rōmānī habērent.   *He asked who were defending the city that the Romans were holding.*

DIRECT COMMAND

In urbe, in quā nātus es, manē!   *Remain in the city, in which you were born!*

INDIRECT COMMAND

Iubet mē in urbe manēre in quā nātus sim.   *He orders me to remain at the city in which I was born.*

Postulāvit ut in urbe manērem in quā nātus essem.   *He demanded that I remain in the city, in which I was born.*

Vocabulary XXV

Third -iō Verbs		Adjectives	
afficiō, -ere, affēcī, affectum	*affect, treat*	immemor, immemoris	*forgetful*
dēficiō, -ere, dēfēcī, dēfectum	*fail; fall away*	memor, memoris	*mindful*
efficiō, -ere, effēcī, effectum	*cause, effect, bring about*	pār, paris	*equal, like*
perficiō, -ere, perfēcī, perfectum	*complete, finish, perfect*		
reficiō, -ere, refēcī, refectum	*repair, restore*		
Noun		**Adverbs**	
līberī, -ōrum, *m.*	*children* (only in plural)	anteā	*before, formerly, previously*
Preposition		deinde	*from there, next, then*
prope (+acc.)	*near*	inde	*from there, thence*
		numquam	*never*
		nūper	*recently*
		nōndum	*not yet*

Exercise XXV

A.

1. Dīxit sē numquam anteā vīdisse illōs līberōs, quī prope stārent.
2. Dīxī mē mūrōs refēctūrum esse postquam cōnsul creātus essem.
3. Dīcit iter, quod faciendum sit, nāvibus facilius quam pede futūrum esse.
4. Dūcēs ab mīlitibus postulāvērunt ut ad lītus prōgrediantur et nāvīs, quās anteā refēcissent, exspectent.
5. Principēs mīlitibus imperāvērunt ut ūnā manērent ut urbem undique expugnāre possent.
6. Memor Gallōs numquam exercitibus Rōmānīs bene ūsōs esse, Caesar iussit eās gentēs, quās in montibus vīcisset, sub iugum mittī.
7. Nisi illae insignēs virtūtēs amīcitiam efficiant, quis eās petendās esse putet?
8. Tandem urbe captā, dūcēs eōs mīsērunt quī cibum aquamque cōpiīs reperīrent.
9. Dīxērunt sē ab amīcitiā nostrā, quae tanta beneficia comparāvisset, dēficere nolle.
10. Sallustius scrīpsit sē, quod vīta, quā fruāmur, brevis sit, memoriam longissimam suī efficere velle.

B.

1. After that task was completed, we were affected by great care and worry.
2. The leaders asked how the storms, about which they had recently heard, were affecting the seas.
3. I hoped that the young men, since they had been affected by the habits of the best teachers, would forgive me more easily.
4. We were informed that the Romans who had gone to Britain had completed the long wall.
5. The consul ordered the soldiers to complete the bridge, which ought to have been made in the winter.
6. The children asked whether they would set out to Rome after the ships had been repaired.
7. Seneca says that virtue is able to bring it about that someone not be wretched.
8. Then he said that he would restore the state which had given him so many benefits.
9. She announced that she was greatly affected by the deeds of the queen, who was the leader of the Carthaginians.
10. He said that he had been so greatly affected by her letters that he seemed to have received a benefit from her rather than given (a benefit) to her.

Lesson XXVI

REVIEW: LESSONS XXII – XXV

INDIRECT COMMANDS: The indirect command is a subordinate clause after a verb indicating a command or a request.

Main Verb	Formula	Example
iubeō, vetō, volō, prohibeō, cōgō, nōlō, patior, cupiō	accusative + infinitive	**Iubet eam sequī.** *He orders her to follow.*
rogō, ōrō, hortor, moneō, obsecrō	accusative + **ut/ne** + subjunctive	**Eam ōrat ut sequātur.** *He begs her to follow.*
imperō, praecipiō, persuadeō	dative + **ut/ne** + subjunctive	**Eī persuadet ut sequātur.** *He persuades her to follow.*
petō, postulō	**ā/ab** + ablative + **ut/ne** + subjunctive	**Ab eā postulat ut sequātur.** *He demands that she follow.*

SUBJUNCTIVE RELATIVE CLAUSES: The following three types of relative clauses use the subjunctive mood: the relative clause of purpose, the relative clause of characteristic, and the relative clause of result.

Construction	Formula	Example
relative clause of purpose	relative pronoun + subjunctive	**Missus est quī urbem caperet.** *He was sent to seize the city.*
relative clause of characteristic	relative pronoun with indefinite antecedent + subjunctive	**Is est quī bene dormiat.** *He is the kind of man who sleeps well.*
relative clause of result	main verb often has **tam, tālis, tantus, ita, sīc,** or **ādeō** + relative pronoun + subjunctive	**Tālis est quem omnēs laudent.** *He is the sort of man that all praise.*

SUPINES: A supine is a verbal noun of the fourth declension used only in the accusative and ablative cases.

The accusative of the supine is used to show purpose with a verb of motion.

> **Vēnī urbem vīsum.**   *I came to see the city.*

In the ablative the supine is used with certain adjectives as an ablative of specification.

> **Mīrābile dictū, vir factus est deus!**   *Amazing to say, the man has become a god!*

SUBORDINATE CLAUSES IN INDIRECT DISCOURSE: A subordinate clause within indirect discourse usually has its verb in the subjunctive mood.

> **Nuntius nuntiāvit lēgātum mortuum esse, quī ad pācem faciendam vēnisset.**
> *The messenger reported that the envoy who had come to make peace had died.*

52

Exercise XXVI

A.

1. Sōlōs eōs quī īram exercēre velint convocās.
2. Potestne tē amāre, quī aliquandō tibī inimīcus fuerit?
3. Hae rēs sunt nōn sōlum malae factū, sed etiam malae audītū.
4. Sunt eī quī Propertium malint. (Quintilian, *Inst. Orat.* 10.1.93)
5. Fingāmus Alexandrum, puerum tantā curā dignum, nōbīs darī ut doceāmus.
6. Existimāvit sua beneficia, quae in caelum ab omnibus sublāta essent, decorī et praesidiō sibi futūra esse.
7. Homō ibi territus, omnī spē vītae āmissā, ōrāvit ut, antequam morerētur, sē cāsum carmine dolēre paterentur.
8. Ipsa nātūra vidētur memoriam velut ducem nōbīs dedisse, quae nōs hortētur ut bona sequāmur.
9. Hortābantur fīnitimōs ut portās aperīrent atque commūnem patriam ab impetū Rōmānōrum dēfendī paterentur.
10. Nōn sumus quibus omnia in terrīs aut mala aut bona videantur.
11. Sī eī māior auctōritās fuisset, princeps senātūs dēlectus esset.
12. Ovidius nōs rogat utrum ille carmina Tibullī tūtus legere possit, aut carmina poetae cuius opus Cynthia sōla fuerit.

B.

1. There are those who say that desire cannot be limited.
2. Let me respond to those who do not wish to make up false rumors.
3. He asked the consuls not to respond with a letter, but to be present themselves at once.
4. There is no one so happy that he would not desire those things.
5. It is slavery not to speak against whom you wish and not to defend whom you wish.
6. Since water was lacking, they came every day to seek aid.
7. If my family were not staying at Rome, I would be with them as a help in this most wretched time.
8. The poet asked whether anyone was able to read the songs of Tibullus safely.
9. How many (people) can say that they will be the same tomorrow?
10. I asked him to stay with me for three days so that he could read my speech.

Lesson XXVII

IMPERSONAL CONSTRUCTIONS

A verb which lacks a personal subject is said to be used impersonally.

INTRANSITIVE VERBS: The Passive Periphrastic of an intransitive verb must be impersonal.

     Nōbīs proficiscendum est.   *We must set out.*

Many verbs are commonly used with an infinitive or a subjunctive clause (with or without **ut**).

Impersonal Verbs with Accusative		Impersonal Verbs with Dative	
necesse est	*it is necessary*	**licet**	*it is permitted*
oportet	*it is fitting*	**placet**	*it is pleasing*

Mē exīre necesse est.

Ut exeam necesse est.   *It is necessary for me to leave. It is necessary that I leave.*

Exeam necesse est.

Tē audīre oportet.

Ut audiās oportet.   *It is fitting that you hear. You ought to listen.*

Audiās oportet.

Nōbīs licet loquī.

(Nōbīs) licet ut loquāmur.   *It is permitted that we speak. We are permitted to speak.*

Licet loquāmur.

Rēgī hoc dīcere placet.

Rēgī ut hoc dicat placet.   *It pleases the king to say this. It is pleasing to the king to say this.*

Rēgī placet hoc dicat.

Vocabulary XXVII

Deponent Verbs		Nouns	
adorior, adorīrī, adortus sum	*attack*	mulier, mulieris, *f.*	*woman*
orior, -īrī, ortus sum	*appear, rise*	tellūs, tellūris, *f.*	*earth, ground, land*
mīror (1)	*be amazed, be surprised, wonder at*	mūnus, mūneris, *n.*	*function, task, gift (of the gods)*
reor, rērī, ratus sum	*imagine, suppose, think*	custōs, custōdis, *m.*	*guard, guardian*
tueor, tuērī, tuitus sum	*observe, protect, scan*		
Impersonal Verbs		Adverbs	
licet, licēre, licuit *or* licitum est	*it is permitted*	paulō	*a little, somewhat*
		posteā	*afterwards*
necesse est	*it is necessary*	rursus	*a second time, backwards, again*
oportet, oportere, oportuit	*it is fitting*		
Adjectives			
ducentī,-ae,-a	*two hundred*	dexter, dextera, dexterum	*right, (as a noun) right hand*
trecentī,-ae,-a	*three hundred*	sinister, sinistra, sinistrum	*left, (as a noun) left hand*

Exercise XXVII

A.

1. Necesse est trecentōs mīlitēs in Britanniam mittī ut illās gentēs contineant.
2. Ut sōlem orientem conspiciāmus nōbīs placet.
3. Tua sum; tua dīcar oportet; Pēnelopē coniunx (wife) semper Ulixis erō. (Ovid, *Heroides* 1.83-84)
4. Quās habeō, dī tueantur opēs! (Ovid, *Heroides*, 16.32)
5. Nōbīs licet ut īrātī sīmus, mīlitibus nōs adortīs et mulieribus līberīsque captīs.
6. Custōdī licet ut interficiat quī rēgī appropinquāre cōnētur.
7. Nōn satis est modo habēre virtūtem - necesse est ut eā utāris.
8. Paulō posteā necesse erit docēre eōs esse custōdēs suae salūtis.
9. Aeneas surrēxit et lūmen solis orientis mīrābātur.
10. Neptūnō placet ut mulierēs mūnera in mare rursus ponant, antequam virī ad Graeciam proficiscantur.
11. Animīs sublātīs, nostrī amīcī perīcula avidē ferre constituērunt.
12. Nōn oportet consulēs adoriantur novōs tribūnōs per factiōnem suam.

B.

1. We are permitted to think, but not to act.
2. It is permitted to weep; by weeping we send away our anger.
3. Aeneas wondered at the work of the three hundred men and the city having arisen from the ground.
4. After the war is finished, it is fitting that you return to Rome and to your mother, brothers and friends.
5. It is fitting that the woman looking for her sons and daughters scan the fields.
6. It is pleasing to the man telling (his story) that the old men and girls wonder, and the women listen eagerly to every word.
7. It is fitting for the sailors to leave a gift for the god after they have returned home from the sea.
8. A hard situation forces me to do such things and to protect my territory with a guard.
9. The light of the rising sun is scarcely permitted to go into the woods of Diana.

Lesson XXVIII

CLAUSES OF FEARING

Clauses of fearing, introduced by verbs like **timeō**, **metuō**, or **vereor**, are subordinate clauses beginning with **ut/nē** and having a subjunctive verb which follows the sequence of tenses. Since what one fears will happen is what one hopes will not happen, a positive fear begins with **nē**, but a negative fear begins with **ut** or **nē...nōn**.

Timeō nē rēx moriātur.	*I fear that the king will (may) die.*
Vereor ut hostēs vincantur.	*I fear that the enemy will (may) not be conquered.*
Metuō nē hostēs nōn vincantur.	*I fear that the enemy will (may) not be conquered.*
Timuit nē rēx morerētur.	*He feared that the king might die.*
Timuimus nē rēx mortuus esset.	*We feared that the king had died.*

When a negative verb of fearing introduces a negative clause of fearing, **nē . . . nōn** is used.

Nōn vereor nē hostēs nōn vincantur.	*I do not fear that the enemy will (may) not be conquered.*
Nōn timēbit nē pater auxilium nōn ferat.	*He will not be afraid that his father will not bring help.*

A clause of fearing may also be dependent on a noun of fearing: **timor**, **perīculum**, or **metus**.

Nē rēx moriātur perīculum est.	*There is a danger that the king may die.*

Use of Quīn

A negative **EXPRESSION OF DOUBT** is followed by a subordinate clause introduced by **quīn** with the verb in the subjunctive.

Nōn dubitō quīn in Ītaliam perveniat.	*I do not doubt that he is arriving in Italy.*
Dubium nōn erat quīn lectūra esset.	*There was no doubt that she would read.*
	(lit. *It was not doubtful that...*)

A positive expression of doubt is followed by an indirect question with **num** or **an**.

Dubitō num ītūrus sit.	*I doubt that (whether) he will go.*
Dubitāvimus an exercitus victus esset.	*We doubted that the army had been conquered.*

Vocabulary XXVIII

Nouns		Adjectives	
inimīcitia,-ae, *f.*	*enmity, hostility, unfriendliness*	dīvīnus,-a,-um	*divine, heavenly*
studium,-ī, *n.*	*devotion, eagerness, enthusiasm*	necessārius,-a,-um	*inevitable, necessary*
gravitās, gravitātis, *f.*	*seriousness, severity, weight*	nātūrālis,-e	*by birth, natural*
nūmen, nūminis, *n.*	*consent, nod, divine will*		
Verbs		Adverb	
afferō, afferre, attulī, allātum	*bring, carry toward, convey*	fortasse	*perhaps*
dubitō (1)	*doubt*		
metuō, metuere, metuī, metitum	*fear*		

Exercise XXVIII

A.

1. Ūna salūs victīs (est) nullam spērāre salūtem. (Vergil *Aen.* 2. 354)
2. Veritus est nē sol orīrētur antequam pervēnit domum.
3. Dux dīxit, "Vereor nē dēficiam sub gravitāte operis quod dīvīna vōx mē perficere iubet."
4. Nōn potest esse dubium quīn id sit summum bonōrum omnium. (Cic. *de Fin.* 1.54)
5. Nec quisquam dubitāvit quīn ille verbīs dē multīs locīs ad ea scrībenda ūsūrus esset.
6. Nōn dubitō quīn tibi hoc rūmor celerius (nuntiāverit) quam ullīus nostrum litterae nuntiāverint. (Cicero *ad Att.* 1.15.1)
7. Metuō nē rēficere nōn possīs nāvem dēlētam tempestāte nisi reperiās necessāria.
8. Ōrātiōne habitā, satis mīrārī nōn potuī eius timōrem nē tē, familiam, amīcōs, etiam rem pūblicam dēfēcisset.
9. Cum liber meus bene reciperētur, omnibus grātiās ēgī, metuens nē sim immemor alicuius quī mē iuvit.
10. Mī frāter, tūne id verēris nē ego, īrā aliquā adductus, puerōs ad tē sine litterīs mīserim aut etiam nē tē vidēre nōluerim?
11. Nāve dēlētā, dubitāvi num nūmen esset vērum, sed tamen iter fēcī pede.
12. Cum necesse sit trecentōs mīlitēs mittī in illam terram, tamen metuō nē incitent inimīcitiam populī.
13. Dux dubitāvit an omnia impedimenta essent necessāria ad faciendum iter.

B.

1. I feared that you had not gone out.
2. There is a danger that the ships have not been repaired.
3. He fears that the sun will not rise again.
4. I feared that you would not come quickly.
5. That man said many things about you, which perhaps you feared that I would hear unwilling(ly).
6. He is performing his duty to the state lest others, less wise than he, try to do the same.
7. There is a danger that they may be away even longer.
8. For I fear lest I seem to have wished to save this man so much that I have not spared you at all.
9. They feared that the sun might rise before they had repaired the wall.
10. There is a danger lest your enmities become, from this day, more serious for us and the state, than for you.

Lesson XXIX

THE GENITIVE CASE

A noun in the genitive case can be dependent on a noun, adjective, verb, or **causā/grātiā**.

The possessive genitive is dependent on another noun.

> **Ille est <u>mātris</u> fīlius.**   *He is his <u>mother's</u> son.*

Partitive Genitive

The **PARTITIVE GENITIVE** expresses the whole element from which part is taken.

> **pars <u>turbae</u>**   *part <u>of the crowd</u>*
> **multī <u>mīlitum</u>**   *many <u>of the soldiers</u>*

The pronoun forms **nostrum** and **vestrum** are used for the partitive genitive.

> **Multōs <u>vestrum</u> vīdimus.**   *We saw many <u>of you</u>.*

The partitive genitive is also used with the following indeclinable nouns, substantive adjectives, and pronouns:

satis	*enough*	**nimis**	*too much*	**quantum**	*how much*
plūs	*more*	**parum**	*too little*	**tantum**	*so much*
minus	*less*	**multum**	*much*		

> **Satis <u>cibī</u> habemus.**   *We have enough (of) <u>food</u>.*

The partitive genitive is <u>not</u> used after **omnis**.

> **Nōs omnēs īmus.**   *All of us are going.*

Genitive of Description

The **GENITIVE OF DESCRIPTION** expresses a quality or characteristic. This genitive must be modified by an adjective. The genitive of description is used invariably if the description denotes a number.

> **mūrus <u>quinque pedum</u>**   *a wall <u>of five feet</u> (a five-foot wall)*
> **vir <u>magnae audaciae</u>**   *a man <u>of great boldness</u>*

Objective Genitive

The **OBJECTIVE GENITIVE** is found with the following adjectives and in many noun phrases to show the object of an action or feeling:

avidus	*greedy*	**immemor**	*unmindful, forgetful*	**patiens**	*tolerant*
cupidus	*desirous*	**perītus**	*skilled*	**studiōsus**	*eager*
memor	*mindful*	**imperītus**	*unskilled*		

> **Rēx cupidus <u>imperiī</u> est.**   *The king is desirous <u>of power</u>.*
> **<u>tuī</u> amōre**   *for love <u>of you</u>*
> **propter <u>mortis</u> timōrem**   *on account of fear <u>of death</u>*

meminī and oblīviscor

The verbs **meminī** and **oblīviscor** use the accusative or the genitive for the direct object. **Meminī** is defective, using the perfect tense for present, pluperfect for any past, and future perfect for the future; **oblīviscor** is deponent.

Meminī means *to remember* or *be mindful of*; **oblīviscor** means *to forget* or *disregard*.

> **Tē bene meminī.**   *I remember you well.*
> **Ipse suī meminerat** (Verr. ii. 136)   *He was mindful of himself (of his own interests)*
> **Oblīvīscere caedis atque incendiōrum**(Cat. i. 6)   *Dismiss the slaughter and conflagrations!*
> **Oblītus sum omnia.**   *I have forgotten everything.*

Vocabulary XXIX

Verbs		Adjectives	
experior, experīrī, expertus sum	*experience, test, try*	doctus,-a,-um	*learned*
oblīviscor, oblīviscī, oblītus sum	*forget*	imperītus,-a,-um	*inexperienced,*
meminī, meminisse	*be mindful of, remember*		*unskilled, ignorant*
redeō, -īre, rediī (-īvī), reditum	*go back, return*	prāvus,-a,-um	*crooked, distorted,*
			improper
Nouns		salvus,-a,-um	*safe, unharmed, well*
nimium,-ī, *n.*	*excess*	uterque, utraque, utrumque	*both, each (of two)*
ars, artis, *f.*	*craft, skill, trade*	**Adverb**	
plūs, plūris, *n.*	*more, too much*	nimis	*too, very much*

Exercise XXIX

A.

1. Nē oblītus sīs mē opem allātūrum esse quō maximē necesse sit.
2. Dīxērunt sē satis pecuniae cupiditātī hominis avārissimī fortasse habēre.
3. Palinūrus nauta ipse negat sē diem noctemque in caelō cernere nec viam in mediō marī meminisse.
4. Multī enim omnis aetātis, omnis ordinis in perīculum vocantur et vocābuntur. (Pliny *Ep.* 10.96.9)
5. Vereor nē sit nihil vērī in eīs quae dīcis.
6. P. Mūrēna mediocrī ingeniō sed magnō studiō rērum veterum, litterārum et studiōsus et nōn imperītus, multae industriae et magnī labōris fuit. (Cicero, *Brutus* 237)
7. Sed uterque nostrum cēdere cōgēbātur magnitūdinī animī ōrātiōnisque gravitātī, cum ille maximā laude omnium vestrum dīxit sē quod vellētis esse factūrum. (Cicero, *Philippics* 9.9)
8. Cum parum praesidiī in locīs mūnītīs esset, proximō diē nōbīscum exīre constituit.
9. Cum in istō iūvene ad faciendum animī satis esset, tamen parum auctōritātis ad persuādendum.

B.

1. He asked me how much water was enough for making the journey.
2. Let each one of you obey the king in order that you may return home safe(ly).
3. There are those who are skilled in all bad arts.
4. It is fitting that we always be mindful of our dignity.
5. You seem to me to forget them as easily as I will forget (them).
6. He is a man very skilled at moving tears.
7. Tell me whether you are learned in all things, or, what is greater, experienced (in all things).
8. Each one of us hoped that he would restrain the improper hopes of others by setting out his reasons.

Lesson XXX

REVIEW: LESSONS XXVII – XXIX

IMPERSONAL CONSTRUCTIONS: Many verbs are used impersonally with an infinitive or a subjunctive clause:

Audīre carmina poētae nōbīs placet. (Ut) audiāmus carmina poētae placet.
It is pleasing to us to hear the songs of the poet.

SUMMARY OF INDIRECT CONSTRUCTIONS:

Construction	Main Verb	Formula	Example
Indirect statement	verb of saying, thinking, knowing, telling, perceiving, showing	Accusative + infinitive	**Dīcit patrem ducere.** *He says that the father is leading.*
Indirect question	verb of saying, thinking, knowing, telling, perceiving, showing, asking	interrogative + subjunctive verb	**Sciō quis sit.** *I know who you are.*
Indirect command	**iubeō, vetō, volō, prohibeō, cōgō, nōlō, patior, cupiō**	accusative of person + infinitive	**Iubet eam sequī.** *He orders her to follow.*
	rogō, ōrō, hortor, moneō, obsecrō	Accusative of person + **ut/nē** + subjunctive	**Eam orat ut sequātur.** *He begs her to follow.*
	imperō, praecipiō, persuādeō	dative of person + **ut/nē** + subjunctive verb	**Eī persuādet ut sequātur.** *He persuades her to follow.*
	petō, postulō	**ā/ab** + ablative of person + **ut/nē** + subjunctive	**Ab eā postulat ut sequātur.** *He demands that she follow.*
Clauses of fearing	**timeō, metuō, vereor**	(positive) **nē** + subjunctive	**Metuō nē rēx moriātur.** *I fear that the king may die.*
		(negative) **ut** or **nē ...nōn** + subjunctive	**Metuō nē rēx nōn moriātur.** *I fear that the king may not die.*

GENITIVE USES:

Partitive	the whole from which part is taken	**fīliae huius gentis** **parum discendī**	*daughters of this tribe* *too little learning*
Description	with an adjective	**exercitus quinque mīlia mīlitum**	*an army of 5,000 soldiers*
Objective	with certain adjectives and nouns to show the object of an action or feeling	**perītī docendī** **timor deōrum**	*skilled in teaching* *fear of the gods*

meminī and **oblīviscor:** with genitive or accusative:

Meam patriam mēminerō.   *I will remember my homeland.*
Nōminis suī oblītus est.   *He forgot his own name.*

60

Exercise XXX

A.

1. Oblītīne estis virtūtis quam senātus tam diū laudābat?
2. Tuae virtūtis meminerimus et confīdēmus tē nostrae fideī nōn oblītum esse.
3. Rogāvit num, etiam sī necesse esset eī id facere, nōn tamen sit ignoscendum.
4. Sī quid fēcerit quod nōn licet, lex pūniet; si quid fēcerit quod licet, sed nōn oportet, pater pūniet.
5. Metuērunt ut multī līberōrum domum redīrent.
6. Fortasse haec ars utrīque nostrum mīranda est, sed certē nōn exercenda.
7. Paulō posteā multās hōrās diēī nāvibus reficiendīs et nautīs convocandīs auxiliō ēgimus.
8. Vereor ut imperītus itineris domum redīre salvus possim.
9. Metus est nōbīs maximus nē trecentī nostrōrum virōrum vī maris interfectī sint.
10. Rūrsus magistrī studium legendō puerōrum expertī sunt, cum illī scrīpta Cicerōnis reperīre possent.
11. Omnia fert aetās, animum quoque. Saepe ego longōs
    cantandō puerum meminī mē condere sōlēs. (Vergil *Eclogues* 9.51-52)
12. Prīmum fac (ut) animō fortī atque magnō sis – ita enim nātus, ita ēdūcātus, ita doctus es…ut tibi id
    faciendum sit; deinde spem quoque habeās firmissimam. (Cicero, *ad Familiares* 6.5.4)
13. Omnia vincit amor, et nōs cēdāmus amōrī. (Vergil *Eclogues* 10.69)

B.

1. Do you remember the difficulties that destroyed our ships last year?
2. I was afraid that you were not able either to protect the city or to bring help.
3. This chief has no strength and fears the sight of us, who come only to speak with him.
4. One of the men had gained possession of the standards but was killed (while) returning to our camp.
5. He persuaded me to leave my fatherland and showed me help for the way, which he had buried in the earth.
6. This leader was of great influence among the Gauls, because they wondered at his strength and bravery.
7. Rumor prefers to report the invented and the distorted rather than the true.
8. We will teach you how those things, which appear to be useful and are not (useful), are hostile to virtue.

Readings and Notes

The readings which follow are from Julius Caesar's *De Bello Gallico*, book 1, chapters 1-29. Each reading is followed by two levels of notes: the first contains vocabulary, arranged in the order in which the words appear in the passage. Many of these words will be learned later in the book as part of the vocabulary lesson for another chapter. Proper nouns and words which have close English derivatives are typically not glossed. The second level of notes contains grammatical help and translated phrases and sentences, listed by the line number where they are found.

Reading I: Julius Caesar describes Gaul

Gallia est omnis dīvīsa in partēs trēs, quārum ūnam *incolunt Belgae*, aliam Aquitānī,	1
tertiam quī ipsōrum *linguā* Celtae, nostrā Gallī appellantur. Hī omnēs linguā, *institūtīs*,	2
lēgibus *inter sē differunt*. Gallōs ab Aquitānīs Garumna flūmen, ā Belgīs Matrōna et	3
Sequāna dīvidit. Hōrum omnium fortissimī sunt Belgae.	4

Gallia, -ae, f. *Gaul*   lingua, -ae, f. *language*
incolō, -ere, incoluī, incultum *inhabit*   institūtum, ī, n. *institution*
Belgae, ārum, m. *Belgians*

3. inter sē differunt: *differ from one another*

Reading II: The Helvetians and their leader Orgetorix

Helvētiī quoque reliquōs Gallōs virtūte *praecēdunt*, quod ferē *cotidiānīs* proeliīs cum	1
Germānīs contendunt, cum *(=ubi)* aut suīs fīnibus eōs *prohibent* aut ipsī in eōrum fīnibus	2
bellum gerunt. *Apud* Helvētiōs longē nōbilissimus fuit et *dītissimus* Orgetorix. Is, *M.*	3
Messalā et M. Pūpiō Pisōne consulibus, regnī *cupiditāte inductus, coniūrātiōnem*	4
nōbilitātis fēcit, et cīvitātī *persuāsit ut* dē fīnibus suīs cum omnibus copiīs *exīrent.*	5

Helvētiī, -ōrum, m. *Helvetians (the Swiss)*   dītissimus, -a, -um *wealthiest*
quoque, conj. *also*   cupiditās, tātis, f. *greed* (+ gen.)
reliquus, -a, -um *the rest of*   indūcō, -ere, -dūxī, -ductum *influence*
praecēdō, -ere, -cessī, -cessum *go before, surpass*   coniūrātiō, -ōnis, f. *conspiracy*
cotidiānus, -a, um *daily*   persuadeō, -ēre, persuāsī, persuāsum (+ dat.) *persuade*
prohibeō, -ēre, -uī, -itum *prevent, keep from*   ut, conj. *to*
apud (+ acc.) prep. *among*   exeō, -īre, exiī, exitum *go out, leave*

4. M. Messalā et M. Pūpiō Pisōne consulibus: *in the consulship of Marcus Messala and Marcus Pupius Piso*

Reading III: The Helvetians make plans to move

Hīs rēbus *adductī* et auctōritāte Orgetorīgis permōtī, (Helvētiī) cōnstituērunt ea quae   1
ad proficiscendum pertinērent comparāre, *iūmentōrum* et *carrōrum* quam maximum   2
numerum *coemere*, *sēmentēs* quam maximās facere ut in itinere *cōpia frūmentī*   3
suppeteret, cum *proximīs* cīvitātibus pācem et amīcītiam cōnfirmāre. *Ad eās rēs*   4
cōnficiendās Orgetorix *dēligitur.*   5

addūcō, -ere, addūxī, adductum *influence*   cōpia, -ae, f. *supply*
iūmentum, ī, n. *mule*   frūmentum, ī, n. *grain*
carrus, ī, m. *cart*   suppetō, -ere, suppetīvī, suppetitum *support*
coemō, -ere, coēmī, coemptum *buy*   proximus, -a, -um *nearest*
sēmentis, -is f. *a planting*

---

2. ad proficiscendum: *for setting out*
4. ad eās rēs cōnficiendās: *for accomplishing these things*
5. dēligitur: *he was chosen.* Caesar often uses the historic present, which may be translated by a past tense if the context requires it. Subjunctives dependent upon an historic present will typically follow secondary sequence.

Reading IV: Orgetorix persuades others to join him

Orgetorīx sibi *lēgātiōnem* ad cīvitātēs suscēpit. In eō itinere persuādet Casticō Sequānō   1
cuius pater regnum in Sequānīs multōs annōs obtinuerat et ā senātū populī Rōmānī   2
amīcus appellātus erat, *ut* regnum in cīvitāte suā *occupāret* quod pater ante habuerat;   3
itemque *Dumnorigī* Aeduō frātrī Dīviciācī. *Inter sē fidem* dant, et regnō *occupātō*   4
per trēs potentissimōs ac *firmissimōs* populōs tōtius Galliae sēsē *potīrī* posse sperant.   5

legatiō, -ōnis, f. *embassy*   occupō (1) *seize*
persuādeō, -ēre, persuāsī, persuāsum *persuade* (+ dat.)   firmus, -a, -um *strong*
Dumnōrix, -igis, m. *Dumnorix*   potior, -īrī, potītus sum *gain possession of* (+ gen.)

---

3. ut occupāret: *to seize*
4. inter sē fidem dant: *they exchange assurances*

Reading V: Orgetorix is tried for his plot

Ea res est Helvētiīs *per indicium* ēnūntiāta. Mōribus suīs Orgetorīgem ex *vinclīs*   1
causam dīcere coēgērunt. *Damnātum poenam sequī oportēbat ut ignī cremārētur.*   2
Diē cōnstitūtā causae *dictiōnis* Orgetorix ad *iudicium* omnem suam familiam   3
undique coēgit: per eōs nē causam dīceret sē ēripuit. Cum cīvitās ob eam rem   4
incitāta armīs *iūs suum exsequī* cōnārētur, Orgetorix mortuus est.   5

iudicium, ī, n. *trial*
dictiō, -ōnis, f. *pleading* (of the case)

---

1. per indicium: *through intelligence*
    vinclīs = vinculīs
2. causam dīcere: *to plead his case*
3. Damnātum poenam sequī oportēbat ut ignī cremārētur:
    it was fitting that the punishment of being burned to death be inflicted on him if condemned.
5. iūs exsequī: *to execute punishment*

Reading VI: The Helvetians prepare to depart

Post eius mortem nihilō minus Helvētiī id quod constituerant facere conantur, ut 1
ē fīnibus suīs exeant. Ubi iam sē ad eam rem parātōs esse *arbitrātī sunt*, *oppida* sua 2
omnia, numerō ad *duodecim*, vīcōs ad *quadringentōs*, reliqua prīvāta aedificia 3
incendunt; *frumentum* omne, *praeterquam* quod sēcum portātūrī erant, *combūrunt*; 4
trium mensum mōlīta cibāria sibi *quemque* domō *efferre* iubent. 5

arbitror (1) *think*	praeterquam *other than*
oppidum, -i, n. *town*	combūrō, -ere, combussī, combustum *burn*
duodecim *twelve*	quisque, quaeque, quidque *each*
quadringentōs *four hundred*	efferō, -ferre, extulī, ēlatum *carry out*
frumentum, -i, n. *grain*	

---

5. trium mensium: *for three months*
    mōlīta cibāria: *edible flour*

Reading VII: The routes out of Helvetia described

Erant *omnīnō* itinera duo, quibus itineribus *domō* exire possent: ūnum per Sequānōs, angustum 1
et difficile, inter *montem Iūram* et flūmen *Rhodanum*; alterum per prōvinciam nostram, multō 2
facilius atque *expeditius*, *proptereā* quod inter fīnēs Helvētiōrum et Allobrogum, quī nuper 3
pacātī erant, Rhodanus fluit, isque *nōn nullīs* locīs *vadō* transitur. Extrēmum oppidum 4
Allobrogum est proximumque Helvētiōrum fīnibus *Genava*. Ex eō oppidō pons ad Helvētiōs 5
pertinet. 6

omnīnō, adv. *altogether*	pacō (1) *pacify, subdue*
Rhodanus, ī, m. *the Rhone river*	nōn nullus, -a, -um *not none, some*
expedītus, -a, -um *unobstructed*	vadum, ī, n. *ford*
proptereā, adv. *especially*	Genava, -ae, f. *Geneva*

---

1. domō : *from home*
2. montem Iūram: a mountain ridge between the Rhone and the Rhine Rivers

Reading VIII: Caesar reacts to the news of the Helvetian movement

Caesarī cum id nūntiātum esset, *eōs* per prōvinciam nostram iter facere cōnārī, *mātūrat ab*   1
urbe proficiscī, et *quam maximīs potest itineribus* in Galliam *ulteriōrem* contendit, et ad   2
Genavam pervēnit. *Prōvinciae tōtī* quam maximum potest mīlitum numerum imperat (erat   3
omnīnō in Galliā ulteriōre *legiō ūna*), pontem quī erat ad Genavam iubet *rescindī*. Ubi dē   4
eius adventū Helvētiī certiōrēs factī sunt, lēgātōs ad eum mittunt nōbilissimōs cīvitātis, quī   5
dīcerent *sibi esse in animō* sine ullō *maleficiō* iter per prōvinciam facere, *proptereā quod*   6
aliud iter habērent nullum.   7

mātūrō (1) *hasten*	maleficium, -ī, n. *harm*
ulteriōr, -ius *farther*	proptereā quod *because*
rescindō, -ere, rescidī, rescissum *tear down*	

---

1. Caesarī: indirect object of the **cum** clause
   eōs: Helvetians
   ab urbe: when the city is not named it usually refers to Rome
2. quam maximīs potest itineribus: *by the longest marches possible*
3. prōvinciae tōtī: dative of the source, *from the whole province*
4. legiō ūna: a legion was made up of 4,200 to 6,000 soldiers
6. sibi esse in animō: *that it was their intention*

Reading IX: Caesar buys himself some time

Caesar, quod *memoriā tenēbat L. Cassium* consulem occīsum exercitumque eius ab   1
Helvētiīs *pulsum* et *sub iugum* missum, *concēdendum* nōn putābat; tamen, ut *spatium*   2
intercēdere posset *dum* mīlitēs quōs imperāverat convenīrent, lēgātīs respondit diem   3
sē *ad dēlīberandum* sumptūrum: *sī quid* vellent, *ad Īdūs Aprīlēs* reverterentur. Intereā eā   4
legiōne quam sēcum habēbat mīlitibusque quī ex prōvinciā convēnerant ā lacū Lemannō   5
ad montem Iūram *mīlia passuum decem novem* mūrum in altitūdinem pedum sēdecim   6
fossamque *perdūcit*. Ubi ea diēs quam constituerat cum lēgātīs vēnit et lēgātī ad eum   7
revertērunt, negat sē mōre et exemplō populī Rōmānī posse iter ullī per prōvinciam   8
dare et, sī vim facere cōnentur, *prohibitūrum* ostendit.   9

pellō, -ere, pepulī, pulsus *defeat*	fossa, ae, f. *ditch*
iugum, ī, n. *yoke*	perdūcō, perdūcere, perdūxī, perductum *build*
sumō, -ere, sumpsī, sumptum *take*	exemplum, ī, n. *example*
lacus, ī, m. *lake*	ostendō, -ere, ostendī, ostensum *show*
sēdecim, indecl. *16*	

---

1. memoriā tenēbat: *remembered*
   L. Cassium: *Lucius Cassius*
2. With **pulsum** and the following participles, **esse** must be understood as part of
   the infinitive in indirect statement **sub iugum**: *under the yoke* (symbolizing subjugation)
   concēdendum esse: *that it should be granted*
3. dum + subjunctive: *until*
4. ad dēlīberandum : *for considering*
   sī quid: *if…anything*
   ad Īdūs Aprīlēs: *towards the Ides of April* (April 13th)
6. mīlia passuum decem novem: *19 miles*
9. (sē) prohibitūrum (esse)

Reading X: The Helvetians gain permission from the Sequani to cross their territory

Relinquēbātur ūna per Sequānōs via, quā *Sequānīs invītīs* propter *angustiās* īre nōn   1
poterant. *Hīs* cum suā sponte *persuādēre* nōn possent, lēgātōs ad Dumnorīgem Aeduum   2
mittunt. Dumnorix *grātiā et largitiōne* apud Sequānōs *plūrimum poterat*, et Helvētiīs erat   3
amīcus, quod ex eā cīvitāte Orgetorīgis fīliam in mātrimōnium dūxerat et, cupiditāte regnī   4
addūctus, *novīs rēbus studēbat* et quam plūrimās cīvitātēs *suō beneficiō* habēre *obstrictās*   5
volēbat. Itaque rem suscēpit et *ā Sequānīs impetrat ut* per fīnēs suōs Helvētiōs īre patiantur.   6

angustia, -ae, f. *narrowness*	studeō, studēre, studuī *be eager for* (+ dat.)
persuadeō, -ēre, persuāsī, persuāsum *persuade* (+ dat.)	obstringō, -ere, -strinxī, strictum *to tie, bind to*
novae rēs, novārum rērum *revolution*	

1. relinquēbātur: the subject is ūna via
   Sequānīs invītīs: conditional use of an ablative modified by a participle: *if the Sequani were unwilling.*
3. grātiā et largitiōne: *because of his charisma and generosity*
   plūrimum poterat: *had the most power* (literally, was most able).
5. suō beneficiō...obstrictās: *bound (to him) because of his kindness*
6. ā Sequānīs impetrat ut: *he gained the request from the Sequani that...*

Reading XI: Caesar reacts to news of the Helvetians' plans

Caesarī *renūntiātur Helvētiīs esse in animō* per agrum Sequānōrum et Aeduōrum iter in   1
Santōnum fīnēs facere, quī nōn longē ā Tolōsātium fīnibus absunt, quae cīvitās est in   2
prōvinciā. *Id sī fīeret*, intellegēbat magnō cum perīculō prōvinciae *futūrum ut* hominēs   3
bellicōsōs, populī Rōmānī inimīcōs, locīs *patentibus* maximēque frumentāriīs fīnitimōs   4
habēret. Ob eās causās *eī mūnitiōnī* quam fēcerat *T. Labiēnum* lēgātum *praefēcit*; ipse in   5
Ītaliam magnīs itineribus contendit, duāsque ibi lēgiōnēs cōnscrībit, et trēs quae circum   6
Aquileiam *hiemābant* ex *hībernīs* ēdūcit et, *quā proximum* iter in ulteriōrem Galliam per   7
Alpēs erat, cum eīs quīnque lēgiōnibus īre contendit.   8

pateō, patēre *lie open, lie exposed*	quā (adv.) *where*
hiēmō (1) *winter, spend the winter*	proximus, -a, -um *nearest*
hīberna, -ōrum n. *winter quarters*	

1. renūntiātur: (impersonal) *it is announced*, the subject is the entire clause "Helvētiīs...facere"
   Helvētiīs esse in animō: *that the Helvetians have in mind* (*intend*)
3. id sī fīeret: *if this were to happen*, as frequently in Latin, the conjunction is delayed to the
   second place in the sentence.
   futūrum (esse): *that it would be...*, impersonal indirect statement;
   ut...habēret: *to have*, the whole clause serves as the subject of futūrum
5. eī mūnitiōnī...T. Labiēnum...praefēcit: he put *Titus Labienus...in charge of the fortification*,
   praeficiō takes a dative and an accusative, "to put x (acc.) in charge of y (dat.)."

Reading XII: The Helvetians move into their neighbors' territories

Helvētiī iam per *angustiās* et fīnēs Sequānōrum suās cōpiās trādūxērunt, et in Aeduōrum   1
fīnēs pervēnerant eōrumque agrōs *populābantur*. Aeduī, cum *sē suaque* ab eīs dēfendere   2
nōn possent, lēgātōs ad Caesarem mittunt *rogātum* auxilium. Eōdem tempore *Aeduī Ambarrī,*   3
necessāriī et consanguineī Aeduōrum, Caesarem certiōrem faciunt *sēsē, dēpopulātīs agrīs,*   4
nōn facile ab oppidīs vim hostium prohibēre. Item Allobrogēs, quī trans Rhodanum vīcōs   5
possessiōnēsque habēbant, fugā *sē* ad Caesarem *recipiunt*, et dēmōnstrant sibi *praeter* agrī   6
solum nihil esse reliquī. Quibus rēbus addūctus Caesar *nōn exspectandum sibi statuit dum,*   7
omnibus fortūnīs sociōrum consumptīs, in Santonōs Helvētiī pervenīrent.   8

angustiae, arum f. *passes*	solum, ī n. *soil*
populor (1) *ravage*	dum (+ subjunctive) *until*
dēpopulō (1) *ravage, pillage*	fortūnae, -ārum *reserves*
praeter (+ accusative) *except*	

---

2. sē suaque: *themselves and their (possessions)*
3. rogātum: *to ask*, supine with a verb of motion (mittunt) expressing purpose
   Aeduī…consanguineī: *the Aeduan Ambarri, friends and relatives*
4. sēsē = sē
   dēpopulātīs agrīs: ablative absolute
6. sē…recipiunt: *they retreat*, literally they take themselves back
7. nōn exspectandum sibi statuit: *he decided that he ought not to wait*
8. omnibus…consumptīs: ablative absolute

Reading XIII: Caesar engages the Helvetians

Flūmen est Arar, quod per fīnēs Aeduōrum et Sequānōrum in Rhodanum *influit, incrēdibīlī*   1
lēnitāte, ita ut oculīs in utram partem fluat *iudicārī* nōn possit. Id Helvētiī *ratibus ac*   2
lintribus iunctīs transībant. Ubi *per explōrātōrēs* Caesar certior factus est *trēs* iam *partēs*   3
cōpiārum Helvētiōs id flūmen trādūxisse, quartam ferē partem *citrā* flūmen Ararim   4
reliquam esse, *dē tertiā vigiliā* cum legiōnibus tribus ē castrīs profectus ad eam partem   5
pervēnit, quae *nōndum* flūmen transīerat. Eōs *impedītōs et inopīnantes* aggressus magnam   6
partem eōrum *concīdit*: reliquī *sēsē fugae mandārunt* atque in proximās silvās *abdidērunt.*   7

influō, -ere, -flūxī, -fluctum *flow in*	iungō, -ere, iunxī, iunctum *join*
incrēdibilis, -e *unbelievable, incredible*	explōrātor, -ōris, m. *scout*
lēnitās, -tātis, f. *slowness*	citrā (+ accusative) *on the near side*
iudicō (1) *judge, determine*	nōndum *not yet*
ratis, -is, f. *raft*	concīdō, -ere, -cīsī, -cīsum *kill*
linter, -tris, f. *boat, skiff*	abdō, -ere, abdidī, abditum *hide*

---

3. trēs partēs: *three quarters*
5. dē tertiā vigiliā: *about the third watch*, the night was divided into 4 watches.
6. impedītōs et inopīnantēs: *loaded down and unsuspecting*
7. sēsē fugae mandārunt: (=mandāvērunt), *entrusted themselves to flight*

Reading XIV: A skirmish and some troop movement

Hōc proeliō factō, reliquās copiās Helvētiōrum ut *consequī* posset, pontem in Arare 1
faciendum cūrat atque ita exercitum trādūcit. *Posterō* diē (Helvētiī) castra ex eō locō 2
movent. Idem facit Caesar, equitātumque omnem ad numerum quattuor mīlium, quem 3
ex omnī prōvinciā et Aeduīs atque eōrum sociīs coactum habēbat, praemittit, quī videant 4
quās in partēs hostēs iter faciant. Quī, *cupidius nōvissimum agmen insecūtī, aliēnō* locō 5
cum equitātū Helvētiōrum proelium committunt; et paucī dē nostrīs *cadunt*. Quō proeliō 6
sublātī Helvētiī audācius *subsistere* nōn numquam et nōvissimō agmine proeliō nostrōs 7
lacessere coepērunt. Caesar suōs a proeliō continēbat, ac *satis habēbat in praesentiā* 8
hostem *rapīnīs pabulātiōnibus populatiōnibusque* prohibēre. Ita diēs *circiter* quindecim 9
iter fēcērunt *utī* inter nōvissimum hostium agmen et nostrum prīmum nōn amplius quīnīs 10
aut sēnīs mīlibus passuum *interesset*. 11

consequor *pursue*	subsistō, -sistere, substitī, -- *stand firm*
posterus, -a, -um *next*	lacessō, -ere, lacessīvī, lacessītum *harass*
aliēnus, -a, -um *strange*	coepī, coepisse *began*
cadō, -ere, cecidī, cāsum *fall*	circiter (+ accusative) *about*
tollō, -ere, sustulī, sublātum *uplifted, exhilarated*	utī (= ut) *that*

2. faciendum cūrat: *he saw to building*
5. cupidius nōvissimum agmen insecūtī: *having pursued the rearguard too eagerly*
8. satis habēbat in praesentiā: *had enough (to do) in the present (circumstances)*
9. rapīnīs, pabulātiōnibus populatiōnibusque: *from pillaging and ravaging the crops*
11. interesset: *there was a distance of...*

Reading XV: Caesar looks for the best approach

(Caesar) ab explōrātōribus certior factus hostēs sub monte *consēdisse* mīlia passuum 1
ab *ipsius* castrīs *octo*, quālis esset natura montis et quālis *in circuitū ascensus*, quī 2
cognoscerent mīsit. Renūntiātum est facilem esse. Dē tertiā vigiliā *T.* Labiēnum, lēgātum 3
prō praetōre, cum duābus lēgiōnibus et eīs ducibus quī iter cognōverant summum *iugum* 4
montis ascendere iubet; *quid suī consilī sit* ostendit. Ipse dē quartā vigiliā eōdem itinere 5
quō hostēs ierant ad eōs contendit equitātumque omnem ante sē mīsit. *P.* Considius, quī 6
reī mīlitāris perītissimus habēbātur, cum explōrātōribus praemittitur. 7

consīdō, -ere, -sēdī, -sessum *settle*	iugum, ī, n. *ridge*
ascensus, ūs m. *ascent*	

2. ipsius: *Caesar's*
   in circuitū: *on all sides*
3. T.: *Titius*
4. prō praetōre: *with the rank of praetor*
5. quid suī consilī sit: *what his plan is*
6. P.: *Publius*

Reading XVI: Caesar receives bad intelligence

Prīmā luce, cum summus mons ā Labiēnō tenērētur, *ipse* ab hostium castrīs nōn longius   1
mille et *quingentīs* passibus abesset, *neque*, ut posteā ex captīvīs *comperit*, aut ipsius   2
adventus aut Labiēnī cognitus esset, Considius *equō admissō* ad eum *accurrit*, dīcit montem   3
ab hostibus tenērī: id sē ā Gallicīs armīs atque *insignibus* cognōvisse. Caesar suās cōpiās in   4
proximum collem *subdūcit*, aciem instruit. Labiēnus, ut erat eī praeceptum ā Caesare nē   5
proelium committeret, nisi ipsius cōpiae prope hostium castra vīsae essent, monte occupātō   6
nostrōs *exspectābat* proeliōque *abstinēbat*. Multō dēnique diē per explōrātōrēs Caesar   7
cognōvit et montem ā suīs tenērī, et Helvētiōs castra mōvisse, et Considium timōre   8
perterritum quod nōn vīdisset *prō vīsō sibi renūntiāsse*. Eō diē hostēs sequitur, et mīlia   9
passuum tria ab eōrum castrīs castra pōnit.   10

quingentī, -ae, a *five hundred*
neque *nor*
comperiō, -īre, comperī, compertum *find out*
accurrō, -ere, accurrī, accursum *run up to*

insignia, ōrum, n. *standards*
subdūcō, -ere, -dūxī, ductum *withdraw*
exspectō (1) *wait for*
abstineō, -ēre, abstinuī, abstentum *refrain from*

---

1. ipse: Caesar
3. equō admissō: *with his horse at a gallop*
9. prō vīsō: *as (something he had) seen*
   sibi: to Caesar
   renūntiāsse = renūntiāvisse

Reading XVII: The Romans and the Helvetians prepare for battle

Postridiē eius diēī, quod ā Bibracte, oppidō Aeduōrum longē maximō et *cōpiōsissimō*,   1
nōn *amplius* mīlibus passuum XVIII aberat, reī frūmentāriae *prospiciendum* existimāvit: 2
iter ab Helvētiīs *āvertit* ac Bibracte īre contendit. Ea rēs per fūgitīvōs hostibus nūntiātur.   3
Helvētiī, *seu* quod timōre perterritōs Rōmānōs discēdere ā sē *existimārent, sive eō quod*   4
rē frūmentāriā interclūdī posse confīderent, *commūtātō* consiliō atque itinere *conversō*   5
nostrōs insequī ac *lacessere coepērunt*. Postquam id animum advertit, cōpiās suās Caesar   6
in proximum collem subdūcit, equitātumque quī sustinēret hostium impetum mīsit. Ipse   7
interim *in colle mediō triplicem aciem instrūxit* legiōnum quattuor veterānōrum; sed in   8
summō iugō duās legiōnēs quās in Galliā citeriōre *proximā* conscrīpserat et omnia auxilia   9
collocārī, ac tōtum montem ab eīs quī in *superiōre* aciē constiterant mūnīrī iussit. Helvētiī   10
cum omnibus suīs carrīs secūtī impedimenta in ūnum locum contulērunt; ipsī *confertissimā*   11
aciē, *reiectō* nostrō equitātū, *phalange* factā sub prīmam nostram aciem *successērunt*.   12

cōpiōsus, -a, -um *affluent*
amplior, -ius *more*
āvertō, -ere, avertī, aversum *turn aside*
seu...sive *whether...or*
commūtō (1) *change*
existimō (1) *think*
convertō, -ere, versī, versum *change*
lacessō, -ere, lacessī, lacessītum *harass*

coepī, coepisse *began*
collocō (1) *station, place*
superior, -ius *higher*
confertissimus, -a, -um *very dense*
reiciō, -ere, reiēcī, reiectum *drive back*
phalanx, phalangis, f. *phalanx* (a battle formation of
   infantry)
succēdō, -ere, -cessī, -cessum *move up*

---

1. postridiē eius diēī: *on the day after that day*
2. prospiciendum: *(they) should look for*
4. eō quod: *for the reason that*
8. in colle mediō: *on the mid-point of the hill, half-way up the hill*
9. proximā: *recently*

Reading XVIII: The battle

Caesar prīmum *suō, deinde* omnium ex conspectū *remōtīs* equīs, ut *aequātō* omnium   1
perīculō spem fugae tolleret, *cohortātus* suōs proelium commīsit. Mīlitēs ē locō superiōre   2
pīlīs missīs facile hostium phalangem *perfrēgērunt*. Eā *disiectā, gladiīs dēstrictīs* in eōs   3
impetum fēcērunt. *Gallīs magnō ad pugnam* erat *impedimentō quod plūribus* eōrum *scutīs*   4
ūnō *ictū* pīlōrum *transfīxīs* et *colligātīs*, cum ferrum sē *inflexisset*, neque *ēvellere* neque   5
sinistrā impedītā *satis commodē* pugnāre poterant; *multī ut praeoptārent* scutum manū   6
ēmittere et *nūdō* corpore pugnāre. Tandem vulneribus dēfessī et *pedem referre* et, quod   7
mons *suberat* circiter mille passuum, *eō* sē recipere coepērunt. Captō monte et   8
succēdentibus nostrīs, Boiī et Tulingī, quī agmen hostium *claudēbant* et *nōvissimīs*   9
praesidiō erant, ex itinere nostrōs *latere apertō* agressī *circumvēnēre*, et id *conspicātī*   10
Helvētiī *rursus instāre* et proelium *redintegrāre* coepērunt.   11

deinde *then*	nūdus, -a, -um *bare*
removeō, -ēre, -mōvī, mōtum *remove*	subsum, -esse, -fuī *be near*
aequō (1) *make equal*	eō *to that place, thither*
cohortor (1) *encourage*	succēdō, -ere, -cessī, cessum *move up*
pīlum, ī, n. *spear*	claudō, -ere, clausī, clausum *enclose*
perfringō, -ere, -frēgī, -fractum *smash*	nōvissimus, -a, -um *last*
disiciō, -ere, -iēcī, -iectum *scatter*	praesidium, ī, n. *guard*
ictus, -ūs, m. *blow*	conspicor (1) *catch sight of*
colligō, -ere, -lēgī, -lectum *bound together*	rursus *again*
inflectō, -ere, -flexī, -flectum *bend aside*	instō -āre, -stitī, -statūrus *threaten*
ēvellō, -ere, -vulsī, -vulsum *pull out*	redintegrō (1) *rejoin*
sinister, -tra, -trum *the left*	

---

1. suō: suo equō remōtō
3. gladiīs dēstrictīs: *with drawn swords*
4. Gallīs magnō…impedimentō: double dative *"it was a great hindrance to the Gauls…"*
   ad pugnam: *"to fighting"*
   quod…poterant: this clause is the subject of "erat"; *the fact that*
   plūribus…scutīs…transfīxīs: *several shields being pierced*
6. satis commodē: *very well*
   multi ut praeoptarent *with the result that many preferred*
7. pedem referre: *retreat*
10. latere apertō: *the open (unprotected) flank*
   circumvēnēre: = circumvēnērunt

Reading XIX

Ita *ancipitī* proeliō diū atque acriter *pugnātum est.* Diūtius cum sustinēre nostrōrum impetūs 1
nōn possent, alterī sē, ut coeperant, in montem recēpērunt, alterī ad impedimenta et *carrōs* 2
suōs *sē contulērunt.* Nam hōc tōtō proeliō, cum ab hōrā septimā ad vesperam pugnātum sit, 3
āversum hostem vidēre nēmō potuit. Ad *multam noctem* etiam ad impedimenta pugnātum 4
est. Diū cum esset pugnātum, impedimentīs castrīsque nostrī potītī sunt. Ibi Orgetorīgis filia 5
 atque ūnus ē filiīs captus est. Ex eō proeliō circiter hominum mīlia Cxxx *superfuērunt,* 6
eāque tōtā nocte *continenter* iērunt: nullam partem noctis itinere intermissō in fīnēs 7
Lingōnum diē quartō pervēnērunt. Caesar ad Lingōnās litterās nūntiōsque mīsit, *nē eōs* 8
frūmentō nēve aliā rē iuvārent: quī sī iūvissent, sē eōdem locō quō Helvētiōs *habitūrum.* 9

anceps, ancipitis *doubtful* supersum, -esse, -fuī *be left over, survive*
carrus, ī, m. *cart* continenter *constantly*

1. pugnātum est: *they fought,* impersonal construction, literally *it was fought.*
3. se contulerunt: *they went* (lit., *they took themselves*)
4. ad multam noctem: *until late at night*
8. nē...iūvissent: indirect command, (*saying*) *that they were not to help them with grain or in any other way;* (*and that*)
   if anyone did help...
9. habitūrum: habitūrum esse, infinitive in indirect speech dependent on "litterās nuntiōsque mīsit."

Reading XX: The Helvetians surrender and return home

Helvētiī omnium rērum inopiā adductī lēgātōs dē *dēditiōne* ad Caesarem mīsērunt. In fīnēs 1
suōs, unde erant profectī, revertī iussit. In castrīs Helvētiōrum *tabulae* repertae sunt litterīs 2
Graecīs *confectae,* et ad Caesarem relātae, quibus in tabulīs *nōminātim ratiō* confecta erat, 3
quī numerus domō exīisset eōrum, quī arma ferre possent, et item *separātim* puerī, senēs, 4
mulierēsque. Quārum omnium rērum *summa* erat *capitum* Helvētiōrum mīlia CCLXIII, 5
Tulingōrum mīlia XXXVI, Lātōvīcōrum XIIII, Raurīcōrum XXIII, Boiōrum XXXII; ex hīs quī 6
arma ferre possent, ad mīlia nōnāgintā duo. Summa omnium fuērunt ad mīlia CCCLXVIII. 7
Eōrum quī domum rediērunt *censū habitō,* ut Caesar imperāverat, repertus est numerus 8
mīlium C et decem. 9

dēditiō, -ōnis, f. *surrender* separātim *separately*
tabula, -ae, f. *tablet, writing tablet* summa, -ae, f. *sum*
nōminātim *name by name* caput, capitis, n. *head; person*
ratiō, -ōnis, f. *account*

3. confectae: *written*
8. censū habitō: *having taken a census*

Reading XXI: Vergil's Fourth *Eclogue*, lines 1-7, the return of the Golden Age

Sīcelidēs Mūsae, paulō maiora *canāmus*!	1
Nōn omnīs *arbusta* iūvant humilēsque *myrīcae*;	2
sī canimus *silvās*, silvae sint consule dignae.	3
Ultima Cūmaeī venit iam carminis aetās;	4
magnus ab integrō *saeclōrum* nascitur ordō.	5
iam redit et Virgō, redeunt *Saturnia* regna,	6
iam nova *prōgenies caelō* demittitur *altō*.	7

canō, -ere, cecinī, cantum *sing*
arbustum, -i, n. *orchard*
myrīca, -ae, f. *tamarisk* (a kind of shrub)
ultimus, -a, -um *last, final*

Cūmaeus, -a, -um *Cumaean*
saeclum, -i, n. *age, generation*
Saturnius, -a, -um *Saturnian*
progenies, -eī f. *offspring*

---

3. silvas: direct object of "canimus" *if we sing (about) the forest*
5. saeclōrum: genitive with "ordō"
7. caelō...altō: ablative of place from which

Reading XXII: Vergil's Fourth *Eclogue*, lines 8-14, the birth of a baby

Tu modo nascentī puerō, quō *ferrea* prīmum	1
dēsinet ac *tōtō* surget gens *aurea mundō*,	2
casta fave *Lūcīna*: tuus iam *regnat* Apollo.	3
Tēque adeō decus hoc *aevī*, *tē consule*, inībit,	4
Polliō, et incipient magnī procēdere *mensēs*;	5
tē duce, *sī qua* manent sceleris *uestīgia* nostrī,	6
irrita perpetuā solvent *formīdine* terrās.	7

ferreus, -a, -um *iron, made of iron*
dēsinō, -ere, dēsiī, dēsitum *cease*
aureus, -a, -um *golden*
mundus, -i m. *world*
castus, -a, -um *chaste, pure*
Lūcīna, -ae f. *Juno*
regnō (1) *reign, rule*

adeō *what is more*
aevum, -i, n. *age*
mensis, -is m. *month*
vestīgium, -i n. *trace*
irritus, -a, -um *without effect*
perpetuus, -a, -um *unending*
formīdō, -inis, f. *fear*

---

1. Tu: subject of "fave" (line 3)
2. tōtō..mundō: *through the whole world*, ablative of place where
4. Tē...tē consule: ablative absolute, "tē" repeated for emphasis
6. si qua...vestīgia: *if any traces...*
7. irrita: nominative plural

Reading XXIII: Valerius Maximus, 3.7.4, Livius Salinator spares the Gauls and Ligurians

Liviī Salīnātōris *aeternae* memoriae *tradendus* animus. quī cum Hasdrubālem	1
exercitumque Poenōrum in Umbriā *dēlesset* et eī dīcerētur Gallōs ac Ligurēs ex aciē	2
sine ducibus et signīs *sparsōs* ac *pālantēs* parvā manū *opprimī* posse, respondit in hoc	3
eīs *oportēre* parcī, nē hostibus tantae *clādis* domesticī nuntiī dēessent.	4

aeternus, -a, -um *eternal*
tradō, -ere, tradidī, traditum *hand down, relate*
spargō, -ere, sparsī, sparsum *scatter*
pālō (1) *wander*

opprimō, -ere, oppressī, oppressum *overwhelm*
oportet, ēre, oportuit *be necessary, proper* (impersonal)
clādes, -is f. *disaster.*

---

2. dēlesset = dēlēvisset

Reading XXIV: Sallust describes Catiline

L. Catilīna, nobilī *genere* nātus, fuit magnā vī et animī et corporis, sed ingeniō malō	1
prāvōque. Huic ab *adulescentiā* bella *intestīna caedes rapīnae* discordia cīvilis grāta *fuēre*,	2
ibique *iuventūtem* suam exercuit. Corpus patiens *inediae algoris vigiliae, supra quam*	3
cuīquam credībile est. animus audāx *subdolus varius, cuius rei libet simulator ac*	4
dissimulator, aliēnī *appetens,* suī *profūsus,* ardens in cupiditātibus; satis ēloquentiae,	5
sapientiae parum. vastus animus *immoderāta incrēdibilia* nimis alta semper cupiēbat.	6
hunc post dominationem L. Sullae *libīdō* maxima *invāserat* reī pūblicae capiendae;	7
neque id quibus modīs *assequerētur, dum* sibi regnum parāret, *quicquam pensī habēbat.*	8
Agitābātur magis magisque *in diēs* animus *ferox inopiā reī familiāris* et *conscientiā*	9
scelerum, *quae utraque* eīs *artibus* auxerat, quās *suprā memorāvī.*	10

genus, generis, n. *family*
adulescentia, -ae, f. *adolescence*
intestīnus, -a, -um *internal*
caedes, -is, f. *murder*
rapīna, -ae, f. *pillaging*
iuventūs, -tūtis, f. *youth*
inedia, -ae, f. *fasting*
algor, -is, m. *cold*
vigiliae, -arum, f. *sleeplessness*
subdolus, -a, -um *cunning*
varius, -a, -um *untrustworthy*

appetens, -entis *striving for*
profūsus, -a, -um *profligate*
immoderātus, -a, -um *excessive*
incrēdībilis, -e *fantastic*
libīdō, libidinis, f. *desire*
invādō, -ere, invāsī, invāsum *invade*
ferox, ferōcis *fierce*
conscientia, -ae, f. *guilt*
ars, artis, f. *skill, quality*
suprā *above*
memoro, (1) *mention*

---

1. L. – Lucius
2. fuēre = fuērunt
3. suprā...est: *beyond what is credible to anyone*
4. cuius...dissimulātor: *a phoney and dissembler about anything at all*
8. assequerētur: *he would acquire*
   dum: *so long as*
   quicquam pensī habēbat: *did he consider it of any importance*
9. in diēs: *day after day*
   inopiā reī familiāris: *by the lack of family property*

Rules of Syntax for New Third Steps in Latin

AGREEMENT

THE FIRST RULE OF CONCORD. A verb agrees with its subject in person and number.

> **Ego vocō.** *I call.*   **Tū vocās.** *You call.*   **Puer vocat.** *The boy calls.*

1. A verb with a compound subject (two or more subjects joined by **et**, **-que**, or **atque**) may be plural or may agree with the nearest subject in person and number.
   > **Puer et puella vocant.** *The boy and the girl call.*
   > **Mīlitēs et dux vēnit.** *The leader and (his) troops came.*

2. A verb with compound subjects of different persons will generally agree with the lower person (1ˢᵗ person takes precedence over 2ⁿᵈ and 3ʳᵈ persons, and 2ⁿᵈ over 3ʳᵈ) and will always be plural.
   > **Ego et tū vocāmus.** *You and I call.*   **Tū et puella vocant.** *You and the girl call.*

3. A verb with subjects joined by a disjunction (**aut** or **neque**) is singular.
   > **Puer aut puella vocat.** *The boy or the girl calls.*

4. GAPPING. A verb that belongs to two or more subjects in separate clauses will agree with one and will be understood with the others.
   > **Puer vocat, nōn puella.** *The boy calls, the girl does not (call).*

5. The verb of a relative clause whose subject is a relative pronoun agrees in person and number with the antecedent of the relative pronoun.
   > **Vōs, puellae, quī tristēs estis, amābitis.** *You, girls, who are sad, will love.*

THE SECOND RULE OF CONCORD. An adjective (as well as an adjectival pronoun or participle) agrees with the noun it modifies in case, number, and gender.

> **bonus nauta,** *good sailor;* **bona puella,** *good girl;* **bona arma,** *good weapons.*

1. An attributive adjective that modifies two or more nouns will generally agree with the nearest noun.
   > **ācerrima īra et studium** *the sharpest anger and zeal.*

2. A predicate adjective that modifies two or more nouns will generally be plural but may agree with the nearest or the most important. (Masculine is most important of those with life, neuter of those without life.)
   > **Puer et puella sunt bonī.** *The boy and girl are good.*
   > **Murus et porta dē caelō tacta sunt.** *The wall and the gate are struck by lightning.*

THE THIRD RULE OF CONCORD. The relative pronoun agrees with its antecedent in number and gender; its case is determined by its use in the relative clause.

> **Puella, quam puer amat, est fēlix.** *The girl, whom the boy likes, is happy.*

Apposition. An appositive is a noun describing another noun and agrees with it in case.

> **Hōs librōs, pulchrum dōnum, heri accēpī.** *Yesterday I received these books, a beautiful gift.*

Predicate Noun. With sum and other linking verbs, a noun in the predicate which describes the subject will agree with it in case.

> **Agricola erat vir fortis.** *The farmer was a brave man.*
> **Discipulus bonus esse vidētur etiam pius fīlius.** *The student seems a dutiful son also.*

CASES USAGE

Nominative

1. **Subject**. The subject of a finite verb is in the nominative case.
   Puella vocat. *The girl calls.*

2. **Predicate**. The predicate noun or adjective of a finite form of the verb **sum**, or of a verb of *seeming* or *becoming*, or of a passive verb of *making, choosing, showing, thinking,* or *calling* is in the nominative case.
   Puer servus est. *The boys is a slave.*   **Vir cōnsul factus est.** *The man was made consul.*

Genitive

1. **The Genitive of Possession**. A genitive is used to denote the person or thing to whom or which an object, quality, feeling, or action belongs.
   patria rēgis   *the homeland of the king / the king's homeland*

2. **The Partitive Genitive**. The genitive is used to express the whole element, from which the noun is taken.
   pars turbae   *part of the crowd*
   multī mīlitum   *many of the soldiers*

3. **The Genitive of Description**. The genitive expresses a quality or characteristic. This genitive must be modified by an adjective. The genitive of quality is used for numerical measurements.
   mūrus quinque pedum   *a wall of five feet*
   vir magnae audaciae   *a man of great boldness*

4. **The Objective Genitive**. The genitive is found with many adjectives (**avidus, cupidus, memor, immemor, perītus, imperītus, patiens, studiōsus**) and in many noun phrases to show the object of an action or feeling.
   Rēx cupidus imperiī est.   *The king is desirous of power.*
   tuī amōre   *for love of you*

Dative

1. **Indirect Object**. A noun or pronoun indirectly affected by the action of the verb is in the dative case.
   Rēx arma nautae dat. *The king gives the arms to the sailor.*

2. **Dative with Special Adjectives**. Adjectives denoting *likeness, nearness, fitness, friendliness,* and their opposites take a dative.
   Rēx amīcus mihi est. *The king is friendly to me.*

3. **Datives with Special Verbs**. Certain special verbs take the dative case (**crēdō, faveō, ignoscō, noceō, parcō, pareō, placeō, studeō**).
   Fīliī matribus paruērunt. *The sons obeyed (their) mothers.*

4. **Dative of Possession**. The dative is used with the verb **sum** to show possession and **dēsum** to show lack. The possessor is in the dative; the possession is in the nominative.
   Vōbīs sunt librī. *You have the books.*

5. Dative of Purpose. The dative is used to express *why* or *for what purpose* something is done.
   Senātus erat magnae cūrae. *The senate was a great care.*

6. **Dative of Reference**. The dative shows the person affected by the action or service rendered.
   Hoc mihi fēcit. *He did this for me.*

7. **Double Dative**. The Double Dative is the pairing of the Dative of Purpose and the Dative of Reference in the same clause.
   Hoc auxiliō mihi fēcit. *He did this as a help to me.*

75

Accusative

1. **Direct Object**. The direct object of a transitive verb is in the accusative case.
   Urbem capit. *He captures the city.*

2. **Accusative of Place to Which (Place Whither)**. The object of a prepositional phrase showing motion to or towards something is in the accusative case. These constructions use the prepositions **ad** or **in**. With the names of cities, of small islands, of towns, **domō** and **rūre,** the preposition is regularly omitted.
   In Ītaliam vēnit. *He came to Italy.*

3. **Accusative of Duration of Time**. Duration of time (or time how long?) is expressed by the accusative without a preposition.
   Rēx decem annōs fuit. *He was king for ten years.*

4. **Double Accusatives.** Verbs of *asking, demanding, teaching,* and *concealing* take two accusatives, one of the person, one of the thing.
   Tē illud docuit. *He taught you that.*

5. **Predicate Accusative.** Verbs of *naming, making, taking, choosing,* and *showing* (factitve verbs) take two accusatives, a direct object and its complement. The two accusatives refer to the <u>same</u> person or thing.
   Urbem Rōmam vocāvit. *He called the city Rome.*

6. **Subject Accusative.** The subject of an infinitive is regularly in the accusative.
   Vult rēgīnam dīcere. *He wants the queen to speak.*

7. **Accusative with Prepositions**. The accusative is used with many prepositions, the most important being: **ad, ante, circum, in, inter, ob, per, post, propter, super.**

Ablative

1. **Ablative of Means or Instrument.** The means or instrument by which something is done is expressed by the ablative without a preposition.
   Mūrus saxīs mūnitus est. *The wall was built with stones.*

2. **Ablative of Personal Agent.** The person by whom something is done is expressed by the ablative case with the preposition **ā/ab**.
   Mūrus ā Rōmānīs mūnitus est. *The wall was built by the Romans.*

3. **Ablative of Accompaniment.** Accompaniment is often expressed by **cum** followed by the ablative. **Cum** regularly becomes enclitic with **mē, tē, sē, nōbīs, vōbīs, quō, quā, quibus.**
   Cum sociīs pugnat. *He fights with his comrades.*
   Puerī mēcum pugnant. *The boys fight with me.*

4. **Ablative of Place Where.** Place where or in which is expressed by the ablative with the prepositions **in, pro** and **sub** (and rarely by the accusative with **ad**). With the names of cities, small islands, town and **dōmus** and **rūs**, use the locative case.
   Fāma in caelō volāvit. *Rumor flew in the sky.* (**Ad flūmen stetit**. *He stood at the river.*)

5. **Ablative of Place from Which or Motion Away From**. Place from which or motion away from is expressed by the ablative with the prepositions **ā/ab, dē**, or **ē/ex**. With the names of cities, of small islands, of towns, **domō** and **rūre,** the preposition is regularly omitted.
   Ex urbe vēnit. *He came from the city.*
   Rōmā vēnit. *He came from Rome.*

6. **Ablative of Time When.** Time when is expressed by the ablative without a preposition.
   Eō tempore urbem cēpit. *At that time, he captured the city.*

7. **Ablative of Comparison.** In comparative constructions without **quam**, the second noun or pronoun compared is in the ablative case.

> **Epistula est brevior librō**. *The letter is shorter than the book.*

8. **Ablative of Degree of Difference.** In comparative constructions, the degree or measure of difference in the things compared is expressed by the ablative without a preposition.

> **Mare est multō altius quam flumen.** *The sea is much deeper than the river.*

9. **Ablative of Cause.** The cause or reason for the action is expressed by the ablative without a preposition.

> **Factīs culpātur.** *He is blamed for his deeds.*

10. **Ablative of Manner.** The manner of an action(answers: how?) is expressed in a prepositional phrase consisting of **cum** and an ablative. When the ablative object is modified by an adjective, the **cum** may be omitted. If the **cum** is not omitted it is often placed between the adjective and its object.

> **Epistula cum cūrā scripta est.** *The letter is written with care (carefully).*
> **Epistula magnā cūrā scripta est.** *The letter is written with great care (very carefully).*

11. **Ablative with Special Verbs.** The following verbs and their compounds take an ablative rather than a direct object. (**fungor, fruor, potior, ūtor, vēscor**)

12. **Ablative of Separation.** With verbs of *preventing, depriving, removing, freeing, lacking* etc., the ablative is used. The prepositions **a/ab** or **ē/ex** are sometimes used.

> **Caesar hostīs ā nostrīs fīnibus prohibet.** *Caesar keeps the enemy from our borders.*

13. **Ablative with Prepositions.** The ablative object is used with many prepositions, the most important being: **abs (ab, ā) cum, dē, prae, prō, sine, sub, ex (or ē).**

14. **Ablative of Specification.** To further specify a characteristic of someone or something, the ablative case is used. **Nōmine** is commonly used in this situation.

> **Puer similis patrī fide est.** *The boy is like his father in loyalty.*

15. **Ablative of Description.** The ablative is used to express a descriptive characteristic of a person or thing.

> **Vir magnā virtūte est.** *He is a man of great courage.*

Locative Case

1. With the names of cities, small islands, and towns, and with **domus** and **rūs**, the locative case is used to express place where.

> **Rōmam pugnat.** *He fights at Rome.*

Vocative Case

1. The vocative case is used for direct address and is often offset by commas in English.

> **Venī domum, mī fīlī!** *Come home, my son!*

VERB TENSES

Present

1. The **Present Tense** shows an action as ongoing or states something that applies to all time.
   Puellam vocat. *He is calling / calls / does call the girl.*
   A. **Dum** takes the present tense but shows past action.
      Dum puellam exspectat, mīlitēs pugnāvērunt.
      While he was waiting for the girl, the soldiers fought.

Imperfect

1. The **Imperfect Tense** shows continued or repeated action in the past.
   Vocābat. *He was calling / kept calling / used to call.*

Future

1. The **Future Tense** shows continuing or indefinite action in the future.
   Vocābit. *He will call.*

Perfect

1. The **Perfect Tense**, though it has one form, has two separate uses.
   A. The **Perfect** shows a continuous past action ending in the present. This corresponds with the English present perfect and uses the auxiliary verb "has / have".
      Vocāvit. *He has called.*
   B. The **Aorist** shows the completion of an action with no reference to its duration.
      Vocavit. *He called / did call.*

Pluperfect

1. The **Pluperfect Tense** shows an action completed in the past and corresponds to the English past perfect. It always uses the auxiliary verb "had".
   Vocāverat. *He had called.*

Future Perfect

1. The **Future Perfect Tense** shows the completion of an action in the future.
   Vocāverit. *He will have called.*

VERB MOODS

Indicative

1. The **Indicative Mood** is used to state a fact or ask a question when there is no modification of the verbal idea except tense.
   Puella vocat. *The girl calls.*   **Puella vocābat.** *The girl was calling.*
   Puella vocābit. *The girl will call.*

2. In temporal clauses introduced by **antequam, postquam, ut**, and **ubi** (when), the indicative mood is used.
   Postquam Caesar pervēnit, puerōs vocavit. *After Caesar arrived, he called the boys.*

Subjunctive

1. The **Subjunctive mood** is used mainly in subordinate clauses. It can express command, purpose, result, characteristic, indirect question, or circumstance.

Purpose Clause: A purpose clause is a subordinate clause which gives the reason behind an action. The relative clause of purpose uses a relative pronoun to introduce a purpose clause with a subjunctive verb.

> **Veniō ut audiam.** *I come to hear.*
> **Epistulās scrībit quibus tē laudet.** *He writes letters to praise you.*

Result Clause: A result clause is a subordinate clause which explains the outcome of an action or situation.

> **Rēx tam īrātus est ut fīlius eum timeat.** *The king is so angry that (his) son fears him.*

Cum Clause: **Cum** can be a subordinating conjunction meaning *when, after, since,* or *although*. With causal or concessive clauses and temporal clauses in secondary sequence, a subjunctive verb is used.

> **Cum librum habe, legō.** *When(ever) I have a book, I read.*
> **Cum hostīs videāmus, currimus.** *Since we see the enemy, we run.*
> **Cum hostīs nōn vīdissēmus, tamen currēbāmus.** *Although we had not seen the enemy,*
> *nevertheless we were running.*

2. **Hortatory/Jussive Subjunctive.** The present subjunctive used as the main verb indicates the ideas of encouragement, wish, or command. The hortatory/ jussive subjunctive is translated into English with "let" or "may."

> **Moneāmus rēgem.** *Let us warn the king.*

3. The subjunctive mood is also used to express a negative command using **nē** and the 2nd person perfect.

> **Nē eum cēperītis!** *Don't seize him!*

Imperative

1. The **Imperative Mood** is commonly used to express commands or entreaties.

> **Lege librōs multōs!** *Read many books!*

VERBAL USAGES

Participle

1. **Participle.** A participle is a verbal adjective. As a verb, it may be followed by an object ; as an adjective, it must agree with the noun it modifies in case, number, and gender.

   A. The PRESENT ACTIVE PARTICIPLE shows action at the same time as the main verb.

   > **Puellam sedentem in silvā vīdī.** *I saw the girl sitting in the forest.*

   B. The PERFECT PASSIVE PARTICIPLE shows action before the time of the main verb.

   > **Puella, in silvā vīsa, puerum vocāvit.** *The girl, seen in the forest, called the boy.*

   C. The FUTURE ACTIVE PARTICIPLE shows action that is after the time of the main verb.

   > **Puella, in silvā moritūra, caput tēxit.** *The girl, about to die in the woods, covered her head.*

2. **Ablative Absolute.** The ablative absolute is a Latin phrase describing circumstances surrounding the action of the main clause. It consists of at least two words in the ablative case, usually a noun and a participle. The noun in the ablative absolute cannot be the same as the subject or direct object of the main clause.

   > **Duce vulnerātō, mīlitēs fūgērunt.** *The leader having been wounded, the soldiers fled.*

Infinitive

1. **Complementary Infinitive.** The complementary infinitive is a verb form that completes the meaning of the main verb without a subject accusative.

   A. Verbs needing to be completed include verbs of *being able, deciding, daring, undertaking, beginning, hesitating, learning,* and *fearing.*

      Puella vidēre potest. *The girl is able to see.*

2. **Infinitive of Indirect Statement.** The infinitive is used after verbs of *saying, thinking, knowing, showing, believing,* or *perceiving* to express an indirect statement.

   A. The PRESENT INFINITIVE expresses action at the same time as the main verb.

      Dīcit puellam rēgīnam esse. *He says(that) the girl is the queen.*
      Dixit puellam rēgīnam esse. *He said (that) the girl was the queen.*
      Dīcet puellam rēgīnam esse. *He will say (that) the girl is the queen.*

   B. The PERFECT INFINITIVE expresses action prior to that of the main verb.

      Dīcit puellam rēgīnam fuisse. *He says (that) the girl was the queen.*
      Dixit puellam rēgīnam fuisse. *He said (that) the girl had been the queen.*
      Dīcet puellam rēgīnam fuisse. *He will say (that) the girl would be the queen.*

   C. The FUTURE INFINITIVE expresses action after that of the main verb.

      Dīcit puellam rēgīnam futūram esse. *He says (that) the girl will be the queen.*
      Dixit puellam rēgīnam futūram esse. *He said (that) the girl would be the queen.*
      Dicēt puellam rēgīnam futuram esse. *He will say the girl will be the queen.*

3. **The Infinitive as a Subject.** The infinitive is used as a singular neuter subject.
   Pessimum est bellum fugere. *It is very bad to flee war.*

4. **The Infinitive as an Object.** The infinitive is used as an object of verbs of emotion, will, or desire.
   Vult dīcere. *He wishes to speak.*

Gerunds

1. The **Gerund** is a verbal noun. The gerund functions like a noun in its respective cases. As a verb it can have an object and can be modified by an adverb or prepositional phrase. The object of a gerund will be in the accusative case unless the verb normally takes another case.
   Legendō discimus. *We learn by reading.*

Gerundives

1. The **Gerundive** is a verbal adjective belonging to the 1st/2nd declension. It is always passive in meaning. It is formed like the gerund but has all the endings of an adjective. The gerundive agrees with the noun it modifies in case, number and gender.
   Cupidus bellī gerendī est. *He is desirous of waging war.*

2. **Passive Periphrastic.** The gerundive with a form of **sum** shows necessity or obligation. The gerundive is declined to agree with its subject in case, number, and gender. This is called the passive periphrastic.
   Hoc faciendum erat. *This had to be done.*

Supines

1. The **Supine** is a verbal noun of the fourth declension and is usually formed from the fourth principal part of the verb. It is always neuter singular, but it is used only in the accusative and ablative cases.
    A. The accusative supine is used after verbs of motion to show purpose. It may have a direct object.
       Pugnātum vēnī. *I have come to fight.*
    B. The ablative supine is used after certain adjectives as an ablative of specification.
       mīrābile dictū *amazing to say*

Indirect Discourse

1. **Indirect Statement.** Indirect statements are introduced by verbs of *saying, thinking, knowing, telling, perceiving,* and *showing.* An indirect statement uses an accusative subject and an infinitive verb in place of a nominative subject and a finite verb.
    Dīcō patrem tuum iam dūcere. *I say that your father is already leading.*

2. **Indirect Question.** An indirect question is sentence which reports a question. The sentence often begins with a main verb of *asking, saying, knowing, telling, perceiving,* or *showing* and contains a subordinate clause which is the question. The subordinate clasue is introduced by an interrogative word and contains a subjunctive verb.
    Scīvit quae puellae cantātūrae essent. *He knew which girls would sing.*

3. **Indirect Command.** The indirect command is a subordinate clause after a verb of commanding or requesting. The indirect command begins with **ut** or **ne** and has its verb in the subjunctive.
    Eōs hortātur ut fortiter pugnent. *He urges them to fight well.*

Regular Verbs

INDICATIVE ACTIVE

	First	Second	Third	Third I-stem	Fourth
Present	amō	moneō	tegō	capiō	audiō
	amās	monēs	tegis	capis	audīs
	amat	monet	tegit	capit	audit
	amāmus	monēmus	tegimus	capimus	audīmus
	amātis	monētis	tegitis	capitis	audītis
	amant	monent	tegunt	capiunt	audiunt
Imperfect	amābam	monēbam	tegēbam	capiēbam	audiēbam
	amābās	monēbās	tegēbās	capiēbās	audiēbās
	amābat	monēbat	tegēbat	capiēbat	audiēbat
	amābāmus	monēbāmus	tegēbāmus	capiēbāmus	audiēbāmus
	amābātis	monēbātis	tegēbātis	capiēbātis	audiēbātis
	amābant	monēbant	tegēbant	capiēbant	audiēbant
Future	amābō	monēbō	tegam	capiam	audiam
	amābis	monēbis	tegēs	capiēs	audiēs
	amābit	monēbit	teget	capiet	audiet
	amābimus	monēbimus	tegēmus	capiēmus	audiēmus
	amābitis	monēbitis	tegētis	capiētis	audiētis
	amābunt	monēbunt	tegent	capient	audient
Perfect	amāvī	monuī	tēxī	cēpī	audīvī
	amāvistī	monuistī	tēxistī	cēpistī	audīvistī
	amāvit	monuit	tēxit	cēpit	audīvit
	amāvimus	monuimus	tēximus	cēpimus	audīvimus
	amāvistis	monuistis	tēxistis	cēpistis	audīvistis
	amāvērunt	monuērunt	tēxērunt	cēpērunt	audīvērunt
Pluperfect	amāveram	monueram	tēxeram	cēperam	audīveram
	amāverās	monuerās	tēxerās	cēperās	audīverās
	amāverat	monuerat	tēxerat	cēperat	audīverat
	amāverāmus	monuerāmus	tēxerāmus	cēperāmus	audīverāmus
	amāverātis	monuerātis	tēxerātis	cēperātis	audīverātis
	amāverant	monuerant	tēxerant	cēperant	audīverant
Future Perfect	amāverō	monuerō	tēxerō	cēperō	audīverō
	amāveris	monueris	tēxeris	cēperis	audīveris
	amāverit	monuerit	tēxerit	cēperit	audīverit
	amāverimus	monuerimus	tēxerimus	cēperimus	audīverimus
	amāveritis	monueritis	tēxeritis	cēperitis	audīveritis
	amāverint	monuerint	tēxerint	cēperint	audīverint

INDICATIVE PASSIVE

	First	Second	Third	Third I-stem	Fourth
Present	amor	moneor	tegor	capior	audior
	amāris	monēris	tegeris	caperis	audīris
	amātur	monētur	tegitur	capitur	auditur
	amāmur	monēmur	tegimur	capimur	audīmur
	amāminī	monēminī	tegiminī	capiminī	audīminī
	amantur	monentur	teguntur	capiuntur	audiuntur
Imperfect	amābar	monēbar	tegēbar	capiēbar	audiēbar
	amābāris	monēbāris	tegēbāris	capiēbāris	audiēbāris
	amābātur	monēbātur	tegēbātur	capiēbātur	audiēbātur
	amābāmur	monēbāmur	tegēbāmur	capiēbāmur	audiēbāmur
	amābāminī	monēbāminī	tegēbāminī	capiēbāminī	audiēbāminī
	amābantur	monēbantur	tegēbantur	capiēbantur	audiēbantur
Future	amābor	monēbor	tegar	capiar	audiar
	amāberis	monēberis	tegēris	capiēris	audiēris
	amābitur	monēbitur	tegētur	capiētur	audiētur
	amābimur	monēbimur	tegēmur	capiēmur	audiēmur
	amābiminī	monēbiminī	tegēminī	capiēminī	audiēminī
	amābuntur	monēbuntur	tegentur	capientur	audientur
Perfect	amātus, -a sum	monitus, -a sum	tectus, -a sum	captus, -a sum	audītus, -a sum
	amātus, -a es	monitus, -a es	tectus, -a es	captus, -a es	audītus, -a es
	amātus, -a, -um est	monitus, -a, -um est	tectus, -a, -um est	captus, -a, -um est	audītus, -a, -um est
	amātī, -ae sumus	monitī, -ae sumus	tectī, -ae sumus	captī, -ae sumus	audītī, -ae sumus
	amātī, -ae estis	monitī, -ae estis	tectī, -ae estis	captī, -ae estis	audītī, -ae estis
	amātī, -ae, -a sunt	monitī, -ae, -a sunt	tectī, -ae, -a sunt	captī, -ae, -a sunt	audītī, -ae, -a sunt
Pluperfect	amātus, -a eram	monitus, -a eram	tectus, -a eram	captus, -a eram	audītus, -a eram
	amātus, -a erās	monitus, -a erās	tectus, -a erās	captus, -a erās	audītus, -a erās
	amātus, -a, -um erat	monitus, -a, -um erat	tectus, -a, -um erat	captus, -a, -um erat	audītus, -a, -um erat
	amātī, -ae erāmus	monitī, -ae erāmus	tectī, -ae erāmus	captī, -ae erāmus	audītī, -ae erāmus
	amātī, -ae erātis	monitī, -ae erātis	tectī, -ae erātis	captī, -ae erātis	audītī, -ae erātis
	amātī, -ae, -a erant	monitī, -ae, -a erant	tectī, -ae, -a erant	captī, -ae, -a erant	audītī, -ae, -a erant
Future Perfect	amātus, -a erō	monitus, -a erō	tectus, -a erō	captus, -a erō	audītus, -a erō
	amātus, -a eris	monitus, -a eris	tectus, -a eris	captus, -a eris	audītus, -a eris
	amātus, -a, -um erit	monitus, -a, -um erit	tectus, -a, -um erit	captus, -a, -um erit	audītus, -a, -um erit
	amātī, -ae erimus	monitī, -ae erimus	tectī, -ae erimus	captī, -ae erimus	audītī, -ae erimus
	amātī, -ae eritis	monitī, -ae eritis	tectī, -ae eritis	captī, -ae eritis	audītī, -ae eritis
	amātī, -ae, -a erunt	monitī, -ae, -a erunt	tectī, -ae, -a erunt	captī, -ae, -a erunt	audītī, -ae, -a erunt

SUBJUNCTIVE ACTIVE

	First	Second	Third	Third I-stem	Fourth
Present	amem	moneam	tegam	capiam	audiam
	amēs	moneās	tegās	capiās	audiās
	amet	moneat	tegat	capiat	audiat
	amēmus	moneāmus	tegāmus	capiāmus	audiāmus
	amētis	moneātis	tegātis	capiātis	audiātis
	ament	moneant	tegant	capiant	audiant
Imperfect	amārem	monērem	tegerem	caperem	audīrem
	amārēs	monērēs	tegeres	caperēs	audīrēs
	amāret	monēret	tegeret	caperet	audīret
	amārēmus	monērēmus	tegerēmus	caperēmus	audīrēmus
	amārētis	monērētis	tegerētis	caperētis	audīrētis
	amārent	monērent	tegerent	caperent	audīrent
Perfect	amāverim	monuerim	tēxerim	cēperim	audīverim
	amāverīs	monuerīs	tēxerīs	cēperīs	audīverīs
	amāverit	monuerit	tēxerit	cēperit	audīverit
	amāverīmus	monuerīmus	tēxerīmus	cēperīmus	audīverīmus
	amāverītis	monuerītis	tēxerītis	cēperītis	audīverītis
	amāverint	monuerint	tēxerint	cēperint	audīverint
Pluperfect	amāvissem	monuissem	tēxissem	cēpissem	audīvissem
	amāvissēs	monuissēs	tēxissēs	cēpissēs	audīvissēs
	amāvisset	monuisset	tēxisset	cēpisset	audīvisset
	amāvissēmus	monuissēmus	tēxissēmus	cēpissēmus	audīvissēmus
	amāvissētis	monuissētis	tēxissētis	cēpissētis	audīvissētis
	amāvissent	monuissent	tēxissent	cēpissent	audīvissent

SUBJUNCTIVE PASSIVE

	First	Second	Third	Third I-stem	Fourth
Present	amer	monear	tegar	capiar	audiar
	amēris	moneāris	tegāris	capiāris	audiāris
	amētur	moneātur	tegātur	capiātur	audiātur
	amēmur	moneāmur	tegāmur	capiāmur	audiāmur
	amēminī	moneāminī	tegāminī	capiāminī	audiāminī
	amentur	moneantur	tegantur	capiantur	audiantur
Imperfect	amārer	monērer	tegerer	caperer	audīrer
	amārēris	monērēris	tegerēris	caperēris	audīrēris
	amārētur	monērētur	tegerētur	caperētur	audīrētur
	amārēmur	monērēmur	tegerēmur	caperēmur	audīrēmur
	amārēminī	monērēminī	tegerēminī	caperēminī	audīrēminī
	amārentur	monērentur	tegerentur	caperentur	audīrentur
Perfect	amātus, -a sim	monitus, -a sim	tectus, -a sim	captus, -a sim	audītus, -a sim
	amātus, -a sīs	monitus, -a sīs	tectus, -a sīs	captus, -a sīs	audītus, -a sīs
	amātus, -a, -um sit	monitus, -a, -um sit	tectus, -a, -um sit	captus, -a, -um sit	audītus, -a, -um sit
	amātī, -ae sīmus	monitī, -ae sīmus	tectī, -ae sīmus	captī, -ae sīmus	audītī, -ae sīmus
	amātī, -ae sītis	monitī, -ae sītis	tectī, -ae sītis	captī, -ae sītis	audītī, -ae sītis
	amātī, -ae, -a sint	monitī, -ae, -a sint	tectī, -ae, -a sint	captī, -ae, -a sint	audītī, -ae, -a sint
Pluperfect	amātus, -a essem	monitus, -a essem	tectus, -a essem	captus, -a essem	audītus, -a essem
	amātus, -a essēs	monitus, -a essēs	tectus, -a essēs	captus, -a essēs	audītus, -a essēs
	amātus, -a, -um esset	monitus, -a, -um esset	tectus, -a, -um esset	captus, -a, -um esset	audītus, -a, -um esset
	amātī, -ae essēmus	monitī, -ae essēmus	tectī, -ae essēmus	captī, -ae essēmus	audītī, -ae essēmus
	amātī, -ae essētis	monitī, -ae essētis	tectī, -ae essētis	captī, -ae essētis	audītī, -ae essētis
	amātī, -ae, -a essent	monitī, -ae, -a essent	tectī, -ae, -a essent	captī, -ae, -a essent	audītī, -ae, -a essent

PARTICIPLES, ACTIVE AND PASSIVE

	First	Second	Third	Third I-stem	Fourth
Active					
pres.	amāns, -ntis	monēns, -ntis	tegēns, -ntis	capiēns, -ntis	audiēns, -ntis
perf.	—	—	—	—	—
fut.	amātūrus, -a, -um	monitūrus, -a, -um	tectūrus, -a, -um	captūrus, -a, -um	audītūrus, -a, -um
Passive					
pres.	—	—	—	—	—
perf.	amātus, -a, -um	monitus, -a, -um	tectus, -a, -um	captus, -a, -um	audītus, -a, -um
fut.	amandus, -a, -um	monendus, -a, -um	tegendus, -a, -um	capiendus, -a, -um	audiendus, -a, -um

INFINITIVES, ACTIVE AND PASSIVE

	First	Second	Third	Third I-stem	Fourth
Active					
pres.	amāre	monēre	tegēre	capere	audīre
perf.	amāvisse	monuisse	tēxisse	cēpisse	audīvisse
fut.	amātūrus, -a, -um, -esse	monitūrus, -a, -um, -esse	tectūrus, -a, -um, -esse	captūrus, -a, -um, -esse	audītūrus, -a, -um, -esse
Passive					
pres.	amārī	monērī	tegī	capī	audīrī
perf.	amātus, -a, -um	monitus, -a, -um	tectus, -a, -um	captus, -a, -um	audītus, -a, -um
fut.	amātum īrī	monitum īrī	tectum īrī	captum īrī	auditum īrī

PRESENT IMPERATIVES, ACTIVE AND PASSIVE

	First	Second	Third	Third I-stem	Fourth
Active					
singular	amā	monē	tege	cape	audī
plural	amāte	monēte	tegite	capite	audīte
Passive					
singular	amāre	monēre	tegere	capere	audīre
plural	amāminī	monēminī	tegiminī	capiminī	audīminī

Irregular Verbs

INDICATIVE

	Sum	Volō	Nōlō	Mālō	Eō	Fīō	Ferō	
Present	sum	volō	nōlō	mālō	eō	fīō	ferō	feror
	es	vīs	nōn vīs	māvīs	īs	fīs	fers	ferris
	est	vult	nōn vult	māvult	it	fit	fert	fertur
	sumus	volumus	nōlumus	mālumus	īmus	fīmus	ferimus	ferimur
	estis	vultis	nōn vultis	māvultis	ītis	fītis	fertis	feriminī
	sunt	volunt	nōlunt	mālunt	eunt	fīunt	ferunt	feruntur
Imperfect	eram	volēbam	nōlēbam	mālēbam	ībam	fīēbam	ferēbam	ferēbar
	erās	volēbās	nōlēbās	mālēbās	ībās	fīēbās	ferēbās	ferēbāris
	erat	volēbat	nōlēbat	mālēbat	ībat	fīēbat	ferēbat	ferēbatur
	erāmus	volēbāmus	nōlēbāmus	mālēbāmus	ībāmus	fīēbāmus	ferēbāmus	ferēbāmur
	erātis	volēbātis	nōlēbātis	mālēbātis	ībātis	fīēbātis	ferēbātis	ferēbāminī
	erant	volēbant	nōlēbant	mālēbant	ībant	fīēbant	ferēbant	ferēbantur
Future	erō	volam	nōlam	mālam	ībō	fīam	feram	ferar
	eris	volēs	nōlēs	mālēs	ībis	fīēs	ferēs	ferēris
	erit	volet	nōlet	mālet	ībit	fīet	feret	ferētur
	erimus	volēmus	nōlēmus	mālēmus	ībimus	fīēmus	ferēmus	ferēmur
	eritis	volētis	nōlētis	mālētis	ībitis	fīētis	ferētis	ferēminī
	erunt	volent	nolent	malent	ībunt	fient	ferent	ferentur
Perfect	fuī	voluī	nōluī	māluī	iī		tulī	lātus, -a sum
	fuistī	voluistī	nōluistī	māluistī	īstī		tulistī	lātus, -a es
	fuit	voluit	nōluit	māluit	iit		tulit	lātus, -a, -um est
	fuimus	voluimus	nōluimus	māluimus	iimus		tulimus	lātī, -ae sumus
	fuistis	voluistis	nōluistis	māluistis	īstis		tulistis	lātī, -ae estis
	fuērunt	voluērunt	nōluērunt	māluērunt	iērunt		tulērunt	lātī, -ae, -a sunt
Pluperfect	fueram	volueram	nōlueram	mālueram	ieram		tuleram	lātus, -a eram
	fuerās	voluerās	nōluerās	māluerās	ierās		tulerās	lātus, -a erās
	fuerat	voluerat	nōluerat	māluerat	ierat		tulerat	lātus, -a, -um erat
	fuerāmus	voluerāmus	nōluerāmus	māluerāmus	ierāmus		tulerāmus	lātī, -ae erāmus
	fuerātis	voluerātis	nōluerātis	māluerātis	ierātis		tulerātis	lātī, -ae erātis
	fuerant	voluerant	nōluerant	māluerant	ierant		tulerant	lātī, -ae, -a erant
Future Perfect	fuerō	voluerō	nōluerō	māluerō	ierō		tulerō	lātus, -a erō
	fueris	volueris	nōlueris	mālueris	ieris		tuleris	lātus, -a eris
	fuerit	voluerit	nōluerit	māluerit	ierit		tulerit	lātus, -a, -um erit
	fuerimus	voluerimus	nōluerimus	māluerimus	ierimus		tulerimus	lātī, -ae erimus
	fueritis	volueritis	nōlueritis	mālueritis	ieritis		tuleritis	lātī, -ae eritis
	fuerint	voluerint	nōluerint	māluerint	ierint		tulerint	lātī, -ae, -a erunt

SUBJUNCTIVE

	Sum	Volō	Nōlō	Mālō	Eō	Fīō	Ferō	
Present	sim	velim	nōlim	mālim	eam	fīam	feram	ferar
	sīs	velīs	nōlīs	mālīs	eās	fīas	ferās	ferāris
	sit	velit	nōlit	mālit	eat	fīat	ferāt	ferātur
	sīmus	velīmus	nōlimus	mālīmus	eāmus	fīāmus	ferāmus	ferāmur
	sītis	velītis	nōlītis	mālītis	eātis	fīātis	ferātis	ferāminī
	sint ēs	velint	nōlint	mālint	eant	fīant	ferānt	ferāntur
Imperfect	essem	vellem	nōllem	māllem	īrem	fierem	ferrem	ferrer
	essēs	vellēs	nōllēs	māllēs	īrēs	fierēs	ferrēs	ferrēris
	esset	vellet	nōllet	māllet	īret	fieret	ferrēt	ferrētur
	essēmus	vellēmus	nōllēmus	māllēmus	īrēmus	fierēmus	ferrēmus	ferrēmur
	essētis	vellētis	nōllētis	māllētis	īrētis	fierētis	ferrētis	ferrēminī
	essent	vellent	nōllent	māllent	īrent	fierent	ferrent	ferrentur
Perfect	fuerim	voluerim	nōluerim	māluerim	ierim		tulerim	lātus, -a sim
	fuerīs	voluerīs	nōluerīs	māluerīs	ierīs		tulerīs	lātus, -a sīs
	fuerit	voluerit	nōluerit	māluerit	ierit		tulerit	lātus, -a, -um sit
	fuerīmus	voluerīmus	nōluerīmus	māluerīmus	ierīmus		tulerīmus	lātī, -ae sīmus
	fuerītis	voluerītis	nōluerītis	māluerītis	ierītis		tulerītis	lātī, -ae sītis
	fuerint	voluerint	nōluerint	māluerint	ierint		tulerint	lātī, -ae, -a sint
Pluperfect	fuissem	voluissem	nōluissem	māluissem	īssem		tulissem	lātus, -a essem
	fuissēs	voluissēs	nōluissēs	māluissēs	īss		tulissēs	lātus, -a essēs
	fuisset	voluisset	nōluisset	māluisset	īsset		tulisset	lātus, -a, -um esset
	fuissēmus	voluissēmus	nōluissēmus	māluissēmus	īssēmus		tulissēmus	lātī, -ae essēmus
	fuissētis	voluissētis	nōluissētis	māluissētis	īssētis		tulissētis	lātī, -ae essētis
	fuissent	voluissent	nōluissent	māluissent	īssent		tulissent	lātī, -ae, -a essent

PARTICIPLES

	Sum	Volō	Nōlō	Mālō	Eō	Fīō	Ferō
Active							
pres.	—	volēns, -ntis	nōlēns, -ntis	—	iēns, -ntis	—	ferēns, -ntis
perf.	—	—	—	—	—	—	—
fut.	futūrus, -a, -um	—	—	—	itūrus, -a, -um	—	lātūrus, -a, -um
Passive							
pres.	—	—	—	—	—	—	—
perf.	—	—	—	—	—	—	lātus, -a, -um
(gerundive)	—	—	—	—	eundus, -a, -um	—	ferendus, -a, -um

INFINITIVES

	Sum	Volō	Nōlō	Mālō	Eō	Fīō	Ferō
Active							
pres.	esse	velle	nōlle	mālle	īre	fierī	ferre
perf.	fuisse	voluisse	nōluisse	māluisse	īsse	—	tulisse
fut.	futūrus, -a, -um esse	—	—	—	itūrus, -a, -um esse	—	lātūrus, -a, -um esse
Passive							
pres.	—	—	—	—	īrī	—	ferrī
perf.	—	—	—	—	—	—	lātus, -a, -um esse
Fut.	—	—	—	—	itum īrī	—	lātum īrī

PRESENT IMPERATIVES, ACTIVE AND PASSIVE

	Sum	Volō	Nōlō	Mālō	Eō	Fīō	Ferō
Active							
sing.	es	—	nōlī	—	ī	fī	fer
pl.	este	—	nōlīte	—	īte	fīte	ferte
Passive							
sing.	—	—	—	—	—	—	ferre
pl.	—	—	—	—	—	—	feriminī

Deponent Verbs

INDICATIVE

	First	Second	Third	Third I-stem	Fourth
Present					
	cōnor	vereor	sequor	patior	mentior
	cōnāris	verēris	sequeris	pateris	mentīris
	cōnātur	verētur	sequitur	patitur	mentītur
	cōnāmur	verēmur	sequimur	patimur	mentīmur
	cōnāminī	verēminī	sequiminī	patiminī	mentīminī
	cōnantur	verentur	sequuntur	patiuntur	mentiuntur
Imperfect					
	cōnābar	verēbar	sequēbar	patiēbar	mentiēbar
	cōnābāris	verēbāris	sequēbāris	patiēbāris	mentiēbāris
	cōnābātur	verēbātur	sequēbātur	patiēbātur	mentiēbātur
	cōnābāmur	verēbāmur	sequēbāmur	patiēbāmur	mentiēbāmur
	cōnābāminī	verēbāminī	sequēbāminī	patiēbāminī	mentiēbāminī
	cōnābantur	verēbantur	sequēbantur	patiēbantur	mentiēbantur
Future					
	cōnābor	verēbor	sequar	patiar	mentiar
	cōnāberis	verēberis	sequēris	patiēris	mentiēris
	cōnābitur	verēbitur	sequētur	patiētur	mentiētur
	cōnābimur	verēbimur	sequēmur	patiēmur	mentiēmur
	cōnābiminī	verēbiminī	sequēminī	patiēminī	mentiēminī
	cōnābuntur	verēbuntur	sequentur	patientur	mentientur
Perfect					
	cōnātus, -a sum	veritus, -a sum	secūtus, -a sum	passus, -a sum	mentītus, -a sum
	cōnātus, -a es	veritus, -a es	secūtus, -a es	passus, -a es	mentītus, -a es
	cōnātus, -a, -um est	veritus, -a, -um est	secūtus, -a, -um est	passus, -a, -um est	mentītus, -a, -um est
	cōnātī, -ae sumus	veritī, -ae sumus	secūtī, -ae sumus	passī, -ae sumus	mentītī, -ae sumus
	cōnātī, -ae estis	veritī, -ae estis	secūtī, -ae estis	passī, -ae estis	mentītī, -ae estis
	cōnātī, -ae, -a sunt	veritī, -ae, -a sunt	secūtī, -ae, -a sunt	passī, -ae, -a sunt	mentītī, -ae, -a sunt
Pluperfect					
	cōnātus, -a eram	veritus, -a eram	secūtus, -a eram	passus, -a eram	mentītus, -a eram
	cōnātus, -a erās	veritus, -a erās	secūtus, -a erās	passus, -a erās	mentītus, -a erās
	cōnātus, -a, -um erat	veritus, -a, -um erat	secūtus, -a, -um erat	passus, -a, -um erat	mentītus, -a, -um erat
	cōnātī, -ae erāmus	veritī, -ae erāmus	secūtī, -a erāmus	passī, -ae erāmus	mentītī, -ae erāmus
	cōnātī, -ae erātis	veritī, -ae erātis	secūtī, -ae erātis	passī, -ae erātis	mentītī, -ae erātis
	cōnātī, -ae, -a erant	veritī, -ae, -a erant	secūtī, -ae, -a erant	passī, -ae, -a erant	mentītī, -ae, -a erant
Future Perfect					
	cōnātus, -a erō	veritus, -a erō	secūtus, -a erō	passus, -a erō	mentītus, -a erō
	cōnātus, -a eris	veritus, -a eris	secūtus, -a eris	passus, -a eris	mentītus, -a eris
	cōnātus, -a, -um erit	veritus, -a, -um erit	secūtus, -a, -um erit	passus, -a, -um erit	mentītus, -a, -um erit
	cōnātī, -ae erimus	veritī, -ae erimus	secūtī, -ae erimus	passī, -ae erimus	mentītī, -ae erimus
	cōnātī, -ae eritis	veritī, -ae eritis	secūtī, -ae eritis	passī, -ae eritis	mentītī, -ae eritis
	cōnātī, -āe, -a erunt	veritī, -ae, -a erunt	secūtī, -ae, -a erunt	passī, -ae, -a erunt	mentītī, -ae, -a erunt

SUBJUNCTIVE

	First	Second	Third	Third I-stem	Fourth
Present					
	cōner	verear	sequar	patiar	mentiar
	cōnēris	verēris	sequāris	patiāris	mentiāris
	cōnētur	verētur	sequātur	patiātur	mentiātur
	cōnēmur	verēmur	sequāmur	patiāmur	mentiāmur
	cōnēminī	verēminī	sequāminī	patiāminī	mentiāminī
	cōnentur	verentur	sequāntur	patiāntur	mentiāntur
Imperfect					
	cōnārer	verērer	sequerer	paterer	mentīrer
	cōnārēris	verērēris	sequerēris	paterēris	mentīrēris
	cōnārētur	verērētur	sequerētur	paterētur	mentīrētur
	cōnārēmur	verērēmur	sequerēmur	paterēmur	mentīrēmur
	cōnārēminī	verērēminī	sequerēminī	paterēminī	mentīrēminī
	cōnārentur	verērentur	sequerentur	paterentur	mentīrentur
Perfect					
	cōnātus, -a sim	veritus, -a sim	secūtus, -a sim	passus, -a sim	mentītus, -a sim
	cōnātus, -a sīs	veritus, -a sīs	secūtus, -a sīs	passus, -a sīs	mentītus, -a sīs
	cōnātus, -a, -um sit	veritus, -a, -um sit	secūtus, -a, -um sit	passus, -a, -um sit	mentītus, -a, -um sit
	cōnātī, -ae sīmus	veritī, -ae sīmus	secūtī, -ae sīmus	passī, -ae sīmus	mentītī, -ae sīmus
	cōnātī, -ae sītis	veritī, -ae sītis	secūtī, -ae sītis	passī, -ae sītis	mentītī, -ae sītis
	cōnātī, -ae, -a sint	veritī, -ae, -a sint	secūtī, -ae, -a sint	passī, -ae, -a sint	mentītī, -ae, -a sint
Pluperfect					
	cōnātus, -a essem	veritus, -a essem	secūtus, -a essem	passus, -a essem	mentītus, -a essem
	cōnātus, -a essēs	veritus, -a essēs	secūtus, -a essēs	passus, -a essēs	mentītus, -a essēs
	cōnātus, -a, -um esset	veritus, -a, -um esset	secūtus, -a, -um esset	passus, -a, -um esset	mentītus, -a, -um esset
	cōnātī, -ae essēmus	veritī, -ae essēmus	secūtī, -a essēmus	passī, -ae essēmus	mentītī, -ae essēmus
	cōnātī, -ae essētis	veritī, -ae essētis	secūtī, -ae essētis	passī, -ae essētis	mentītī, -ae essētis
	cōnātī, -ae, -a essent	veritī, -ae, -a essent	secūtī, -ae, -a essent	passī, -ae, -a essent	mentītī, -ae, -a essent

PARTICIPLES

	First	Second	Third	Third I-stem	Fourth
pres.	cōnāns, -ntis	verēns, -ntis	sequēns, -ntis	patiēns, -ntis	mentiēns, -ntis
perf.	cōnātus, -a, -um	veritus, -a, -um	secūtus, -a, -um	passus, -a, -um	mentītus, -a, -um
fut. act.	cōnātūrus, -a, -um	veritūrus, -a, -um	secūtūrus, -a, -um	passūrus, -a, -um	mentītūrus, -a, -um
(gerundive)	conandus, -a, -um	verendus, -a, -um	sequendus, -a, -um	patiendus, -a, -um	mentiendus, -a, -um

INFINITIVES

	First	Second	Third	Third I-stem	Fourth
pres.	cōnārī	verērī	sequī	patī	mentīrī
perf.	cōnātus, -a, -um esse	veritus, -a, -um esse	secūtus, -a, -um esse	passus, -a, -um esse	mentītus, -a, -um esse
fut.	cōnātūrus, -a, -um esse	veritūrus, -a, -um esse	secūtūrus, -a, -um esse	passūrus, -a, -um esse	mentītūrus, -a, -um esse

PRESENT IMPERATIVES

	First	Second	Third	Third I-stem	Fourth
sing.	cōnāre	verēre	sequere	patere	mentīre
pl.	cōnāminī	verēminī	sequiminī	patiminī	mentīminī

Five Noun Declensions

	First (F / M)	Second (M / N)		Third (M / F / N)		Third I-stem (M / F / N)		Fourth (M / N)		Fifth (M / F)
	F	M	N	M	N	F	N	M	N	F
Singular										
Nom.	puella	dominus	verbum	mīles	opus	nāvis	mare	gradus	cornū	rēs
Gen.	puellae	dominī	verbī	mīlitis	operis	nāvis	maris	gradūs	cornūs	reī
Dat.	puellae	dominō	verbō	mīlitī	operī	nāvī	marī	graduī	cornū	reī
Acc.	puellam	dominum	verbum	mīlitem	opus	nāvem	mare	gradum	cornū	rem
Abl.	puellā	dominō	verbō	mīlite	opere	nāve	marī	gradū	cornū	rē
Plural										
Nom.	puellae	dominī	verba	mīlitēs	opera	nāvēs	maria	gradūs	cornua	rēs
Gen.	puellārum	dominōrum	verbōrum	mīlitum	operum	nāvium	marium	graduum	cornuum	rērum
Dat.	puellīs	dominīs	verbīs	mīlitibus	operibus	nāvibus	maribus	gradibus	cornibus	rēbus
Acc.	puellās	dominōs	verba	mīlitēs	opera	nāvīs	maria	gradūs	cornua	rēs
Abl.	puellīs	dominīs	verbīs	mīlitibus	operibus	nāvibus	maribus	gradibus	cornibus	rēbus

Adjective Declensions

FIRST AND SECOND DECLENSION

	Singular			Plural		
	M	F	N	M	F	N
Nom.	bonus	bona	bonum	bonī	bonae	bona
Gen.	bonī	bonae	bonī	bonōrum	bonārum	bonōrum
Dat.	bonō	bonae	bonō	bonīs	bonīs	bonīs
Acc.	bonum	bonam	bonum	bonōs	bonās	bona
Abl.	bonō	bonā	bonō	bonīs	bonīs	bonīs

	Singular			Plural		
	M	F	N	M	F	N
Nom.	sacer	sacra	sacrum	sacrī	sacrae	sacra
Gen.	sacrī	sacrae	sacrī	sacrōrum	sacrārum	sacrōrum
Dat.	sacrō	sacrae	sacrō	sacrīs	sacrīs	sacrīs
Acc.	sacrum	sacram	sacrum	sacrōs	sacrās	sacra
Abl.	sacrō	sacrā	sacrō	sacrīs	sacrīs	sacrīs

	Singular			Plural		
	M	F	N	M	F	N
Nom.	miser	misera	miserum	miserī	miserae	misera
Gen.	miserī	miserae	miserī	miserōrum	miserārum	miserōrum
Dat.	miserō	miserae	miserō	miserīs	miserīs	miserīs
Acc.	miserum	miseram	miserum	miserōs	miserās	misera
Abl.	miserō	miserā	miserō	miserīs	miserīs	miserīs

93

THIRD DECLENSION

Three Terminations

	Singular			Plural		
	M	F	N	M	F	N
Nom.	ācer	ācris	ācre	ācrēs	ācrēs	ācria
Gen.	ācris	ācris	ācris	ācrium	ācrium	ācrium
Dat.	ācrī	ācrī	ācrī	ācribus	ācribus	ācribus
Acc.	ācrem	ācrem	ācre	ācrīs, -ēs	ācrīs, -ēs	ācria
Abl.	ācrī	ācrī	ācrī	ācribus	ācribus	ācribus

Two Terminations

	Singular		Plural	
	M/F	N	M/F	N
Nom.	omnis	omne	omnēs	omnia
Gen.	omnis	omnis	omnium	omnium
Dat.	omnī	omnī	omnibus	omnibus
Acc.	omnem	omne	omnīs, -ēs	omnia
Abl.	omnī	omnī	omnibus	omnibus

One Termination

	Singular		Plural	
	M/F	N	M/F	N
Nom.	fēlīx	fēlīx	fēlīcēs	fēlīcia
Gen.	fēlīcis	fēlīcis	fēlīcium	fēlīcium
Dat.	fēlīcī	fēlīcī	fēlīcibus	fēlīcibus
Acc.	fēlīcem	fēlīx	fēlīcīs, -ēs	fēlīcia
Abl.	fēlīcī	fēlīcī	fēlīcibus	fēlīcibus

Participle Declensions

First Conjugation

	Singular		Plural	
	M/F	N	M/F	N
Nom.	amāns	amāns	amantēs	amantia
Gen.	amantis	amantis	amantium	amantium
Dat.	amantī	amantī	amantibus	amantibus
Acc.	amantem	amāns	amantīs, -ēs	amantia
Abl.	amantī	amantī	amantibus	amantibus

Second Conjugation

	Singular		Plural	
	M/F	N	M/F	N
Nom.	monēns	monēns	monentēs	monentia
Gen.	monentis	monentis	monentium	monentium
Dat.	monentī	monentī	monentibus	monentibus
Acc.	monentem	monēns	monentīs, -ēs	monentia
Abl.	monentī	monentī	monentibus	monentibus

Third Conjugation

	Singular		Plural	
	M/F	N	M/F	N
Nom.	dūcēns	dūcēns	dūcentēs	dūcentia
Gen.	dūcentis	dūcentis	dūcentium	dūcentium
Dat.	dūcentī	dūcentī	dūcentibus	dūcentibus
Acc.	dūcentem	dūcēns	dūcentīs, -ēs	dūcentia
Abl.	dūcentī	dūcentī	dūcentibus	dūcentibus

Third Conjugation I-stem

	Singular		Plural	
	M/F	N	M/F	N
Nom.	capiēns	capiēns	capientēs	capientia
Gen.	capientis	capientis	capientium	capientium
Dat.	capientī	capientī	capientibus	capientibus
Acc.	capientīs	capiēns	capientīs, -ēs	capientia
Abl.	capientī	capientī	capientibus	capientibus

Fourth Conjugation

	Singular		Plural	
	M/F	N	M/F	N
Nom.	audiēns	audiēns	audientēs	audientia
Gen.	audientis	audientis	audientium	audientium
Dat.	audientī	audientī	audientibus	audientibus
Acc.	audientīs	audiēns	audientīs, -ēs	audientia
Abl.	audientī	audientī	audientibus	audientibus

COMPARATIVE ADJECTIVE

	Singular		Plural	
	M/F	**N**	**M/F**	**N**
Nom.	longior	longius	longiōrēs	longiōra
Gen.	longiōris	longiōris	longiōrum	longiōrum
Dat.	longiōrī	longiōrī	longiōribus	longiōribus
Acc.	longiōrem	longius	longiōrēs	longiōra
Abl.	longiōre	longiōre	longiōribus	longiōribus

IRREGULAR COMPARISON OF ADJECTIVES

Positive		Comparative		Superlative	
bonus, -a, -um	*good*	melior, melius	*better*	optimus, -a, -um	*best*
malus, -a, -um	*bad*	peior, peius	*worse*	pessimus, -a, -um	*worst*
magnus, -a, -um	*great*	maior, maius	*greater*	maximus, -a, -um	*greatest*
parvus, -a, -um	*small*	minor, minus	*smaller*	minimus, -a, -um	*smallest*
multus, -a, -um	*much, many*	sg. plūs *(neuter noun only)*	*more*	plūrimus, -a, -um	*most, very many*
		pl. plūrēs, plūra	*several, more*		

Comparison of Adverbs

REGULAR COMPARISON OF ADVERBS

Positive		Comparative		Superlative	
ācriter	*keenly*	ācrius	*more keenly*	ācerrimē	*very keenly*
altē	*deeply*	altius	*more deeply*	altissimē	*very deeply*
facile	*easily*	facilius	*more easily*	facillimē	*very easily*
miserē	*unhappily*	miserius	*more unhappily*	miserrimē	*very unhappily*
sapienter	*wisely*	sapientius	*more wisely*	sapientissimē	*very wisely*

IRREGULAR COMPARISON OF ADVERBS

Positive		Comparative		Superlative	
bene	*well*	melius	*better*	optimē	*best*
male	*badly*	peius	*worse*	pessimē	*worst*
magnopere	*greatly*	magis	*more (quality)*	maximē	*most, especially*
parum	*too little*	minus	*less*	minimē	*least*
multum	*much*	plūs	*more (quantity)*	plūrimum	*most, very much*
diū	*for a long time*	diūtius	*for a longer time*	diūtissimē	*for the longest time*

Pronoun Declensions

PERSONAL PRONOUNS

		1st person	2nd person	3rd person		
Singular	Nom.	ego	tū	is	ea	id
	Gen.	meī	tuī	eius	eius	eius
	Dat.	mihi	tibi	eī	eī	eī
	Acc.	mē	tē	eum	eam	id
	Abl.	mē	tē	eō	eā	eō
Plural	Nom.	nōs	vōs	eī	eae	ea
	Gen.	nostrum, nostrī	vestrum, vestrī	eōrum	eārum	eōrum
	Dat.	nōbīs	vōbīs	eīs	eīs	eīs
	Acc.	nōs	vōs	eōs	eās	ea
	Abl.	nōbīs	vōbīs	eīs	eīs	eīs

REFLEXIVE PRONOUNS

		1st person	2nd person	3rd person
Singular	Nom.	—	—	—
	Gen.	meī	tuī	suī
	Dat.	mihi	tibi	sibi
	Acc.	mē	tē	sē (sēsē)
	Abl.	mē	tē	sē (sēsē)
Plural	Nom.	—	—	—
	Gen.	nostrī	vestrī	suī
	Dat.	nōbīs	vōbīs	sibi
	Acc.	nōs	vōs	sē (sēsē)
	Abl.	nōbīs	vōbīs	sē (sēsē)

RELATIVE PRONOUNS

	Singular			Plural		
	M	**F**	**N**	**M**	**F**	**N**
Nom.	quī	quae	quod	quī	quae	quae
Gen.	cuius	cuius	cuius	quōrum	quārum	quōrum
Dat.	cuī	cuī	cuī	quibus	quibus	quibus
Acc.	quem	quam	quod	quōs	quās	quae
Abl.	quō	quā	quō	quibus	quibus	quibus

Demonstrative

Hic, Haec, Hoc

	Singular			Plural		
	M	F	N	M	F	N
Nom.	hic	haec	hoc	hī	hae	haec
Gen.	huius	huius	huius	hōrum	hārum	hōrum
Dat.	huic	huic	huic	hīs	hīs	hīs
Acc.	hunc	hanc	hoc	hōs	hās	haec
Abl.	hōc	hāc	hōc	hīs	hīs	hīs

Ille, Illa, Illud

	Singular			Plural		
	M	F	N	M	F	N
Nom.	ille	illa	illud	illī	illae	illa
Gen.	illīus	illīus	illīus	illōrum	illārum	illōrum
Dat.	illī	illī	illī	illīs	illīs	illīs
Acc.	illum	illam	illud	illōs	illās	illa
Abl.	illō	illā	illō	illīs	illīs	illīs

Is, Ea, Id

	Singular			Plural		
	M	F	N	M	F	N
Nom.	is	ea	id	eī	eae	ea
Gen.	eius	eius	eius	eōrum	eārum	eōrum
Dat.	eī	eī	eī	eīs	eīs	eīs
Acc.	eum	eam	id	eōs	eās	ea
Abl.	eō	eā	eō	eīs	eīs	eīs

Īdem, Eadem, Idem

	Singular			Plural		
	M	F	N	M	F	N
Nom.	īdem	eadem	idem	eīdem	eaedem	eadem
Gen.	eiusdem	eiusdem	eiusdem	eōrundem	eārundem	eōrundem
Dat.	eīdem	eīdem	eīdem	eīsdem	eīsdem	eīsdem
Acc.	eundem	eandem	idem	eōsdem	eāsdem	eadem
Abl.	eōdem	eādem	eōdem	eīsdem	eīsdem	eīsdem

Iste, Ista, Istud

	Singular			Plural		
	M	F	N	M	F	N
Nom.	iste	ista	istud	istī	istae	ista
Gen.	istīus	istīus	istīus	istōrum	istārum	istōrum
Dat.	istī	istī	istī	istīs	istīs	istīs
Acc.	istum	istam	istud	istōs	istās	ista
Abl.	istō	istā	istō	istīs	istīs	istīs

Intensive

Ipse, Ipsa, Ipsum

	Singular			Plural		
	M	**F**	**N**	**M**	**F**	**N**
Nom.	ipse	ipsa	ipsum	ipsī	ipsae	ipsa
Gen.	ipsīus	ipsīus	ipsīus	ipsōrum	ipsārum	ipsōrum
Dat.	ipsī	ipsī	ipsī	ipsīs	ipsīs	ipsīs
Acc.	ipsum	ipsam	ipsum	ipsōs	ipsās	ipsa
Abl.	ipsō	ipsā	ipsō	ipsīs	ipsīs	ipsīs

Numerals

Arabic	Roman Numeral	Cardinal	Ordinal
1	I	ūnus, -a, -um	prīmus, -a, -um
2	II	duo, duae, duo	secundus, -a, -um
3	III	trēs, tria	tertius, -a, -um
4	IV	quattuor	quārtus, -a, -um
5	V	quinque	quīntus, -a, -um
6	VI	sex	sextus, -a, -um
7	VII	septem	septimus, -a, -um
8	VIII	octo	octāvus, -a, -um
9	IX	novem	nōnus, -a, -um
10	X	decem	decimus, -a, -um
100	C	centum	centēsimus, -a, -um

Classified Vocabulary

Verbs

1st Conjugation

adligō (1), *bind, tie*
amō (1), *like, love*
appellō, (1), *accost, address, name*
appropinquō, (1), *approach*
cantō (1), *sing*
clāmō (1), *shout*
confirmō (1), *encourage, strengthen*
comparō (1) , *achieve, gather, prepare*
cōnor (1), *attempt, try*
convocō (1), *call together*
creō (1), *create, elect*
dēlīberō (1), *consider, deliberate*
dēplōrō (1), *lament, mourn*
dēvorō (1), *devour, swallow*
errō (1), *make a mistake, wander*
exanimō (1), *exhaust*
excitō (1), *awaken, rouse*
existimō (1), *consider, regard, think*
expugnō (1), *storm*
exspectō (1), *look out*
habitō (1), *dwell, live in*
hortor (1), *encourage*
ignōrō (1), *have no knowledge of, demand*
imperō (1), *order, obtain (by asking)*
importō (1), *bring in, carry in*
incitō (1), *arouse, urge on*
iuvō, -āre, iūvī, iūtum, *help*
laudō (1), *praise*
līberō (1), *free, liberate*
memorō (1), *bring up, mention*
mīror (1), *be amazed, be surprised, wonder at*
monstrō (1), *show*
mūtō (1), *change, transform*
nārrō (1), *tell, relate*
nūntiō (1), *announce, report*
obsecrō (1), *beg, beseech*
occupō (1), *seize*
optō (1), *desire*
orō (1), *beg, beseech*
parō (1), *prepare*
portō (1), *carry*
postulō (1), *demand*
praestō, -āre, praestitī, praestatum, *exhibit, show*
pugnō (1), *fight*
puto (1), *consider, think*
rogō (1), *ask*
servō (1), *guard, save, watch over*
spērō (1), *hope*
stō, -āre, stetī, statum, *stand*
superō (1), *surpass*
temptō (1), *test, try*

turbō (1), *disturb, stir up*
vetō, -āre, vetuī, vetitum, *forbid, order . . . not*
vītō (1), *avoid, escape*
vocō (1), *call*
volō (1), *fly*
vulnerō (1), *hurt, wound*

2nd Conjugation

ardeō, -ēre, arsī, arsūrus, *be inflamed, blaze, burn*
augeō, -ēre, auxī, auctum, *increase*
contineō, -ēre, continuī, contentum, *contain, hold together, sustain*
dēleō, -ēre, dēlēvī, dēlētum, *destroy*
doceō, -ēre, docuī, doctum, *teach*
doleō, -ēre, doluī, dolitum, *grieve*
exerceō, -ēre, exercuī, exercitum, *train*
faveō, -ēre, fāvī, fautum (+dat.), *favor, support*
fleō, flēre, flēvī, flētum, *weep*
habeō -ēre, habuī, habitum, *consider, have, hold*
iubeō, iubēre, iussī, iussum, *bid, command, order*
maneō, -ēre, mānsī, mānsum, *remain, stay*
moneō, -ēre, monuī, monitum, *advise, warn*
moveō, -ēre, mōvī, mōtum, *move*
noceō, nocēre, nocuī, nocitum (+dat.), *harm*
obtineō, -ēre, obtinuī, obtentum , *hold, obtain*
pāreō, -ēre, pāruī, pāritum (+dat), *obey*
persuadeō, -ēre, persuasī, persuasum (+dat.), *persuade*
pertineō, -ēre, pertinuī, pertentum, *extend, pertain*
placeō, -ēre, placuī, placitum (+dat.), *be pleasing*
prohibeō, -ēre, prohibuī, prohibitum, *deny, keep off, prevent*
reor, rērī, ratus sum, *imagine, suppose, think*
respondeō, -ēre, respondī, responsum, *answer, respond*
retineō, -ēre, retinuī, retentum, *hold back, restrain*
sedeō, -ēre, sēdī, sessum, *sit*
studeō, -ēre, studuī, ----, (+dat.) *be eager for, desire*
sustineō, -ēre, sustinuī, sustentum, *hold (up), sustain*
teneō, -ēre, tenuī, tentum, *contain, hold*
terreō, -ēre, terruī, territum, *frighten*
timeō, timēre, timuī, -----, *be afraid of, fear*
tueor, tuērī, tuitum, *observe, protect, scan*
vereor, verērī, veritus, *fear, respect*
videō, -ēre, vīdī, vīsum, *see, (pass.) appear, be seen, seem*

3rd Conjugation

abscīdō, -ere, -cīdī, -cīsum, *cut away, cut off*
accēdō, -ere, accessī, accessum, *approach, come up to, go towards*
accipiō, -ere, -cēpī, -ceptum, *receive*
accurrō, -ere, accursī, accursum, *run to*
addūcō, -ere, addūxī, adductum, *lead to, influence*
admittō, -ere, admīsī, admissum, *admit, allow*
agō, -ere, ēgī, actum, *deal with, do, drive, treat*
āmittō, -ere, āmīsī, āmissum, *lose, send away*

animadvertō, -ere, animadvertī, animadversum, *notice, pay attention to*

ascendō, -ere, ascendī, ascēnsum, *ascend*

cēdō, -ere, cessī, cessum, *go, yield*

cernō, -ere, crēvī, crētum, *decide, discern, perceive*

cogō, -ere, coēgī, coactum, *compel, drive together, collect, force, gather*

colloquor, colloquī, collocūtus sum, *converse*

committō, -ere, commīsī, commissum, *engage, entrust*

comprehendō, -ere, -hendī, -hensum, *grasp, seize*

concēdō, -ere, concessī, concessum, *grant, yield*

condō, -ere, condidī, conditum, *bury, found (a city)*

confīdō, -ere, confīsus sum, (semi-deponent), *trust*

conscrībō, -ere, conscrīpsī, conscrīptum, *enlist, enroll*

cōnsequor, cōnsequī, cōnsecūtus sum, *follow, gain, pursue*

cōnsistō, -ere, cōnstitī, cōnstitum, *stop*

cōnstituō, -ere, cōnstituī, cōnstitūtum, *decide, determine, establish*

cōnsulō, -ere, cōnsuluī, cōnsultum, *consult, resolve*

contegō, -ere, contēxī, contēctum, *cover*

contendō, -ere, contendī, contentum, *compete, hurry, make effort, march, strive*

crēdō, -ere, crēdidī, crēditum (dat.), *believe, entrust*

currō, -ere, cucurrī, cursum, *hasten, run*

dēdūcō, -ere, dēdūxī, dēductum, *draw (a weapon), lead away, remove*

dēfendō, -ere, dēfendī, dēfēnsum, *defend*

dēligō, -ere, dēlēgī, dēlectum, *choose*

dēpōnō, -ere, dēposuī, dēpositum, *put down*

dēscendō, -ere, dēscendī, dēscēnsum, *descend*

dīcō, -ere, dīxī, dictum, *say, speak, tell*

dīmittō, -ere, dīmīsī, dīmissum, *dismiss, send away*

discēdō, -ere, discessī, discessum, *depart, leave, withdraw*

discō, -ere, didicī,----, *learn*

dūcō, -ere, dūxī, ductum, *lead*

ēdō, -ere, ēdidī, ēditum, *give out, lead out, unsheath*

ērumpō, -ere, ērūpī, ēruptus, *break out, burst out*

excēdō, -ere, excessī, excessum, *depart, go out*

excipio, -ere, excēpī, exceptum, *greet, receive*

exigō, -ere, exēgī, exactum, *collect, demand, drive out, finish (a life)*

expōnō, -ere, exposuī, expositum, *explain, expose*

extrahō, -ere, extrāxī, extrāctum, *drag out*

exuō, -ere, exuī, exūtum, *put off, take off*

fingō, -ere, finxī, fictus, *compose, fashion, imagine, make, make up*

fruor, fruī, fructus sum (+abl.), *enjoy, profit from*

fungor, fungī, functus sum (+abl.), *perform*

gerō, gerere, gessī, gestum, *carry on*

ignoscō, -ere, ignōvī, ignōtum (+dat.), *forgive*

incēdō, -ere, incessī, incessum, *go in*

incendō, -ere, incendī, incensum, *burn, outrage, set fire to*

inclūdō, -ere, inclūsī, inclūsum, *enclose, imprison, shut up*

incolō, -ere, incoluī, ----, *inhabit*

indūcō, -ere, indūxī, inductum, *influence, lead in*

induō, -ere, induī, indūtum, *clothe*

induō, -ere, induī, indūtum, *put on*

inrumpō, -ere, inrūpī,inruptum, *burst in*

intellegō, -ere, intellēgī, intellectum, *understand*

interclūdō, -ere, interclūsī, interclūsum, *block, shut off, stop*

lābor, lābī, lapsus sum, *collapse, slip*

legō, -ere, lēgī, lēctum, *choose, pick out, read*

loquor, loquī, locūtus sum, *speak, talk*

mergō, -ere, mersī, mersum, *plunge, sink*

mittō, -ere, mīsī, missum, *send*

nanciscor, nanciscī, nactus sum, *get, obtain*

nascor, nascī, nātus sum, *be born*

oblīviscor, oblīviscī, oblītus sum, *forget*

offendō, -ere, offendī, offēnsum, *offend*

ostendō, -ere, ostendī, ostentum, *stretch out before, display, show*

parcō, -cere, pepercī,----(+dat.), *spare*

perdūcō, -ere, perdūxī, perductum, *lead through*

petō, -ere, petivī, petītum, *ask for, seek*

pōnō, -ere, posuī, positum, *place, put, set up*

praecipiō, -ere, praecēpī, praeceptum, *advise, direct, order, set out*

quaerō, -ere, quaesīvī, quaesītum, *ask, seek*

recipiō, -ere, recēpī, receptum, *accept, receive*

reddō, -ere, reddidi, redditum, *give back*

redīgō, -ere, redēgī, redactum, *drive back*

regō, -ere, rēxī, rēctum, *rule*

relinquō, -ere, relīquī, relictum, *leave, leave behind*

remittō, -ere, remīsī, remissum, *send back*

revertō, -ere, revertī, ---- (usu. deponent in pres.), *return, turn back*

scrībō, -ere, scrīpsī, scrīptum, *write*

sequor, sequī, secutus sum, *follow*

solvō, -ere, solvī, solūtum, *release, unbind, loosen, untie*

sūmō, -ere, sūmpsī, sūmpsum, *take up*

surgō, -ere, surrēxī, surrēctum, *rise, stretch upward, swell*

suscipiō, -ere, suscēpī, susceptum, *support, take up, undertake*

tegō, -ere, tēxī, tēctum, *conceal, cover, shelter*

tendō, -ere, tetendī, tentum, *extend, proceed, stretch out*

tollō, tollere, sustulī, sublātum, *lift, raise*

trādō, -ere, trādidī, trāditum, *hand across, hand down*

trādūcō, -ere, trāduxī, trāductum, *lead across*

trahō, -ere, trāxī, trāctum, *drag*

transīgō, -ere, transēgī, transactum, *accomplish, finish, pierce, run through*

ūtor, ūtī, ūsus sum (+abl.), *enjoy, experience, use*

vertō, -ere, vertī, versum, *turn*

vescor, vescī, ---- (+abl.), *eat, feed on*

vincō, -ere, vīcī, victum, *conquer, defeat*

vīvō, -ere, vīxī, vīctum, *live*

volvō, -ere, volvī, volūtum, *roll*

3rd Conjugation I-stem

afficiō, -ere, affēcī, affectum, *affect, do to, move, treat*

aggredior, aggredī, aggressus sum, *approach, attack*

capiō, -ere, cēpī, captum, *capture, seize, take*

conficiō, -ere, confēcī, confectum, *accomplish, finish, make ready* conicio, -ere, coniēcī, coniectum, *cast, hurl, throw, throw together*

conspiciō, -ere, conspexī, conspectum, *catch sight of, observe, spot*

cupiō, -ere, cupīvī, cupītum, *desire, long for, wish*

dēficiō, -ere, dēfēcī, dēfectum, *fail, fall away*

despiciō, -ere, despexī, despectum, *look down on*

efficiō, -ere, effēcī, effectum, *cause, effect, bring about*

ēgredior, ēgredī, ēgressus sum, *go out, leave*

ēripiō, -ere, ēripuī, ēreptum, *rescue, snatch*

faciō, -ere, fēcī, factum, *do, make*

fugiō, -ere, fūgī, fugitūrus, *avoid, flee, run away*

incipiō, -ere, incēpī, inceptum, *begin*

inficiō, -ere, infēcī, infectum, *dye, stain*

inspiciō, -ere, inspexī, inspectum, *look into or upon*

interficio, -ere, -fēcī, -fectum, *kill*

morior, morī, mortuus sum, *die*

patior, patī, passus sum, *endure, experience, suffer*

perficiō, -ere, perfēcī, perfectum, *complete, finish, perfect*

perspiciō, -ere, perspexī, perspectum, *examine, observe*

prōgredior, prōgredī, prōgressus sum, *advance, go forward, march forward*

reficiō, -ere, refēcī, refectum, *repair, restore*

4th Conjugation

adorior, adorīrī, adortus sum, *attack*

aperiō, īre, aperuī, apertum, *open, reveal, uncover*

audiō, -īre, audīvī, audītum, *hear, listen to*

conveniō, īre, convēnī, conventum, *come together, convene, meet*

dormiō, - īre, dormīvī, dormitum , *sleep*

experior, experīrī, expertus sum, *experience, test, try*

finiō, -īre, finīvī/finiī, finitum, *define, limit*

inveniō, -īre, invēnī, inventum, *come upon, find*

mentior, mentīrī, mentītus sum, *tell a lie*

mūniō, -īre, mūnīvī, mūnītum, *fortify, build*

nesciō, nescīre, nescīvī/nesciī, nescītus, *not know*

orior, -īrī, ortus sum, *rise, appear*

perveniō, -īre, pervēnī, perventum, *arrive, come to*

potior, -īrī, potītum sum, *gain possession of*

puniō, -īre, pūnīvī, pūnītum, *punish*

reperiō, -īre, repperī, repertum, *discover, find (by looking)*

sciō, -īre, scīvī (or sciī), scītum, *know*

sentiō, -īre, sēnsī, sēnsum, *feel, perceive*

veniō, -īre, vēnī, ventum, *come*

Irregular

abeō, abīre, abiī (-īvī), abītum,, *go away*

absum, abesse, āfuī, āfutūrus, *be away*

adeō, adīre, adiī (-īvī), aditum, *go toward, go to*

adsum, adesse, adfuī, adfutūrus, *be present*

afferō, afferre, attulī, allātum, *bring, carry toward, convey*

conferō, conferre, contulī, collātum, *bring together, (with sē) go*

dēsum, dēesse, dēfuī, dēfutūrus (+dat.), *be lacking, fail*

differō, differre, distulī, dīlātum, *defer, differ, scatter*

do, dare, dedī, datum, *give*

eō, īre, iī(īvī), itum, *go*

exeō, -īre, exīvī/exiī, exītum, *go out, withdraw*

ferō, ferre, tulī, lātum, *bear, bring, carry, endure*

fiō, fiērī, factus sum, *be made, become, happen*

ineō, -īre, iniī (inīvī), initum, *go in, enter, adopt (plan)*

mālō, mālle, māluī, -----, *prefer*

meminī, meminisse, *be mindful of, remember*

nōlō, nōlle, nōluī, -----, *be unwilling, not to want, not to wish*

perferō, perferre, pertulī, perlātum, *endure, report*

possum, posse, potuī, -----, *be able, can*

praetereō, -īre, preaterivī/-iī, praeteritum, *go past, skip*

redeō, -īre, rediī (-īvī), reditum, *go back, return*

referō, referre, retulī, relatum, *bring back, carry back, relate*

subeō, -īre, subiī (subīvī), subitum, *undergo*

sum, esse, fuī, futūrus, *be*

tollō tollere, sustulī, sublātum, *lift, raise*

volō, velle, voluī, -----, *want, wish*

Impersonals

licet, licēre, licuit or licitum est, *it is permitted*

necesse esse, *it is necessary*

oportet, oportere, oportuit, *it is fitting*

Nouns

1st Declension: Feminine

amīcitia,-ae, f., *friendship*

aqua, -ae f., *water*

causa, -ae f., *cause*

cōpia, cōpiae f., *abundance, supply,* pl. *provisions, troops*

cūra, -ae f., *care, concern, worry*

dea, -ae f., *goddess*

diligentia, -ae, f., *diligence*

dextera, -ae, f., *right hand*

ēloquentia,-ae f., *eloquence*

epistula, -ae f., *letter*

fāma, -ae f., *glory, reputation, rumor*

familia, familiae f., *family, household slaves*

fīlia, -ae f., *daughter*

flamma, -ae f., *flame*

forma, formae f., *form*

fortūna, -ae f., *fortune, luck*

fuga, -ae f., *escape, flight*

galea, -ae f., *helmet*

gloria, gloriae f., *fame, glory*

gratia, -ae f., *favor* (pl.) *thanks*

hōra, -ae f., *hour*

inimīcitia,-ae f., *enmity, hostility, unfriendliness*

inopia, inopiae f., *lack*

insula, -ae f., *island*

invidia, -ae f., *envy, hatred, jealousy*

īra, -ae f., *anger, wrath*

lacrima, -ae f., *tear*

littera,-ae, f., *letter (of the alphabet),* (pl.). *letter, literature*

memoria, memoriae f., *memory*

mora, -ae f., *delay*

nātūra,-ae f., *character, nature*

101

ōra, -ae f., *edge, rim, shore*
patria, -ae, *native land*
pecūnia,-ae, f., *money*
poena, -ae f., *punishment*
porta, -ae f., *gate*
prōvincia,-ae, f., *province*
puella, -ae f., *girl*
rēgia, -ae f., *palace*
rēgīna, -ae f., *queen*
sententia,-ae, f., *opinion*
silva, -ae f., *forest, woods*
sinistra, -ae f., *left hand*
terra, -ae f., *country, earth, land*
umbra, -ae f., *ghost, shadow*
unda, -ae f., *wave*
vespera,-ae f., *evening*
via, -ae f., *road, way*
vīta, -ae f., *life*

1st Declension: Masculine

agricola, -ae m., *farmer*
incola, -ae m., *inhabitant*
nauta, -ae m., *sailor*
pīrāta, -ae m., *pirate*
poēta, -ae m., *poet*
scrība, -ae m., *secretary, writer*

2nd Declension: Masculine

ager, agrī m., *field*
amīcus, -ī m., *friend*
animus, -ī m., *spirit, mind* (pl.) *bravery*
annus, -ī m., *year*
avus, -ī m., *grandfather*
campus, -ī m., *field, plain, playing field*
cibus,-ī, m., *food*
deus, -ī m., *god*
discipulus, -ī m., *student*
discus, ī m., *discus*
dominus, -ī m., *master*
equus, ī m., *horse*
fīlius, -ī m., *son*
gladius, -ī m., *sword*
lēgātus,-ī, m., *envoy, legate*
liber, librī m., *book*
līberī,-ōrum m., *children*
locus, -ī m., (loca, -ōrum n. pl.), *place*
lūdus, -ī m., *game, sport*
magister, magistrī m., *teacher*
modus, -ī m., *manner, way*
mūrus, -ī m., *wall*
numerus,-ī, m., *number*
nūntius, -ī m., *messenger*
oculus, -ī m., *eye*
populus,-ī, m., *people*
puer, puerī m., *boy*
servus, -ī m., *slave*
socius, -ī m., *ally*

somnus, ī m., *sleep*
tribūnus,-ī, m., *tribune*
umerus, -ī m., *shoulder*
ventus, ī m., *wind*
vesper, vesperis m., *evening*
vīcus,-ī, m., *village*
vir, virī m., *man*

2nd Declension: Neuter

arma, -ōrum n. pl., *arms*
aurum, -ī n., *gold*
auxilium,-ī, n., *aid, help*
bellum, ī n., *war*
beneficium,-ī, n., *favor, help, kindness, support, benefit, service*
caelum, -ī n., *air, heaven, sky*
castra, -ōrum n., pl., *camp*
collum, -ī n., *neck*
cōnsilium, -ī n., *plan*
donum, -ī n., *gift*
factum, ī n., *deed*
fātum, -ī n., *fate*
ferrum, -ī n., *iron, sword*
forum,-ī n., *forum, marketplace*
gaudium,-ī, n., *joy, gladness*
impedīmentum,-ī, m., *hindrance,* (pl.). *baggage*
imperium, -ī n., *power, rule*
ingenium,-ī n., *character, innate quality*
monstrum, -ī n., *monster*
negōtium,-ī n., *business*
nimium,-ī n., *excess*
officium,-ī n., *duty, office*
ōrāculum, -ī n., *oracle*
perīculum, -ī n., *danger, peril*
praemium,-ī n., *prize, reward*
praesidium,-ī n., *assistance, defense, protection*
rēgnum, -ī n., *kingdom*
saxum, -ī n., *rock, stone*
signum,-ī n., *sign, signal, standard*
spatium,-ī n., *room, space*
studium,-i n., *devotion, eagerness, enthusiasm, keenness*
tantum,-ī n., *so much*
tēlum, ī n., *javelin, weapon*
tergum, -ī n., *back*
verbum, -ī n., *word*
vinculum,-ī n., *chain, fetter, bond*

3rd Declension: Feminine

aetās,-tātis, f., *age*
arbor, arbōris, f., *tree*
ars, artis f., *craft, skill, trade*
arx, arcis,f., *citadel*
auctōritās,-tātis, f., *authority, influence*
celeritās, celeritātis, f., *speed, swiftness*
cīvitās,-tātis, f., *citizenship, state*
continens, continentis f., *mainland*
cupiditās,-tātis, f., *desire, greed*
difficultās,-tātis, f., *difficulty*

factiō, factiōnis, f., *faction*
facultās, facultātis f., *ability, opportunity, power, skill*
falx, falcis, f., *sickle, sword (curved)*
famēs, famis f., *famine, hunger*
forte (in abl.), *by chance*
gēns, gentis (-ium) f., *nation, tribe*
gravitās, gravitātis f., *hardness, seriousness, severity, weight*
hiems, hiemis f., *winter*
laus, laudis f., *praise*
lēx, lēgis f., *law*
lībertās,-tātis, f., *freedom*
lūx, lūcis f., *light*
māter, mātris f., *mother*
mens, mentis (-ium) f., *intention, mind*
mors, mortis (-ium) f., *death*
mulier, mulieris f., *woman*
multitūdō, multitūdinis f., *crowd, multitude*
nāvis, nāvis (-ium) f., *ship*
nox, noctis (-ium) f., *night*
ops, opis f., *power, (pl.) resources*
ōrātiō, ōrātiōnis f., *speech*
pars, partis (-ium) f., *direction, part*
pax, pacis, f., *peace*
plebs, plebis f., *common people, plebs*
potestās,-tātis, f., *power*
quiēs, quiētis f., *quiet, rest, sleep*
ratiō, ratiōnis f., *reason, theory*
salus, salūtis f., *safety(personal), well-being*
sēdēs, sēdis f., *abode, seat*
servitūs, servitūtis f., *slavery*
sollicitūdō, sollicitūdinis f., *care, worry*
soror, sorōris f., *sister*
tellūs, tellūris f., *earth, ground, land*
tempestās, tempestātis f., *storm, tempest, weather*
urbs, urbis (-ium) f., *city*
uxor, uxōris f., *wife*
virgō, virginis f., *maiden*
virtūs, virtūtis f *courage, excellence, strength, virtue*
vīs, vīs f. (pl. vīrēs, vīrium), *force, power, (pl.) strength*
vōx, vōcis f., *voice*

3rd Declension: Masculine

amor, amōris, m., *love*
clāmor, clāmōris, m., *noise, shout*
cōnsul, cōnsulis m., *consul*
custōs, custōdis, m., *guard, guardian, protector*
dolor, dolōris m., *grief, pain*
dux, ducis m., *leader*
eques, equitis m., *horseman, (pl.) cavalry*
fīnis, -is (-ium) m., *end, (pl.) territory*
frāter, frātris m., *brother*
furor, -ōris m., *fury, rage*
homō, hominis m., *human, man*
honor, honōris m., *honor, esteem, office*
hostis, hostis (-ium) m., *enemy*
ignis, -is (ium) m., *fire*
iuvenis, -is m., *youth, young man*

labor, labōris m., *hardship, labor, work*
māiōrēs, -um m., *ancestors*
mīles, mīlitis m., *soldier*
mōns, montis (-ium) m., *mountain*
mōs, mōris, m., *custom, (pl.). behavior, character*
nēmō, nēminis m., *no one, nobody*
ordō, ordinis m., *order, rank*
pater, patris m., *father*
pavor, pavōris m., *panic, terror*
pēs, pedis m., *foot*
pōns, pontis (-ium) m., *bridge*
princeps, principis m., *chief, leader*
rēx, rēgis m., *king*
rūmor, rūmōris m., *rumor*
sanguis, sanguinis m., *blood*
senex, senis m., *old man*
sōl, sōlis, m., *sun*
spontē, (abl. only), *of one's own accord, voluntarily*
terror, terrōris m., *fear, terror*
timor, timōris m., *fear*
vātēs, vātis m., *prophet, seer*

3rd Declension: Masculine and Feminine

adulēscēns, adulēscentis m./f., *youth*
anguis, -is m./f., *serpent, snake*
cīvis, cīvis (-ium) m/f, *citizen*
comes, comitis m./f., *companion*
coniunx, coniugis m./f., *spouse*
infans, infantis (-ium) m./f., *infant*

3rd Declension: Neuter

aes, aeris n., *bronze, copper*
agmen, agminis n., *column (of men)*
caput, capitis n., *head*
carmen, carminis n., *song*
certāmen, certāminis n., *contest, struggle*
corpus, corporis n., *body*
decus, decoris n., *dignity, glory, honor*
genus, -eris n., *kind, sort*
iter, itineris n., *journey, road, way*
iūs, iūris n., *right, law*
lītus, lītoris n., *beach, coast, shore*
lūmen, lūminis n., *light*
mare, maris (ium) n., *sea*
moenia, -ium n. pl., *walls*
mūnus, mūneris n., *function, task, gift (of the gods)*
nōmen, nōminis n., *name*
nūmen, nūminis n., *consent, nod, will (divine)*
onus, oneris n., *burden*
opus, operis n., *task, work*
ōs, oris n., *mouth*
pectus, pectoris n., *breast, chest, heart*
plūs, plūris n., *more, too much*
rūs, rūris n., *country, countryside*
scelus, sceleris n., *crime*
sīdus, sīderis n., *star*
tempus, tempōris n., *time*

4th Declension: Feminine

domus, -ūs, f., *home, household*
manus, -ūs f., *band, hand*

4th Declension: Masculine

adventus,-ūs, m., *approach, arrival*
cāsus, -ūs m., *chance, fall, misfortune*
cōnspectus,-ūs, m., *sight*
cursus,-ūs, m., *course*
exercitus, -ūs m., *army*
flūctus, -ūs m., *wave, flood, sea*
fremitus, -ūs m., *groan, roar, rumble*
fructus, -ūs m., *benefit, enjoyment, fruit*
gradus, -ūs m., *step*
ictus, -ūs m., *blow, strike*
impetus,-ūs, m., *attack, attack*
magistrātus,-ūs, m., *magistracy, magistrate*
metus,-ūs, m., *fear*
reditus, -ūs m., *return*
senātus, -ūs m., *senate*
sinus, -ūs m., *bosom, embrace*
ūsus, -ūs m., *application, practice, skill, use*

4th Declension: Neuter

cornū, -ūs n., *horn, wing (of an army)*

5th Declension

diēs, -ēī, m., *day*
fidēs, -eī, f., *faith, loyalty*
rēs, reī f., *affair, matter, thing, situation*
speciēs, -ēī, f., *appearance, sight*
spēs, speī, f., *hope*

Indeclinable

nefās (indecl.) n., *evil, wrong*
nihil (indecl.) n., *nothing*

Proper Nouns

Aethiōps, Aethiopis, m., *Ethiopian*
Aquītānia, -ae, f., *province in S. W. Gaul*
Asia, -ae, f., *Asia*
Britannia, -ae, f, *Britain*
Brundisium, ī, n. *Brundisium*
Caesar, Caesaris, m., *Gaius Julius Casear*
Cathāgō, -inis, *Carthage*
Cicerō, Ciceronis, m., *M. Tullius Cicero*
Diana, -ae, f., *Diana*
Gorgo(n), Gorgonis, f., *Gorgon*
Helvētius, ī, m., *Swiss person*
Ītalia, -ae, f., *Italy*
Iuppiter, Iovis, m., *Jupiter*
Livius, Liviī, m., *Titus Livius*
Medusa, -ae, f., *Medusa*
Minerva, - ae, f., *Minerva*
Neptūnus, -ī, m., *Neptune*
Olympus, -ī, m., *Mount Olympus*

Pompeius Magnus, Pompeiī Magnī, m., *Pompey*
Rōma, -ae, f., *Rome*
Sicilia, -ae, f., *Sicily*
Valerius Maximus, Valeriī Maximī, m., *Valerius Maximus*
Vergilius, Vergiliī, m., *Publius Vergilius Maro*

Adjectives

1st and 2nd Declension

aeger, aegra, aegrum, *sick*
aequus, aequa, aequum, *even, fair, flat, level*
aliēnus,-a,-um, *foreign, unrelated*
alius, -a, -um, *another, other*
alter, altera, alterum, *the other (of 2)*
altus, -a, -um, *deep, high, tall*
amīcus, -a, -um, *friendly*
angustus,-a,-um,, *narrow*
antīquus, -a, -um, *ancient*
aptus,-a,-um, *appropriate*
āter, ātra, ātrum, *black, dark*
avidus,-a,-um, *eager, greedy*
beātus, -a, -um, *blessed, happy*
bellus,-a,-um, *fine, handsome, nice, pretty*
bonus, -a, -um, *good*
cārus, -a, -um, *dear*
certus, -a, -um, *certain, set*
cēterī, -ae, -a, *the remaining, the rest*
cupidus,-a,-um, *eager, greedy, longing*
desertus, -a, -um, *deserted*
dexter, dextera, dexterum, *right*
dignus,-a,-um, *worthy*
dīvīnus,-a,-um, *divine, heavenly*
dīvus, -a, -um, *divine*
doctus,-a,-um, *learned*
falsus,-a,-um, *mistaken, untrue*
fessus, -a, -um, *exhausted, tired*
finitimus,-a,-um, *neighboring*
firmus,-a,-um, *firm, resolute, strong*
grātus, -a, -um, *pleasing*
idōneus, -a, -um, *suitable*
ignāvus, -a, -um, *idle, lazy*
imperītus,-a,-um, *ignorant, inexperienced, unskilled*
īmus,-a,-um, *at the foot of, bottom of, deepest, lowest*
inimīcus,-a,-um, *hostile, unfriendly*
inīquus,-a,-um, *uneven, unfair*
integer, integra, integrum, *untouched, whole*
invītus,-a,-um, *unwilling*
īrātus, -a, -um, *angry*
laetus, -a, -um, *happy, joyful*
līber, lībera, līberum, *free*
ligneus, -a, -um, *wooden*
longus, -a, -um, *long*
magicus, -a, -um, *magical*
magnus, -a, -um, *great, large*
malus, -a, -um, *bad, evil, wicked*
maximus, -a, -um, *most*
meritus, -a, -um, *deserved, due*

meus, -a, -um, *mine, my*
minimus, -a, -um, *smallest, very small*
miser, misera, miserum, *unhappy, wretched*
multus, -a, -um, *many, much*
necessārius,-a,-um, *inevitable, necessary*
neuter, neutra, neutrum, *neither*
noster, nostra, nostrum, *our*
nōvissimus,-a,-um, *last, most recent*
novus, -a, -um, *new*
nullus, -a, -um, *no, none, not any*
optimus, -a,-um, *best, very good*
parvus, -a, -um, *little, small*
paucī, -ae, -a, *few*
perītus,-a,-um, *experienced, skilled*
pessimus, -a, -um, *worst*
pius, -a, -um, *devoted, dutiful, loyal*
plurimus, -a, -um, *most, very many*
prāvus,-a,-um, *crooked, distorted, improper*
prīmus, -a, -um, *first*
propinquus,-a,-um, *near, neighboring*
proximus, -a, -um, *next*
pūblicus, -a, -um, *public*
pulcher, pulchra, pulchrum, *beautiful*
reliquus,-a,-um, *remaining, rest*
sacer, sacra, sacrum, *holy*
salvus,-a,-um, *safe, unharmed, well*
secundus, -a, -um, *second*
sinister, sinistra, sinistrum, *left*
sōlus, -a, -um, *alone, only, sole*
studiōsus,-a,-um, *devoted, eager, zealous*
summus,-a,-um, *highest, top of*
tantus,-a,-um, *so great*
tardus,-a,-um, *late, slow*
tōtus, -a, -um, *whole, entire*
tranquillus, -a, -um, *calm, tranquil*
tūtus, -a, -um, *safe, safe*
tuus, -a, -um, *your, yours* (sg.)
ullus, -a, -um, *any*
ūmidus,-a,-um, *damp, moist*
uter, utra, utrum, *which (of two)*
uterque, utraque, utrumque, *both, each (of two)*
vacuus, -a, -um, *empty*
vērus,-a,-um, *true*
vester, vestra, vestrum, *your, yours* (pl.)
vīvus,-a,-um, *alive*

3rd Declension: 3 Terminations

ācer, ācris, ācre, *fierce, keen, sharp*
celer, celeris, celere, *quick, swift*

3rd Declension: 2 Termination

brevis, -e, *brief, short*
commūnis,-e, *common, general, shared*
difficilis, -e, *difficult*
dissimilis, -e, *dissimilar, unlike*
dulcis, -e, *sweet*

facilis, -e, *easy*
fidēlis,-e, *faithful, loyal*
fortis, -e, *brave, strong*
gracilis, -e, *graceful, slender*
gravis, -e, *heavy, serious*
horribilis, -e, *horrible*
humilis, -e, *humble, low*
incolumis,-e, *safe, unharmed*
insignis,-e, *distinguished, prominent*
māior, maius, *greater, better*
minor, minus, *smaller*
mīrābilis,-e, *amazing, remarkable, wonderful*
nātūrālis,-e, *by birth, natural*
nōbilis,-e, *noble*
omnis, -e, *all, every*
peior, peius, *worse*
similis, -e, *like, similar*
tālis,-e, *such*
trīstis, -e, *sad*
turpis, -e, *disgraceful, shameful*
ūtilis, -e, *useful*

3rd Declension: 1 Termination

audāx, audācis, *bold*
dīligēns,-ntis, *careful*
fēlīx, fēlīcis, *happy*
immemor, immemoris, *forgetful, huge*
ingens, ingentis, *vast*
memor, memoris, *mindful*
pār, paris, *equal, like*
patien, -entis, *hardy, patient, tolerant*
potens,-ntis, *capable, powerful*
prūdens,-ntis, *prudent, sensible*
sapiēns, sapientis, *wise*
vetus, veteris, *old*

Reflexive Adjectives

meus, -a, -um, *mine, my own*
noster, nostra, nostrum, *our own*
suus, -a, -um, *his, her, its, their own*
tuus, -a, -um, *your (sg.) own*
vester, vestra, vestrum, *your (pl.) own*

Proper Adjectives

Belgius, -a, -um, *Belgian*
Celtus, -a, -um, *Celtic*
Gallus, -a, -um, *Gaul, Gallic*
Germānus, -a, -um, *German*
Helvētius, -a, -um, *Swiss*
Poenus, -a, -um, *Carthaginian, Punic*
Rōmānus, -a, -um, *Roman, Roman*

Indeclinable

satis, *enough*
tot, *so many*

Interrogative

quālis,-e, *what kind of?, what sort of?*
quantus,-a,-um, *how great?, how much?*
quī, quae, quod, *which?, what?*
quot, *how many?*

Pronouns

Personal and Reflexive

ego, *I*
is, ea, id, *he, she, it*
nōs, *we*
suī (gen. sg.), *himself, herself, itself, themselves*
tū, *you (sg.)*
vōs, *you (pl.)*

Relative

quī, quae, quod, *that, which, who*

Demonstrative

hic, haec, hoc, *this (pl.) these*
īdem, eadem, idem, *same*
ille, illa, illud, *that, (pl.) those*
is, ea, id, *this, that*
iste, ista, istud, *that (of yours)*

Indefinite

aliquis, aliquid, *any*
quīdam, quaedam, quoddam, *certain*
quisque, quaeque, quidque, *each*

Intensive

ipse, ipsa, ipsum, *himself, herself, itself, themselves, myself, yourself, ourselves, yourselves; very*

Interrogative

quis, quid, *who? what?*

Adverbs

adeō, *so, to such an extent*
adhūc, *still, to this point, yet*
aegrē, *painfully, with difficulty*
aliquandō, *anytime, sometime*
anteā, *before, formerly*
anteā, *previously*
audacter, *boldly*
bene, *well*
clam, *secretly*
confestim, *immediately*
cottīdiē, *daily*
crās, *tomorrow*
deinde, *from there, next, then*
dēsuper, *above, from above*
diū, *for a long time*
diūtissimē, *for a very long time, for the longest time*

diūtius, *for a longer time*
eō, *to that place*
ferē, *almost, nearly*
fortasse, *perhaps*
forte, *accidently*
frustrā, *in vain*
graviter, *seriously*
haud, *not at all*
herī, *yesterday*
hīc, *here*
hinc, *from here, from this place*
hodiē, *today*
hūc, *to this place, hither*
iam, *already, now*
ibī, *there*
inde, *from there, thence*
interim, *meanwhile*
ita, *so, thus*
itaque, *and so*
item, *likewise*
iterum, *again*
libenter, *freely, willingly*
longē, *far*
magis, *more*
magnopere, *greatly*
maximē, *very greatly*
modo, *just, only, merely*
mox, *soon*
multum, *much*
nimis, *too, very much*
nōn, *not*
nōndum, *not yet*
numquam, *never*
nunc, *now*
nūper, *recently*
omnīnō, *altogether, entirely*
paene, *almost, practically*
parum, *too little*
paulō, *a little, somewhat*
posteā, *afterwards*
praesertim, *especially*
prīmō, *at first*
quam (+ superlative), *as...as possible*
quam, *than*
quondam, *at one time, formerly, once*
rursus, *a second time, backwards, again*
saepe, *often*
semper, *always*
sīc, *so, thus*
statim, *at once, immediately*
subitō, *suddenly*
tam, *so*
tandem, *at length, finally*
tum, *at that time, then*
tunc, *at that time, then*
umquam, *ever*
ūnā, adv, *together*

undique, *everywhere, from all sides, on all sides*
velut/velutī, *even as, just as*
vix, *hardly, scarcely*

Interrogative

cur, *why?*
quamdiū, *how long?*
quandō, *when?*
quō, *to where?, whither?*
quotiēns, *how often?*
unde, *from where?, whence?*

Prepositions

With the Ablative

ā, ab, *away from ,by, away*
cum, *along with, with*
dē, *about, concerning, down from*
ē, ex, *from, out of*
in, *in, on*
prō, *in front of, on behalf of*
sine, *without*
sub, *under*

With the Accusative

ad, *at, to*
ad, *towards*
circum, *around*
ante, *before*
apud, *among, at the house of, in the presence of*
contrā, *opposite, toward*
in, *into, onto, against,*
inter, *among, between*
ob, *because of, on account of*
per, *through, by*
post, *after*
praeter, *along, by, in front of, past*
prope, *near*
propter, *on account of, because of*
super, *above, in a higher position, over*
trāns, *across*

Conjunctions

ac/atque, *and*
antequam, *before*
at, *but*
aut, *or*
aut...aut, *either...or*
autem, *but, however, moreover*
dum, *while*
enim, *for*
et, *and*
etiam, *also, even*
igitur, *therefore*
nam, *for*
nec/neque, *and...not, nor*
neque...neque, *neither...nor*

nōn modo ... sed etiam, *not only ... but also*
postquam, *after*
-que, *and*
quod, *because*
sed, *but*
tamen, *nevertheless, still, yet*
ubi, *when, where*
ut (+ ind.), *as* (+ subj.), *in order that, so that, with the result that*

Numerals

Cardinal

ūnus, -a, -um, *one*
duo, duae, duo, *two*
trēs, tria, *three*
quattuor, *four*
quinque, *five*
sex, *six*
septem, *seven*
octo, *eight*
novem, *nine*
decem, *ten*
centum, *hundred*
ducentī,-ae,-a, *two hundred*
trecentī,-ae,-a, *three hundred*

Ordinal

prīmus, -a, -um, *first*
secundus, -a, -um, *second*
tertius, -a, -um, *third*

Idioms

aes aliēnum, *debt*
causam habēre, *have a reason*
cōnsilium capere, *adopt a plan*
dē... agere, *debate about, talk about*
in mātrimōnium ducere, *marry*
sē ēripere, *escape*
fac ut, *bring it about that*
iter facere, *make a journey, march*
fīdēs pūblica, *safe conduct*
bellum gerere, *wage war*
gratiās agere (+dat.), *give thanks, thank*
causam habēre, *have a reason*
iter facere, *make a journey, march*
in mentem venīre, *come to mind*
mōs maiōrēs, *tradition*
ōrātionem habēre, *give a speech*
poenās dare, *pay a penalty*
quam prīmum, *as soon as possible*
fīdēs pūblica, *safe conduct*
sē recipere, *retreat*
rēs pūblica, reī pūblicae f., *state*
utor bene, *treat well*
vītam agere , *lead a life*

Vocabulary

Nouns: The nominative singular of each noun is given followed by the genitive singular. For regular nouns of the first, second, fourth and fifth declension, only the genitive singular ending is given (e.g. **mūrus, -ī**). Where the stem cannot be determined from the nominative singular form, as in some second declension nouns and in the third declension, the full form of the genitive singular is given. Third I-stem nouns are indicated in the lists by (**-ium**).

Adjectives: Adjectives whose stems can be determined from the nominative singular masculine form appear as the nominative masculine singular with the endings for the other genders (e.g., **bonus, -a, -um; trīstis, -e**). Adjectives whose stems cannot be determined from the nominative singular masculine are written out fully: all three genders in the case of the adjectives of three or two terminations (e.g., **āter, ātris, ātre; melior, melius**); the nominative and genitive singulars in the case of adjectives of one termination (e.g., **fēlīx, fēlīcis**).

Verbs: The first person singular present indicative active of each verb is listed. If the verb is a regular first conjugation verb, a numeral follows to indicate its conjugation (**laudō** (1), *I praise*). Principal parts of second, third, and fourth conjugation verbs and irregular verbs are given in full, save that only the last three letters of the infinitive are typically written out.

Words introduced in *New First Steps In Latin* and *New Second Steps in Latin* are followed by an asterisk (*). Words introduced in *New Third Steps in Latin* chapters are marked with the lesson number in Roman numerals in square brackets [I].

LATIN – ENGLISH VOCABULARY

A

ā, ab (+ abl.), *away from, by, from**

abeō, abīre, abiī (-īvī), abītum,, *go away* [XX]

abscīdō, -ere, -cīdī, -cīsum, *cut away, cut off**

absum, abesse, āfuī, āfutūrus, *be away**

ac, *and**

accēdō, -ere, accessī, accessum, *approach, come up to, go towards* [IX]

accipiō, -ere, -cēpī, -ceptum, *receive**

accurrō, -ere, accursī, accursum, *run to**

ācer, ācris, ācre, *fierce, keen, sharp**

ad (+ acc.), *at, to, towards**

addūcō, -ere, addūxī, adductum, *lead to, influence* [X]

adeō, adv., *to such an extent, so* [IV]

adeō, adīre, adiī (-īvī), aditum, *go to* [XX]

adhūc, adv., *still, to this point, yet* *

adligō (1), *bind, tie**

admittō, -ere, admīsī, admissum, *admit, allow* [IX]

adorior, adorīrī, adortus sum, *attack* [XXVII]

adsum, adesse, adfuī, adfutūrus, *be present**

adulēscēns, adulēscentis m./f., *youth**

adventus, -ūs, m, *arrival, approach,* [I]

aeger, aegra, aegrum, *sick**

aegrē, adv., *painfully, with difficulty**

aequus, aequa, aequum, *even, level, fair, flat* [XX]

aes, aeris n., *copper, bronze* [XIII]

aes aliēnum, *debt* [XIII]

aetās, -tātis, f., *age,* [II]

Aethiōps, Aethiopis m., *Ethiopian,*

afferō, afferre, attulī, allātum, *bring, carry toward, convey* [XXVIII]

afficiō, -ere, affēcī, affectum, , *treat, affect* [XXV]

ager, agrī m., *field**

aggredior, aggredī, aggressus sum, *approach, attack* [V]

agmen, agminis n., *column (of men)**

agō, -ere, ēgī, actum, *deal with, do, drive, treat**

dē … agere , *talk about, debate about**

gratias agere (+dat), *thank, give thanks**

vītam agere, *lead a life**

agricola, -ae m., *farmer**

aliēnus, -a, -um, *unrelated, foreign* [XX]

aliquandō, adv., *sometime, anytime* [XXIII]

aliquis, aliquid, *anyone, anything* [XVII]; *someone, something*

alius, -a, -um, *another, other**

alter, altera, alterum, *the other (of 2)**

altus, -a, -um, *deep, high* *tall,*

amīcitia, -ae, f., *friendship* [III]

amīcus, -a, -um, *friendly**

amīcus -ī m., *friend*

āmittō, -ere, āmīsī, āmissum, *send away, lose* [IX]

amō (1), *like, love**

amor, amōris, m., *love* [XII]

Andromeda, -ae f., *Andromeda**

anguis, -is m./f., *serpent, snake**

angustus, -a, -um, *narrow* [V]

animadvertō, -ere, animadvertī, animadversum, *notice, pay attention to* [III] animus, -ī m., *spirit, mind, (pl) bravery* *

annus, -ī m., *year**

ante (+ acc.), *before**

anteā, adv., *formerly, before, previously* [XXV]

antequam, conj., *before**

antīquus, -a, -um, *ancient**

aperiō, īre, aperuī, apertum, *open, uncover, reveal* [XXIII]

appellō, (1), *accost, address, name* [I]

appropinquō, (1), *approach* [XV]

aptus, -a, -um, *appropriate* [XX]

apud (+acc.), *among, at the house of, in the presence of* [X]

Aquitania, -ae f., *province in S. W. Gaul*

aqua, -ae f., *water**

arbor, arbōris, f., *tree* [XII]

arca, -ae f., *ark, box, chest**

ardeō, -ēre, arsī, arsūrus, *be inflamed, blaze, burn**

arma, -ōrum n. pl., *arms**

ars, artis f., *skill, craft, trade* [XXIX]

arx, arcis,f., *citadel* [XIII]

ascendō, -ere, ascendī, ascēnsum, *ascend, climb*

Asia, -ae f., *Asia,*

at, conj., *but**

āter, ātra, ātrum, *black, dark**

ac/atque, conj., *and**

auctōritās, -tātis, f., *authority, influence* [II]

audacter, adv., *boldly**

audāx, audācis, *bold**

audiō, -īre, audīvī, audītum, *hear, listen to**

augeō, -ēre, auxī, auctum, *increase* [X]

aurum, -ī n., *gold**

aut, conj., *or**

aut...aut, conj., *either...or**

autem, conj., *but, however, moreover**

auxilium, -ī, n., *aid, help* [XXII]

avidus, -a, -um, *eager, greedy* [VII]

avus, -ī m., *grandfather**

B

beātus, -a, -um, *blessed, happy**

bellum, ī n., *war**

bellus, -a, -um, *pretty, handsome, fine, nice* [XVIII]

bene, adv., *well**

ūtor bene, *treat well*

beneficium, -ī n., *service, benefit, kindness, favor, help, support* [XXIII]

bonus, -a, -um, *good**

brevis, -e, *brief, short**

C

caelum, -ī n., *air, heaven, sky**

Caesar, Caesaris m., *Gaius Julius Casear*

calamitās, calamitātis f. *calamity* [I]

campus, -ī m., *field, plain, playing field**

cantō (1), *sing**

capiō, -ere, cēpī, captum, *capture, seize, take**

caput, capitis n., *head**

carmen, carminis n., *song**

Cathāgō, -inis, *Carthage*

cārus, -a, -um, *dear**

castra, -ōrum n. pl., *camp**

cāsus, -ūs m., *chance, fall, misfortune**

causa, -ae f., *cause,*

causam habēre, *have a reason,*

cēdō, -ere, cessī, cessum, *yield, go* [IX]

celer, celeris, celere, *quick, swift**

celeritās, celeritātis, f., *swiftness, speed* [X]

centum (indecl.), *hundred**

cernō, -ere, crēvī, crētum, *decide, discern, perceive**

certāmen, certāminis n., *contest, struggle**

certiōrem facere, *inform*

certus, -a, -um, *certain, set* [VII]

cēterī, -ae, -a, *the remaining, the rest**

cibus, -ī, m., *food* [VIII]

Cicerō, Ciceronis m., *M. Tullius Cicero*

circum (+ acc.), *around**

cīvis, cīvis (-ium) m./f., *citizen**

cīvitās, -tātis, f., *state, citizenship* [II]

clam, adv., *secretly* [I]

clāmō (1), *shout**

clāmor, clāmōris, m., *noise, shout* [IX]

cogō, -ere, coēgī, coactum, *compel, drive together, force, collect, gather* [XIV]

colloquor, colloquī, collocūtus sum, *converse* [VII]

collum, -ī n., *neck**

comes, comitis m./f., *companion**

confirmō (1), *encourage, strengthen* [I]

committō, -ere, commīsī, commissum, *entrust, engage, commit* [IX]

commūnis, -e, *common, shared, general* [XIV]

comparō (1) *prepare, gather, achieve, acquire* [III]

comprehendō, -ere, -hendī, -hensum, *grasp, seize**

concēdō, -ere, concessī, concessum, *yield, grant* [IX]

condō, -ere, condidī, conditum, *found (a city), bury* [XIII]

conferō, conferre, contulī, collātum , *bring together, (with sē) go**

confestim, adv., *immediately* [I]

conficiō, -ere, confēcī, confectum, *finish, accomplish, make ready* [XIX]

confidō, -ere, confisus sum, (semi-deponent), *trust* [XVII]

coniciō, -ere, coniēcī, coniectum, *cast, hurl, throw, throw together**

coniunx, coniugis m./f., *spouse**

cōnor (1), *attempt, try**

cōnscrībō, -ere, conscrīpsī, conscrīptum, *enlist, enroll* [XIII]

cōnsequor, cōnsequī, cōnsecūtus sum, *follow, pursue, gain, acquire* [XVII]

cōnsilium, -ī, n., *plan**

cōnsilium capere, *adopt a plan*

cōnsistō, -ere, cōnstitī, cōnstitum, *stop**

cōnspectus, -ūs, m., *sight* [I]

conspiciō, -ere, conspexī, conspectum, *spot, observe, catch sight of* [XVIII]

cōnstituō, -ere, cōnstituī, cōnstitūtum, *decide, determine, establish**

cōnsul, cōnsulis m., *consul**

cōnsulō, -ere, cōnsuluī, cōnsultum, *consult, resolve**

contegō, -ere, contēxī, contēctum, *cover**

contendō, -ere, contendī, contentum, *compete, hurry, make effort, march, strive**

continens, continentis f., *mainland**

contineō, -ēre, continuī, contentum, *contain, sustain, hold together* [II]

contrā, *opposite, facing, toward* [XVII]

conveniō, -īre, convēnī, conventum, *meet, come together, convene* [XII]

convocō (1), *call together* [XXIII]

cōpia, cōpiae f., *supply, abundance,* (pl.) *troops, provisions* [XVII]

cornū, -ūs, n., *horn, wing(of an army)**

corpus, corporis, n., *body**

cottīdiē, adv., *daily* [XXIII]

crās, adv., *tomorrow**

crēdō, -ere, crēdidī, crēditum, *entrust, believe* [XV]

creō (1), *create, elect* [X]

cum (+ abl.), *along with, with**

cupiditās, -tātis, f., *greed, desire* [II]

cupidus, -a, -um, *eager, longing, greedy, desirous* [XVIII]

cupiō, -ere, cupīvī, cupītum, *wish, desire, long for* [XXIII]

cur, adv., *why?* [VIII]

cūra, -ae f., *care, concern, worry**

currō, -ere, cucurrī, cursum, *hasten, run**

cursus, -ūs, m., *course* [I]

custōs, custōdis, m., *guard, guardian, protector* [XXVII]

D

dē (+ abl.), *about, concerning, down from**

dē... agere, *talk about**

dea, -ae f., *goddess**

decem (indecl.), *ten**

decus, decoris n., *honor, glory, dignity* [XVII]

dēdūcō, -ere, dēdūxī, dēductum, *lead away, remove, draw (a weapon)* [X]

dēfendō, -ere, dēfendī, dēfēnsum, *defend**

dēficiō, -ere, dēfēcī, dēfectum, *fail, fall away* [XXV]

deinde, adv., *then, next, from there* [XXV]

dēleō, -ēre, dēlēvī, dēlētum, *destroy**

dēlīberō (1), *consider, deliberate* [XVIII]

dēligō, -ere, dēlēgī, dēlectum, *choose* [III]

dēplōrō (1), *lament, mourn**

dēpōnō, -ere, dēposuī, dēpositum, *put down**

dēscendō, -ere, dēscendī, dēscēnsum, *descend**

desertus, -a, -um, *deserted**

despiciō, -ere, despexī, despectum, *look down on* [XVIII]

dēsum, dēesse, dēfuī, dēfutūrus, *be lacking, lack, fail* [XV]

dēsuper, adv., *above, from above**

deus, -ī m. (*pl.* dī), *god**

dēvorō (1), *devour, swallow**

dexter, dextera, dexterum, *right,* (subst.)*right hand* [XXVII]

Diana, -ae f., *Diana,*

dīcō, -ere, dīxī, dictum, *say, speak, tell**

diēs, -ēī m., *day**

differō, differre, distulī, dilātum, *scatter, defer, differ* [II]

difficilis, -e, *difficult**

difficultās, -tātis, f., *difficulty* [II]

dignus, -a, -um, (+ abl.) *worthy* [V]

dīligēns, -ntis, *careful* [I]

diligentia, -ae f., *diligence**

dīmittō, -ere, dīmīsī, dīmissum, *send away, dismiss* [IX]

discēdō, -ere, discessī, discessum, *depart, leave, withdraw* [XVII]

discipulus, -ī m., *student**

discō, -ere, didicī, ----, *learn* [XVIII]

discus, ī m., *discus**

dissimilis, -e, *dissimilar, unlike**

diū, adv., *for a long time**

diūtissimē (superl. of diū), adv., *for the longest time, for a very long time**

diūtius (compara. of diū), adv., *for a longer time**

dīvīnus, -a, -um, *divine, heavenly* [XXVIII]

dīvus, -a, -um, *divine**

do, dare, dedī, datum, *give**

poenās dare, *pay a penalty**

doceō, -ēre, docuī, doctum, *teach**

doctus, -a, -um, *learned* [XXIX]

doleō, -ēre, doluī, dolitum, *grieve* [XXIII]

dolor, dolōris m., *grief, pain**

dominus, -ī m., *master**

domus, -ūs, f, *home, household**

donum, -ī n., *gift**

dormiō, - īre, dormīvī, dormitum , *sleep**

dubitō, dubitāre, dubitāvī, dubitātum [XXVIII]

ducentī, -ae, -a, *two hundred* [XXVII]

dūcō, -ere, dūxī, ductum, *lead**

in mātrimōnium ducere, *marry**

dulcis, -e, *sweet**

dum, conj., *while**

duo, duae, duo, *two**

dux, ducis m., *leader**

E

ē, ex (+ abl.), *from, out of**

ēdō, -ere, ēdidī, ēditum, *give out**

ēdūcō, -ere, ēdūxī, ēductum, *lead out, unsheath**

efficiō, -ere, effēcī, effectum, *effect, cause, bring about* [XXV]

ego, *I**

ēgredior, ēgredī, ēgressus sum, *go out, leave* [V]

ēloquentia, -ae f., *eloquence* [XIX]

enim, conj., *for**

eō, adv., *to that place**

eō, īre, iī(īvī), itum, *go**

epistula, -ae f., *letter**

eques, equitis m., *horseman,* (pl.) *cavalry* [XIV]

equus, ī m., *horse**

ēripiō, -ere, ēripuī, ēreptum, *snatch, rescue* [V]

sē ēripere, *escape* [V]

errō (1), *make a mistake, wander**

ērumpō, -ere, ērūpī, ēruptus, *burst out, break out* [XIV]

et, conj., *and**

110

etiam, conj., *also, even**

ex, ē (+abl.), *from, out of**

exanimō (1), *exhaust**

excēdō, -ere, excessī, excessum, *depart, go out**

excipio, -ere, excēpī, exceptum, *receive, greet* [IV]

excitō (1), *awaken, rouse**

exeō, -īre, exīvī/exiī, exītum, *go out, withdraw* [XX]

exerceō, -ēre, exercuī, exercitum, *train* [XXIII]

exercitus, -ūs m., *army**

exigō, -ere, exēgī, exactum, *drive out, demand, collect, finish (a life)* [XIV]

existimō (1), *consider, regard, think* [XXIII]

experior, experīrī, expertus sum, *experience, test, try* [XXIX]

expōnō, -ere, exposuī, expositum, *expose, explain* [XIII]

expugnō (1), *storm* [XXIII]

exspectō (1), *look out**

extrahō, -ere, extrāxī, extrāctum, *drag out**

exuō, -ere, exuī, exūtum, *put off, take off**

F

facilis, -e, *easy**

faciō, -ere, fēcī, factum, *do, make**

fac ut, *bring it about that*

iter facere, *make a journey, march**

factiō, factiōnis f., *faction* [IX]

factum, ī n., *deed**

facultās, facultātis f., *ability, power, skill, opportunity* [X]

falsus, -a, -um, *untrue, mistaken* [XXIV]

falx, falcis f., *sickle, sword (curved)**

fāma, -ae f., *glory, reputation, rumor**

famēs, famis f., *hunger, famine**

familia, familiae f., *household slaves, family* [XVII]

fātum, -ī n., *fate**

faveō, -ēre, fāvī, fautum (+dat.), *favor, support* [XV]

fēlīx, fēlīcis, *happy**

ferē, adv., *nearly, almost* [II]

ferō, ferre, tulī, lātum, *bear, bring, carry, endure**

ferrum, -ī n., *iron, sword**

fessus, -a, -um, *exhausted, tired**

fidēlis, -e, *faithful, loyal* [VIII]

fidēs, -eī f, *faith, loyalty*, trust*

fidēs pūblica, fideī pūblicae f., *safe conduct*

fīlia, -ae f., *daughter**

fīlius, -ī m., *son**

fingō, -ere,finxī, fictus, *compose, fashion, make, imagine, make up* [XXIV]

fīniō, -īre, finīvī/finiī, finitum, *limit, define* [XXIII]

fīnis, -is (-ium) m., *end, (pl.) territory**

finitimus, -a, -um, *neighboring* [VIII]

fiō, fiērī, factus sum, *be made, become, happen* [X]

firmus, -a, -um, *strong, firm, resolute* [IV]

flamma, -ae f., *flame**

fleō, flēre, flēvī, flētum, *weep* [XXIII]

flūctus, -ūs m., *flood, sea, wave**

forma, formae f., *form* [XVII]

fortasse, adv., *perhaps* [XXVIII]

forte, adv., *accidently, by chance* [XXIII]

fortis, -e, *brave, strong**

fortūna, -ae f., *fortune, luck**

forum, -ī n., *forum, marketplace* [V]

frāter, frātris m., *brother**

fremitus, -ūs m., *groan, roar, rumble**

fructus, -ūs m., *benefit, enjoyment, fruit**

fruor, fruī, fructus sum (+abl.), *enjoy, profit from* [XIII]

frustrā, adv., *in vain* [XX]

fuga, -ae f., *escape, flight**

fugiō, -ere, fūgī, fugitūrus, *avoid, flee, run away, escape**

fungor, fungī, functus sum (+abl.), *perform* [XIII]

furor, -ōris m., *fury, rage**

G

galea, -ae f., *helmet**

Gallus, -a, -um, *Gaul, Gallic,*

gaudium, ī n., *gladness, joy* [XXIII]

gēns, gentis (-ium) f., *nation, tribe**

genus, -eris n., *kind, sort**

gerō, gerere, gessī, gestum, *carry on, manage**

bellum gerere, *wage war**

gladius, -ī m., *sword**

gloria, gloriae f, *glory, fame* [XVII]

Gorgo(n), Gorgonis f., *Gorgon**

gracilis, -e, *graceful, slender**

gradus, -ūs m., *step**

gratia, -ae f., *favor, pl. thanks**

gratiās agere (+dat.), *give thanks, thank**

grātus, -a, -um, *pleasing**

gravis, -e, *heavy, serious**

gravitās, gravitātis f., *weight, severity, hardness, seriousness* [XXVIII]

graviter, adv., *seriously,*

H

habeō -ēre, habuī, habitum, *consider, have, hold**

ōrātiōnem habēre, *give a speech* [IX]

causam habēre, *have a reason,*

habitō (1), *dwell, live**

harēna, -ae f., *sand**

haud, adv., *not at all* [I]

heri, adv., *yesterday**

hic, haec, hoc, *this, (pl.) these* *

hīc, adv., *here, in this place* [XX]

hiems, hiemis f., *winter* [XVIII]

hinc, adv., *from here, from this place* [XX]

hodiē, adv., *today**

homō, hominis m, *human, man**

honor, honōris m., *honor, esteem, office* [V]

hōra, -ae f., *hour**

horribilis, -e, *horrible**

hortor (1), *encourage* [XXII]

hostis, hostis (-ium) m., *enemy**

hūc, adv., *hither, to this place* [XX]

humilis, -e, *humble, low**

I

iam, adv., *already, now**

ibī, adv., *there**

ictus, -ūs m., *blow, strike**

īdem, eadem, idem, *same**

idōneus, -a, -um, *suitable**

igitur, adv., *therefore, then**

ignāvus, -a, -um, *idle, lazy**

ignis, -is (ium) m., *fire**

ignōrō (1), *have no knowledge of**

ignoscō, -ere, ignōvī, ignōtum (+dat.), *forgive* [XV]

ille, illa, illud, *that, (pl.) those**

immemor, immemoris, *forgetful* [XXV]

impedīmentum, -ī, n., *hindrance, (pl.). baggage* [V]

imperītus, -a, -um, *inexperienced, unskilled, ignorant* [XXIX]

imperium, -ī n., *power, rule**

imperō (1), *order, demand* [XXII]

impetrō (1), *obtain (by asking)* [X]

impetus, -ūs, m., *attack* [I]

importō (1), *bring in, carry in* [XXIII]

īmus, -a, -um, *deepest, lowest, bottom of* [XVIII]

in (+abl.), *in, on,* (+acc.), *into, onto, against**

incēdō, -ere, incessī, incessum, *go in**

incendō, -ere, incendī, incensum, *set fire to, outrage, burn* [III]

incipiō, -ere, incēpī, inceptum, *begin**

incitō (1), *urge on, arouse* [V]

inclūdō, -ere, inclūsī, inclūsum, *enclose, imprison, shut up**

incola, -ae m., *inhabitant**

incolō, -ere, incoluī, ----, *inhabit* [VIII]

incolumis, -e, *safe, unharmed* [XIV]

inde, adv., *from there, thence* [XXV]

indūcō, -ere, indūxī, inductum, *lead in, influence* [XII]

induō, -ere, induī, indūtum, *clothe, put on**

ineō, -īre, iniī (inīvī), initum, *go in, enter, adopt (plan)* [XX]

infans, infantis (-ium) m./f., *infant**

inficiō, -ere, infēcī, infectum, *dye, stain**

ingenium, -ī n., *innate quality, character* [XIX]

ingens, ingentis, *huge, vast**

inimīcitia, -ae f., *enmity, unfriendliness, hostility* [XXVIII]

inimīcus, -a, -um, *hostile, unfriendly* [VII]

inīquus, -a, -um, *uneven, unfair* [XX]

inopia, inopiae f., *lack* [XVII]

inrumpō, -ere, inrūpī, inruptum, *burst in**

insignis, -e, *distinguished, prominent* [XIV]

inspiciō, -ere, inspexī, inspectum, *look into or upon**

insula, -ae, f., *island* [III]

integer, integra, integrum, *whole, untouched* [XVIII]

intellegō, -ere, intellēgī, intellectum, *understand* [III]

inter (+acc.), *among, between**

interclūdō, -ere, interclūsī, interclūsum, *shut off, block, stop* [XIII]

interficio, -ere, -fēcī, -fectum, *kill**

interim, adv., *meanwhile* [XIV]

inveniō, -īre, invēnī, inventum, *come upon, find* [XII]

invidia, -ae f., *envy, hatred, jealousy**

invītus, -a, -um, *unwilling* [VII]

Iove (abl. sg. of Iuppiter), *Jupiter,*

ipse, ipsa, ipsum, *-self**

īra, -ae f., *anger, wrath**

īrātus, -a, -um, *angry**

is, ea, id, *he, she, it, that, this**

iste, ista, istud, *that (of yours)**

ita, adv., *so, thus* [IV]

Ītalia, -ae f., *Italy,*

itaque, adv., *and so [X]*

item, adv., *likewiseIV*

iter, itineris n., *journey, road, way**

    iter facere, *make a journey, march**

iterum, adv., *again**

iubeō, iubēre, iussī, iussum, *bid, command, order**

Iuppiter, Iovis m., *Jupiter**

iūs, iūris n., *law, right**

iuvenis, -is m., *youth, young man* [XVIII]

iuvō, -āre, iūvī, iūtum, *help* [XIX]

L

labor, labōris m., *hardship, labor, work**

lābor, lābī, lapsus sum, *collapse, slip**

laborō (1), *work, labor*

lacrima, -ae f., *tear**

laetus, -a, -um, *happy, joyful**

laudō (1), *praise**

laus, laudis f., *praise* [XVII]

lēgātus, -ī m., *legate, envoy, ambassador* [VIII]

legō, -ere, lēgī, lēctum, *choose, pick out, read**

libenter, adv., *freely, willingly**

līber, lībera, līberum, *free**

liber, librī m, *book**

līberī, -ōrum m.pl., *children* [XXV]

līberō (1), *free, liberate* [XIII]

lībertās, -tātis, f., *freedom* [II]

licet, licēre, licuit or licitum est, *it is permitted* [XXVII]

ligneus, -a, -um, *wooden**

littera, -ae, f., *letter (of the alphabet),* (pl.) *letter, literature* [III]

lītus, lītoris n., *beach, coast, shore**

Livius, Liviī m., *Titus Livius,*

locus, -ī , m., (loca, -ōrum n. pl.), *place**

longē, adv., *far**

longus, -a, -um, *long**

loquor, loqui, locūtus sum, *speak, talk* [VII]

lūdus, -ī m., *game, sport**

lūmen, lūminis n., *light**

lūx, lūcis f., *light**

M

magicus, -a, -um, *magical*

magis (comp. of magnopere), *more**

magister, magistrī m., *teacher**

magistrātus, -ūs, m., *magistracy, magistrate* [I]

magnopere, adv., *greatly**

magnus, -a, -um, *large, great**

māior, maius (comp. of magnus), *greater**

māiōrēs, -um f. pl., *ancestors* [V]

mālō, mālle, māluī, -----, *prefer**

malus, -a, -um, *bad, evil, wicked**

maneō, -ēre, mānsī, mānsum, *remain, stay**

manus, -ūs f., *band, hand**

mare, maris (ium) n., *sea**

māter, mātris f., *mother**

maximē (superl. of magnopere), adv., *very greatly**

maximus, -a, -um (superl. of magnus), *most**

Medusa, -ae f., *Medusa*

melior, melius (comp. of bonus), *better**

meminī, meminisse, *remember, be mindful of* [XXIX]

memor, memoris, *mindful* [XXV]

memoria, memoriae f., *memory* [XVII]

memorō (1), *mention, bring up* [XXIV]

mens, mentis (-ium) f., *mind, intention**

   in mentem venīre, *come to mind**

mentior, mentīrī, mentītus sum, *tell a lie**

mergō, -ere, mersī, mersum, *plunge, sink**

meritus, -a, -um, *deserved, due**

metuō, metuere, metuī, metitum [XXVII]

metus, -ūs, m., *fear* [I]

meus, -a, -um, *mine, my**

mīles, mīlitis m., *soldier**

Minerva, - ae f., *Minerva,*

minimus, -a, -um (superl. of parvus), *smallest**

minor, minus (comp. of parvus), *smaller**

mīrābilis, -e, *remarkable, amazing, wonderful* [XXIV]

mīror (1), *be amazed, wonder at, be surprised at* [XXVII]

miser, misera, miserum, *unhappy, wretched**

mittō, -ere, mīsī, missum, *send**

modo, adv., *just, merely, only* [XXII]

modus, -ī m., *manner, way**

moenia, -ium n. pl., *walls**

moneō, -ēre, monuī, monitum, *advise, warn**

mōns, montis (-ium) m., *mountain**

monstrō (1), *show**

monstrum, -ī n., *monster**

mora, -ae f., *delay**

morior, morī, mortuus sum, *die**

mors, mortis f. (-ium), *death**

mōs, mōris m., *custom, , (pl.) character, behavior* [V]

   mōs maiōrum, m., *tradition* [V]

moveō, -ēre, mōvī, mōtum, *move**

mox, adv., *soon**

mulier, mulieris f., *woman* [XXVII]

multitūdō, multitūdinis f., *crowd, multitude* [IX]

multum, adv., *much**

multus, -a, -um, *many, much**

mūniō, -īre, mūnīvī, mūnītum, *build, fortify**

mūnus, mūneris n., *function, task, gift (of the gods)* [XXVII]

mūrus, -ī m., *wall**

mūtō (1), *change, transform**

N

nam, conj., *for**

nanciscor, nancisci, nactus sum, *acquire, get, obtain* [VII]

narrō (1), *tell, relate* [XII]

nascor, nascī, nātus sum, *be born* [VII]

nātūra, -ae f., *nature, character* [XV]

nātūrālis, -e, *natural, by birth* [XXVIII]

nauta, -ae m., *sailor**

nāvis, nāvis (-ium) f., *ship**

-ne (introduces a question), VIII

nec/neque, *and...not, nor* *

necessārius, -a, -um, *necessary, inevitable* [XXVIII]

necesse esse, *it is necessary* [XXVII]

nefās (indecl.) n., *evil, wrong* [XXIV]

negō (1), *say...not, deny*

negōtium, -ī n., *business* [XIII]

nēmō, nēminis m., *no one, nobody**

Neptūnus, -ī m., *Neptune**

neque/nec, *and...not, nor* *

neque...neque, *neither...nor**

nesciō, nescīre, nescīvī/nesciī, nescītus, *not know* [XII]

neuter, neutra, neutrum, *neither**

nihil (indecl.) n., *nothing**

nimis, adv., *too, very much* [XXIX]

nimium, -ī n., *excess* [XXIX]

nōbilis, -e, *noble* [VIII]

noceō, nocēre, nocuī, nocitum (+dat.), *harm* [XV]

nōlō, nōlle, nōluī, -----, *be unwilling, not to want, not to wish**

nōmen, nōminis n., *name**

nōn, adv., *not**

nōn modo ... sed etiam, *not only ... but also**

nōndum, adv., *not yet* [XXV]

nōnne (introduces a question expecting "yes" answer), *surely* [VIII]

nōs, *we**

noster, nostra, nostrum, *our**

novem (indecl.), *nine**

nōvissimus, -a, -um, *most recent, last,*

novus, -a, -um, *new**

nox, noctis (-ium) f., *night**

nullus, -a, -um, *no, not any, none**

num (introduces a question expecting "no" answer), *surely... not* [VIII]

nūmen, nūminis n., *nod, consent, will (divine)* [XXVIII]

numerus, -ī, m., *number* [IV]

numquam, adv., *never* [XXV]

nunc, *now**

nūntiō (1), *announce, report**

nūntius, -ī m., *messenger**

nūper, adv., *recently* [XXV]

O

ob (+acc), *because of, on account of**

oblīviscor, oblīviscī, oblītus sum, *forget* [XXIX]

obsecrō (1), *beseech, beg [XXII]*

obtineō, -ēre, obtinuī, obtentum, *hold, obtain* [II]

occīdō, -ere, occīdī, occīsum, *kill, slaughter*
occupō (1), *seize**
octo (indecl.), *eight**
oculus, -ī m., *eye**
offendō, -ere, offendī, offēnsum, *offend**
officium, -ī n., *duty, office* [XIII]
Olympus, -ī, m., *Mount Olympus*
omnīnō, adv., *entirely, altogether* [VIII]
omnis, -e, *all, every**
onus, oneris n., *burden**
oportet, oportere, oportuit, *it is fitting* [XXVII]
oppidum, ī, n., *town*
ops, opis, f., *power,* (pl.)*resources* [XIII]
optimus, -a, -um (superl. of bonus), *best**
optō (1), *desire**
opus, operas, n., *task, work**
ōra, -ae f., *edge, rim, shore**
ōrāculum, -ī n., *oracle**
ōrātiō, ōrātiōnis, f., *speech* [IX]
ōrātionem habēre, *give a speech* [IX]
ordō, ordinis, m., *order, rank* [XVII]
orior, -īrī, ortus sum, *rise, appear* [XXVII]
ōrō (1), *beseech, beg* [XXII]
ōs, oris, n., *mouth**
ostendō, -ere, ostendī, ostentum, *stretch out before, show, display* [XV]

P

paene, adv., *practically, almost* [II]
pār, paris, *equal, like* [XXV]
parcō, -cere, pepercī, ----, *spare* [XV]
pāreō, -ēre, pāruī, pāritum (+dat), *obey* [XV]
parō (1), *prepare**
pars, partis (-ium) f, *direction, part**
parum, *too little**
parvus, -a, -um, *little, small**
pater, patris m., *father**
patien, -entis, *tolerant, hardy, patient*
patior, patī, passus sum, *endure, experience, suffer**
patria, -ae f., *native land**
paucī, -ae, -a, *few**
paulō, adv., *a little, somewhat* [XXVII]
pavor, pavōris m., *panic, terror**
pax, pacis, f., *peace* [III]
pectus, pectoris n., *breast, chest, heart**.
pecūnia, -ae, f., *money* [III]
peior, peius (comp. of malus), *worse**
per (+ acc.), *through, by,*
perdūcō, -ere, perdūxī, perductum, *lead through**
perferō, perferre, pertulī, perlātum, *endure, report* [II]
perficiō, -ere, perfēcī, perfectum, *finish, complete, perfect* [XXV]
perīculum, -ī, n., *danger, peril* [V]
perītus, -a, -um, *skilled, experienced* [XV]
Perseus, Perseī, m., *Perseus*
perscrībo, -scrībere, -scrīpsī, -scriptum, *write out*

perspiciō, -ere, perspexī, perspectum, *examine, observe* [XVIII]
persuadeō, -ēre, persuasī, persuasum, *persuade* [XXII]
pertineō, -ēre, pertinuī, pertentum, *pertain, extend* [II]
perveniō, -īre, pervēnī, perventum, *come to, arrive* [XII]
pēs, pedis m., *foot**
pessimus, -a, -um (superl. of malus), *worst, very bad**
petō, -ere, petivī, petītum, *ask for, seek**
pīrāta, -ae m., *pirate**
pius, -a, -um, *devoted, dutiful, loyal**
placeō, -ēre, placuī, placitum, *be pleasing* [XV]
plebs, plebis f., *plebs, common people* [XVII]
plurimus, -a, -um (superl. of multus), *most, very many**
plūs, plūris n., *more, too much* [XXIX]
poena, -ae f., *punishment**
poenās dare, *pay a penalty**
Poenus, -a, -um, *Carthaginian, Punic*
poēta, -ae m., *poet**
Pompeius Magnus, Pompeiī Magnī m., *Pompey**
pōnō, -ere, posuī, positum, *place, put, set up**
pōns, pontis (-ium) m., *bridge**
populus, -ī, m., *people* [IV]
porta, -ae f., *gate**
portō (1), *carry**
possum, posse, potuī, -----, *be able, can**
post (+acc.), *after**
posteā, adv., *afterwards* [XXVII]
postquam, conj., *after**
postulō (1), *demand* [XXII]
potens, -ntis, *capable, powerful* [I]
potestās, -tātis, f., *power* [II]
potior, -īrī, potītum sum, *gain possession of* [XIII]
praecipiō, -ere, praecēpī, praeceptum, *direct, advise, order* [IV]
praemium, -ī n., *prize, reward* [XXIII]
praesertim, adv., *especially, particularly* [XIV]
praesidium, -ī n., *protection, assistance, defense* [V]
praestō, -āre, praestitī, praestatum, *exhibit, show**
praeter (+acc.), *past, by, along, in front of* [XII]
praetereō, -īre, preaterivī/-iī, praeteritum, *go past, skip* [XX]
prāvus, -a, -um, *distorted, crooked, improper* [XXIX]
prīmō, adv., *at first**
quam prīmum, *as soon as possible*
prīmus, -a, -um, *first**
princeps, principis m., *leader, chief* [XVII]
prō (+abl.), *in front of, on behalf of**
proelium, -ī, n., *battle* [V]
proficiscor, proficiscī, profectus sum, *set out* [VII]
prōgredior, prōgredī, prōgressus sum, *advance, go forward, march forward**
prohibeō, -ēre, prohibuī, prohibitum, *keep off, prevent, deny* [XIII]
prope (+acc.), *near* [XXV]
propinquus, -a, -um, *near, neighboring* [V]
propter (+acc.), *on account of , because of**
prōvincia, -ae, f., *province* [III]
proximus, -a, -um, *next**

prūdens, -ntis , *prudent, sensible* [I]
pūblicus, -a, -um, *public**
    fidēs pūblica, fideī pūblicae f., *safe conduct*
puella, -ae f., *girl**
puer, puerī m, *boy**
pugnō (1), *fight**
pulcher, pulchra, pulchrum, *beautiful**
pūniō, -īre, pūnīvī, pūnītum, *punish**
puto (1), *consider, think**

Q

quaerō, -ere, quaesīvī, quaesītum, *ask, seek**
quālis, -e, *what sort of?, what kind of?* [VIII]
quam (+ superlative), *as...as possible**
quam, adv., *than**
quam prīmum, *as soon as possible*
quamdiū, adv., *how long?* [VIII]
quandō, adv., *when?* [VIII]
quantus, -a, -um, *how great?, how much?* [VIII]
quattuor (indecl.), *four**
-que, *and**
quī, quae, quod (rel. pron), *that, which, who**
quīdam, quaedam, quoddam, *a certain* [XIX]
quiēs, quiētis f., *quiet, rest, sleep**
quinque (indecl.), *five**
quis, quid (interr. pron.), *who?, what?* [VIII]
quisque, quaeque, quidque, *each* [XIV]
quō, adv., *to where?, whither?* [VIII]
quod, conj., *because**
quōmodo, adv., *how*
quondam, adv., *at one time, formerly, once**
quot (indecl. adj.), *how many?* [VIII]
quotiēns, adv., *how often?* [VIII]

R

ratiō, ratiōnis f., *reason, theory* [IX]
recipiō, -ere, recēpī, receptum, *receive, accept* [IV]
    sē recipere, *retreat* [IV]
reddō, -ere, reddidi, redditum, *give back**
redeō, -īre, rediī (-īvī), reditum, *go back, return* [XXIX]
redīgō, -ere, redēgī, redactum, *drive back**
reditus, -ūs m., *return**
referō, referre, rettulī, relātum, *bring back, carry back, relate* [XIX]
reficiō, -ere, refēcī, refectum, *repair, restore* [XXV]
rēgia, -ae f., *palace**
rēgīna, -ae f., *queen**
rēgnum, -ī n., *kingdom**
regō, -ere, rēxī, rēctum, *rule**
relinquō, -ere, relīquī, relictum, *leave, leave behind**
reliquus, -a, -um, *rest, remaining* [V]
remittō, -ere, remīsī, remissum, *send back* [IX]
reor, rērī, ratus sum, *think, suppose, imagine* [XXVII]
reperiō, -īre, repperī, repertum, *find (by looking), discover* [XIX]
rēs, reī f., *affair, matter, thing, situation**
rēs pūblica, reī pūblicae f., *state**

respondeō, respondēre, respondī, responsum, *answer, respond* [XXIII]
retineō, -ēre, retinuī, retentum, *hold back, restrain* [II]
revertō, -ere, revertī, ---- (usu, deponent in pres.), *turn back, return* [XIV]
rēx, rēgis m., *king**
rogō (1), *ask**
Rōma, -ae f., *Rome*
Rōmānus, -a, -um, *Roman*
rūmor, rūmōris m., *rumor* [XII]
rūrsus, adv., *again, backwards, a second time* [XXVII]
rūs, rūris n., *countryside, country* [VII]

S

sacer, sacra, sacrum, *holy**
saepe, adv., *often**
salūs, salūtis f., *safety (personal), well-being* [XXII]
Sallustius, ī, *Sallust*
salvus, -a, -um, *well, safe, unharmed* [XXIX]
sanguis, sanguinis m., *blood**
sapiēns, sapientis, *wise**
satis (indecl. adj.), *enough* [XIV]
saxum, -ī n., *rock**
saxum, -ī n., *stone**
scelus, sceleris n., *crime**
sciō, -īre, scīvī (or sciī), scītum, *know* [XIX]
scrība, -ae m., *secretary, writer**
scrībō, -ere, scrīpsī, scrīptum, *write**
sē (acc./abl. of suī), *-self**
secundus, -a, -um, *second**
sed, conj., *but**
sedeō, -ēre, sēdī, sessum, *sit**
sēdēs, sēdis f., *abode, seat**
semper, adv., *always**
senātor, ōris m., *senator*
senātus, -ūs m., *senate**
Seneca, -ae, m., *Seneca*
senex, senis m., *old man* [XIX]
sententia, -ae, f., *opinion* [III]
sentiō, -īre, sēnsī, sēnsum, *feel, perceive**
septem (indecl.), *seven**
sequor, sequī, secutus sum, *follow**
servitūs, servitūtis f., *slavery* [IX]
servō (1), *guard, save, watch over**
servus, -ī m., *slave**
sex (indecl), *six**
sibi (dat. of reflexive suī), *-self**
sīc, adv., *so, thus* (modifies verbs only)[IV]
Sicilia, -ae f., *Sicily,*
sīdus, sīderis n., *star**
signum, -ī n., *sign, standard, signal* [V]
silva, -ae f., *forest, woods**
similis, -e, *like, similar**
sine (+abl.), *without**
sinister, sinistra, sinistrum, *left*, (subst) *left hand* [XXVII]
sinus, -ūs m., *bosom, embrace**
socius, -ī m., *ally**

sōl, sōlis, m., *sun* [XIII]

sollicitūdō, sollicitūdinis f., *worry, care* [IX]

sōlus, -a, -um, *alone, only, sole**

solvō, -ere, solvī, solūtum, *release, unbind, loosen, untie* [XIV]

somnus, ī m., *sleep**

soror, sorōris f., *sister**

spatium, -ī n., *space, room* [XXIII]

speciēs, -ēī f., *appearance, sight**

speculum, -ī n., *looking glass, mirror**

spērō (1), *hope* [III]

spēs, speī f., *hope**

spontē (abl. only), *voluntarily, of one's own accord* [X]

statim, adv., *at once, immediately**

stō, -āre, stetī, statum, *stand**

studeō, -ēre, studuī, ----, *be eager for, desire* [XV]

studiōsus, -a, -um, *eager, zealous, devoted* [XVIII]

studium, -i n., *keenness, eagerness, enthusiasm, devotion* [XXVIII]

sub (+abl.), *under, at the foot of**

subeō, -īre, subiī (subīvī), subitum, *undergo**

subitō, adv., *suddenly**

suī (gen. sg.), *-self**

sum, esse, fuī, futūrus, *be**

summus, -a, -um, *highest, top of* [XV]

sūmō, -ere, sūmpsī, sūmptum, *take up* [XIV]

super (+acc), *above, in a higher position, over**

superō (1), *surpass* [XIII]

surgō, -ere, surrēxī, surrēctum, *rise, stretch upward, swell**

suscipiō, -ere, suscēpī, susceptum, *support, take up, undertake* [IV]

sustineō, -ēre, sustinuī, sustentum, *sustain, hold (up)* [II]

suus, -a, -um, *his, her, its, their own**

T

tālis, -e, *such* [IV]

tam, adv., *so* (modifies adj. and adv. only)[IV]

tamen, adv., *nevertheless, yet, still**

tandem, adv., *at length, finally**

tantum, -ī n., *so much,*

tantus, -a, -um, *so great* [IV]

tardus, -a, -um, *slow, late* [XVIII]

tegō, -ere, tēxī, tēctum, *conceal, cover, shelter**

tellūs, tellūris f., *earth, ground, land* [XXVII]

tēlum, ī n., *javelin, weapon**

tempestās, tempestātis f., *storm, tempest, weather**

temptō (1), *test, try* [I]

tempus, tempōris n., *time**

tendō, -ere, tetendī, tentum, *extend, proceed, stretch out**

teneō, -ēre, tenuī, tentum, *contain, hold**

tergum, -ī n., *back**

terra, -ae f., *country, earth, land**

terreō, -ēre, terruī, territum, *frighten**

terror, terrōris m., *fear, terror**

tertius, -a, -um, *third**

timeō, timēre, timuī, -----, *be afraid of, fear**

timor, timōris m., *fear**

tollō, tollere, sustulī, sublātum, *lift, raise* [XVIII]

tot, adj. (indecl.), *so many* [IV]

tōtus, -a, -um, *entire, whole**

trādō, -ere, trādidī, trāditum, *hand across, hand down* *

trādūcō, -ere, trāduxī, trāductum, *lead across* [XII]

trahō, -ere, trāxī, trāctum, *drag**

tranquillus, -a, -um, *calm, tranquil**

trāns (+acc.), *across**

transīgō, -ere, transēgī, transactum, *accomplish, finish, pierce, run through**

trecentī, -ae, -a, *three hundred* [XXVII]

trēs, tria, *three**

tribūnus, -ī, *tribune* [VIII]

tribūnus mīlitum, *military tribune*

trīstis, -e, *sad**

tū, *you (sg.)**

tueor, tuērī, tuitum, *scan, observe, protect* [XXVII]

tum, adv., *at that time, then**

tunc, adv., *at that time, then**

turbō (1), *disturb, stir up**

turpis, -e, *disgraceful, shameful* [XIV]

tūtus, -a, -um, *safe* [XVIII]

tuus, -a, -um, *your, yours**

U

ubi, , adv., *when, where**

ullus, -a, -um, *any**

umbra, -ae f., *ghost, shadow**

umerus, -ī m., *shoulder**

ūmidus, -a, -um, *moist, damp* [XXIV]

umquam, adv., *ever* [VII]

ūnā, adv., *together* [XIV]

unda, -ae f., *wave**

unde, adv., *from where, whence* [VIII]

undique, adv, *everywhere, on all sides, from all sides* [III]

ūnus, -a, -um, *one**

urbs, urbis (-ium) f., *city**

ūsus, -ūs m., *application, practice, skill, use**

ut (+ subj.), *so that, in order that, with the result that* [II] (+ ind.), *as**

fac ut, *bring it about that,*

uter, utra, utrum, *which (of two)**

uterque, utraque, utrumque, *each (of two), both* [XXIX]

ūtilis, -e, *useful**

ūtor, ūtī, ūsus sum (+abl.), *use, enjoy, experience* [XIII]

ūtor bene, *treat well,*

utrum, conj., *whether* [VIII]

utrum ... annōn, *whether...or not* [VIII]

utrum ... an, *whether...or* [VIII]

uxor, uxōris, f., *wife**

V

vacuus, -a, -um, *empty**

Valerius Maximus, Valeriī Maximī. m., *Valerius Maximus*

vātēs, vātis m., *prophet, seer**

velut/velutī, adv., *just as, even as* [XXIV]

veniō, -īre, vēnī, ventum, *come**

in mentem venīre, *come to mind**

ventus, ī m., *wind**

verbum, -ī n., *word**

vereor, verērī, veritus, *fear, respect**

Vergilius, Vergiliī m., *Publius Vergilius Maro*

vertō, -ere, vertī, versum, *turn**

vērus, -a, -um, *true* [XII]

vescor, vescī, ---- (+abl.), *feed on, eat* [XIII]

vesper, vesperis m., *evening* [XVIII]

vespera, -ae f., *evening* [XVIII]

vester, vestra, vestrum, *your, yours**

vetō, -āre, vetuī, vetitum, *forbid, order . . . not**

vetus, veteris, *old* [XXIV]

via, -ae f., *road, way**

vīcus, -ī, m., *village* [IV]

videō, -ēre, vīdī, vīsum, *see, (pass.) be seen, seem, appear **

vincō, -ere, vīcī, victum, *conquer, defeat**

vinculum, -ī n., *bond, chain, fetter* [V]

vir, virī m., *man**

virgō, virginis f., *maiden**

virtūs, virtūtis f, *courage, strength, excellence, virtue* [IX]

vīs, vīs f. (pl. vīrēs, vīrium), *violence, force, (pl.) strength* [VII]

vīta, -ae f., *life**

vītam agere , *lead a life**

vītō (1), *avoid, escape**

vīvō, -ere, vīxī, vīctum, *live**

vīvus, -a, -um, *alive* [VII

vix, adv., *hardly, scarcely**

vocō (1), *call**

volō (1), *fly**

volō, velle, voluī, -----, *want, wish**

volvō, -ere, volvī, volūtum, *roll**

vōs, *you (pl.)**

vōx, vōcis f., *voice**

vulnerō (1), *hurt, wound**

ENGLISH – LATIN VOCABULARY

A

ability, facultās, facultātis f. [X]

abode, sēdēs, sēdis f., *

about, dē (+ abl.),*

above, dēsuper, adv., super (+acc.), *

abundance, cōpia, cōpiae f. [XVII]

accept, recipiō, -ere, recēpī, receptum [IV]

accidently, forte, *

accomplish, conficiō, -ere, confēcī, confectum [XIX], transīgō, -ere, transēgī, transactum, *

accost, appellō, (1) [I]

achieve, comparō (1) [III]

acquire, compārō (1); cōnsequor, cōnsequī, consecutus sum; nanciscor, nanciscī, nactus sum

across, trāns (+acc.)

address, appellō, (1) [I]

admit, admittō, -ere, admīsī, admissum [IX]

adopt (plan), ineō, -īre, inīvī/iniī, initum [XX], cōnsilium capere,

advance, prōgredior, prōgredī, prōgressus sum *

advise, moneō, -ēre, monuī, monitum, * praecipiō, -ere, praecēpī, praeceptum [IV]

affair, rēs, reī f., *

affect, afficiō, -ere, affēcī, affectum [XXV]

after, post (+acc.), *postquam, adv. *

afterwards, posteā, adv. [XXVII]

again, iterum, adv. * rūrsus, adv. *

against, in (+acc.), *

age, aetās,-tātis, f. [II]

aid, auxilium,-ī, n. [XXII]

air, caelum, -ī n., *

alive, vīvus,-a,-um [VII]

all, omnis, -e, *

allow, admittō, -ere, admīsī, admissum [IX]

ally, socius, -ī m., *

almost, ferē, adv. [II], paenē, adv. [II]

alone, sōlus, -a, -um *

along, praeter (+acc.) [XII], *(with),* cum (+ abl.), *

already, iam, adv., *

also, etiam, *

altogether, omnīnō, adv. [VIII]

always, semper, *

amazing, mīrābilis,-e [XXIV]

among, apud (+acc.) [X], inter (+acc.), *

ancestors, māiōrēs, -um,

ancient, antīquus, -a, -um, *

and, ac/atque, *et, *-que, *

and so, itaque, adv. [X]

and…not, nec/neque, *

Andromeda, Andromeda, -ae f.,

anger, īra, -ae f., *

angry, īrātus, -a, -um, *

announce, nūntiō (1), *

another, alius, -a, -um, *

answer, respondeō, respondēre, respondī, responsum [XXIII]

any, ullus, -a, -um, *

anything, aliquis, aliquid [XVII]

anytime, aliquandō, adv. [XXIII]

appear, orior, -īrī, ortus sum [XXVII], videō, -ēre, vīdī, vīsum, (pass.) *

appearance, speciēs, -ēī f., *

application, ūsus, -ūs m., *

approach (noun), adventus,-ūs, m. [I]

approach (verb), accēdō, -ere, accessī, accessum, * aggredior, aggredī, aggressus sum [V], appropinquō, (1) [XV]

appropriate, aptus,-a,-um [XX]

ark, arca, -ae f., *

arms, arma, -ōrum n. pl., *

army, exercitus, -ūs m., *

117

around, circum (+ acc.), *

arouse, incitō (1) [V]

arrival, adventus,-ūs, m [I]

arrive, perveniō, -īre, pervēnī, perventum [XII]

as, ut (+ ind.), *

as soon as possible, quam prīmum,

as...as possible, quam (+ superlative), *

ascend, ascendō, -ere, ascendī, ascēnsum

Asia, Asia, -ae f.

ask, quaerō, -ere, quaesīvī, quaesītum, *rogō (1), *

ask for, petō, -ere, petivī, petītum, *

assistance, praesidium,-ī n. [V]

at, ad (+ acc.), *

at first, prīmō, *

at length, tandem, *

at once, statim, *

at one time, quondam, *

at that time, tum, *tunc, *

at the foot of, īmus,-a,-um [XVIII]

at the house of, apud (+ acc.) [X]

attack (noun), impetus,-ūs, m. [I]

attack (verb), adorior, adorīrī, adortus sum [XXVII],
    aggredior, aggredī, aggressus sum [V]

attempt, cōnor (1), *

authority, auctōritās,-tātis, f., [II]

avid, avidus, -a, -um

avoid, fugiō, -ere, fūgī, fugitūrus, * vītō (1), *

awaken, excitō (1), *

away, ab, ā (+ abl.), *

away from, ā, ab (+ abl.), *

B

back, tergum, -ī n., *

backwards, rursus [XXVII]

bad, malus, -a, -um, *

baggage, impedīmentum,-ī, n. (pl.) [V]

band, manus, -ūs f., *

battle, proelīum,-ī, n. [V]

be, sum, esse, fuī, futūrus, *

be able, possum, posse, potuī, -----, *

be afraid of, timeō, timēre, timuī, -----, *

be amazed, mīror (1) [XXVII]

be away, absum, abesse, āfuī, āfutūrus, *

be born, nascor, nascī, nātus sum [VII]

be eager for, studeō, -ēre, studuī, ---- [XV]

be inflamed, ardeō, -ēre, arsī, arsūrus, *

be lacking, dēsum, dēesse, dēfuī, dēfutūrus [XV]

be made, fiō, fiērī, factus sum [X]

be mindful of, meminī, meminisse [XXIX]

be pleasing, placeō, -ēre, placuī, placitum [XV]

be present, adsum, adesse, adfuī, adfutūrus, *

be seen , videō, -ēre, vīdī, vīsum, *

be surprised, mīror (1) [XXVII]

be unwilling, nōlō, nōlle, nōluī, -----, *

beach, lītus, lītoris n., *

bear, ferō, ferre, tulī, lātum, *

beautiful, pulcher, pulchra, pulchrum, *

because, quod, *

because of, ob (+acc), * propter (+acc.), *

become, fiō, fiērī, factus sum [X]

before, ante (+ acc.), * anteā, adv. [XXV], antequam, conj.*

beg, obsecrō (1) [XXII], orō (1) [XXII]

begin, incipiō, -ere, incēpī, inceptum, *

behavior, mōs, mōris (pl.) [V]

believe, crēdō, -ere, crēdidī, crēditum [XV]

benefit, beneficium, -ī n., * fructus, -ūs m., *

beseech, obsecrō (1) [XXII], orō (1) [XXII]

best, optimus, -a,-um (superl. of bonus), *

better, melior, melius (comp. of bonus), *

between, inter (+acc.), *

bid, iubeō, iubēre, iussī, iussum, *

bind, adligō (1), *

black, āter, ātra, ātrum, *

blaze, ardeō, -ēre, arsī, arsūrus, *

blessed, beātus, -a, -um, *

block, interclūdō, -ere, interclūsī, interclūsum [XIII]

blood, sanguis, sanguinis m., *

blow, ictus, -ūs m., *

body, corpus, corporis n., *

bold, audāx, audācis, *

boldly, audacter,

bond, vinculum, -ī n., *

book, liber, librī m, *

bosom, sinus, -ūs m., *

both, uterque, utraque, utrumque [XXIX]

bottom of, īmus,-a,-um [XVIII]

box, arca, -ae f., *

boy, puer, puerī m, *

brave, fortis, -e, *

bravery (pl.), animus, -ī m., *

break out, ērumpō, -ere, ērūpī, ēruptus [XIV]

breast, pectus, pectoris n., *

bridge, pōns, pontis (-ium) m., *

brief, brevis, -e, *

bring, afferō, afferre, attulī, allātum [XXVIII], ferō, ferre, tulī,
    lātum, *

bring about, efficiō, efficere, effēcī, effectum [XXV]

bring back, referō, referre, rettulī, relātum [XIX]

bring in, importō (1) [XXIII]

bring it about that, fac ut

bring together, conferō, conferre, contulī, collātum , *

bring up, memorō (1) [XXIV]

bronze, aes, aeris, n. [XIII]

brother, frāter, frātris m., *

build, mūniō, -īre, mūnīvī, mūnītum, *

burden, onus, oneris n., *

burn, ardeō, -ēre, arsī, arsūrus, * incendō, -ere, incendī,
    incensum [III]

burst in, inrumpō, -ere, inrūpī,inruptum, *

burst out, ērumpō, -ere, ērūpī, ēruptus [XIV]

bury, condō, -ere, condidī, conditum [XIII]

business, negōtium,-ī n. [XIII]

but, at*

but, autem, * sed, *

by, ā, ab (+ abl.), * per, praeter (+acc.) [XII]
by birth, nātūrālis,-e [XXVIII]
by chance, forte [XXIII]

C

calamity, calamitās, calamitātis f., [II], cāsus, ūs, m.
call, vocō (1), *
call together, convocō (1) [XXIII]
calm, tranquillus, -a, -um, *
camp, castra, -ōrum n. pl., *
can, possum, posse, potuī, -----, *
capable, potens,-ntis [I]
capture, capiō, -ere, cēpī, captum, *
care, cūra, -ae f., * sollicitūdō, sollicitūdinis f. [IX]
careful, dīligēns,-ntis, [I]
carry, ferō, ferre, tulī, lātum, * portō (1), *
carry back, referō, referre, rettulī, relātum [XIX]
carry in, importō (1) [XXIII]
carry on, gerō, gerere, gessī, gestum, *
carry toward, afferō, afferre, attulī, allātum [XXVIII]
Carthage, Cathāgō, -inis, f.
Carthaginian, Poenus, -a, -um,
cast, coniciō, -ere, coniēcī, coniectum, *
catch sight of, conspiciō, -ere, conspexī, conspectum [XVIII]
cause (noun), causa, -ae f.,
cause (verb), efficiō, -ere, effēcī, effectum [XXV]
cavalry, eques, equitis m. [XIV]
certain, quīdam, quaedam, quoddam [XIX], certus,-a, -um [VII]
chain, vinculum,-ī n. [V]
chance, cāsus, -ūs m., *
change, mūtō (1), *
character, ingenium,-ī n. [XIX], nātūra,-ae f. [XV], mōs, mōris (pl.) [V]
chest (box), arca, -ae f., *
chest (breast), pectus, pectoris n., *.
chief, princeps, principis m. [XVII]
children, līberī,-ōrum m. [XXV]
choose, dēligō, -ere, dēlēgī, dēlectum [III], legō, -ere, lēgī, lēctum, *
Cicero, M. Tullius Cicero, Cicerō, Ciceronis m.,
citadel, arx, arcis, f. [XIII]
citizen, cīvis, cīvis (-ium) m./f., *
citizenship, cīvitās,-tātis, f. [II]
city, urbs, urbis (-ium) f., *
climb, ascendō, -ere, ascendī, ascensum
clothe, induō, -ere, induī, indūtum, *
coast, lītus, lītoris n., *
collapse, lābor, lābī, lapsus sum, *
collect, cogō, -ere, coēgī, coactum [XIV], exigō, -ere, exēgī, exactum [XIV]
column (of men), agmen, agminis n., *
come, veniō, -īre, vēnī, ventum, *
come to, perveniō, -īre, pervēnī, perventum [XII]
come to mind, in mentem venīre, *
come together, conveniō, īre, convēnī, conventum [XII]
come up to, accēdō, -ere, accessī, accessum, *

come upon, inveniō, -īre, invēnī, inventum [XII]
command, iubeō, iubēre, iussī, iussum, *
commit, committo, -ere, -mīsī, -missum
common, commūnis,-e [XIV]
common people, plebs, plebis f. [XVII]
companion, comes, comitis m./f., *
compel, cogō, -ere, coēgī, coactum, *
compete, contendō, -ere, contendī, contentum, *
complete, perficiō, -ere, perfēcī, perfectum [XXV]
compose, fingō, -ere,finxī, fictus [XXIV]
conceal, tegō, -ere, tēxī, tēctum, *
concern, cūra, -ae f., *
concerning, dē (+ abl.), *
conquer, vincō, -ere, vīcī, victum, *
consent, nūmen, nūminis n. [XXVIII]
consider, dēlīberō (1) [XVIII], existimō (1) [XXIII], habeō -ēre, habuī, habitum, * puto (1), *
consul, cōnsul, cōnsulis m., *
consult, cōnsulō, -ere, cōnsuluī, cōnsultum, *
contain, contineō, -ēre, continuī, contentum [II], teneō, -ēre, tenuī, tentum, *
contest, certāmen, certāminis n., *
convene, conveniō, īre, convēnī, conventum [XII]
converse, colloquor, colloquī, collocūtus sum [VII]
convey, afferō, afferre, attulī, allātum [XXVIII]
copper, aes, aeris n., *
country(versus city), rūs, rūris n.[VII]
country, terra, -ae f., *
countryside, rūs, rūris [VII]
courage, virtūs, virtūtis f, *
course, cursus,-ūs, m. [I]
cover, contegō, -ere, contēxī, contēctum, * tegō, -ere, tēxī, tēctum, *
craft, ars, artis f. [XXIX]
create, creō (1) [X]
crime, scelus, sceleris n., *
crooked, prāvus,-a,-um [XXIX]
crowd, multitūdō, multitūdinis f. [IX]
custom, mōs, mōris [V]
cut away, abscīdō, -ere, -cīdī, -cīsum, *
cut off, abscīdō, -ere, -cīdī, -cīsum, *

D

daily, cottīdiē, adv. [XXIII]
damp, ūmidus,-a,-um [XXIV]
danger, perīculum,-ī [V]
dark, āter, ātra, ātrum, *
daughter, fīlia, -ae f., *
day, diēs, -ēī m, *
deal with, agō, -ere, ēgī, actum, *
dear, cārus, -a, -um, *
death, mors, mortis f. (-ium), *
debate about, dē ... agere , *
debt, aes aliēnum [XIII]
decide, cernō, -ere, crēvī, crētum, * cōnstituō, -ere, cōnstituī, cōnstitūtum, *
deed, factum, ī n., *

deep, altus, -a, -um, *

deepest, īmus,-a,-um [XVIII]

defeat, vincō, -ere, vīcī, victum, *

defend, dēfendō, -ere, dēfendī, dēfēnsum, *

defense, praesidium,-ī n. [V]

defer, differō, differre, distulī, dīlātum [II]

define, fīniō, -īre, fīnīvī/fīniī, fīnitum [XXIII]

delay, mora, -ae f., *

deliberate, dēlīberō (1) [XVIII]

demand, exigō, -ere, exēgī, exactum [XIV], imperō (1) [XXII], postulō (1) [XXII]

deny, prohibeō, -ēre, prohibuī, prohibitum [XIII]

depart, discēdō, -ere, discessī, discessum, * excēdō, -ere, excessī, excessum, *

descend, dēscendō, -ere, dēscendī, dēscēnsum,

deserted, desertus, -a, -um

deserved, meritus, -a, -um, *

desire (noun), cupid
ita s,-tātis, f. [II]

desire (verb), cupiō, -ere, cupīvī, cupītum [XXIII], optō (1), * studeō, studēre, studuī, ---- [XV]

desirous, cupidus, -a, -um (+ gen.)

destroy, dēleō, -ēre, dēlēvī, dēlētum, *

determine, cōnstituō, -ere, cōnstituī, cōnstitūtum, *

devoted, pius, -a, -um, * studiōsus,-a,-um [XVIII]

devotion, studium,-i n. [XXVIII]

devour, dēvorō (1), *

Diana, Diana, -ae f.

die, morior, morī, mortuus sum, *

differ, differō, differre, distulī, dīlātum [II]

difficult, difficilis, -e, *

difficulty, difficultās,-tātis, f. [II]

dignity, decus, decoris n. [XVII]

diligence, diligentia, -ae

direct, praecipiō, -ere, praecēpī, praeceptum [IV]

direction, pars, partis (-ium) f. , *

discern, cernō, -ere, crēvī, crētum, *

discover, reperiō, -īre, repperī, repertum [XIX]

discus, discus, ī m., *

disgraceful, turpis,-e [XIV]

dismiss, dīmittō, -ere, dīmīsī, dīmissum [IX]

display, ostendō, -ere, ostendī, ostentum [XV]

dissimilar, dissimilis, -e, *

distinguished, insignis,-e [XIV]

distorted, prāvus,-a,-um [XXIX]

disturb, turbō (1), *

divine, dīvīnus,-a,-um [XXVIII], dīvus, -a, -um, *

do, agō, -ere, ēgī, actum, * faciō, -ere, fēcī, factum, *

do to, adficiō, -ere, -fēcī, -fectum, *

doubt, dubitō (1) [XXVIII]

down from, dē (+ abl.), *

drag, trahō, -ere, trāxī, trāctum, *

drag out, extrahō, -ere, extrāxī, extrāctum, *

draw (a weapon), dēdūcō, -ere, dēdūxī, dēductum [X]

drive, agō, -ere, ēgī, actum, *

drive back, redīgō, -ere, redēgī, redactum, *

drive out, exigō, -ere, exēgī, exactum [XIV]

drive together, cōgō, -ere, coēgī, coactum, *

due, meritus, -a, -um, *

dutiful, pius, -a, -um, *

duty, officium,-ī n. [XIII]

dwell, habitō (1), *

dye, inficiō, -ere, infēcī, infectum, *

E

each, quisque, quaeque, quidque [XIV]

each (of two), uterque, utraque, utrumque [XXIX]

eager, avidus,-a,-um [VII], cupidus,-a,-um [XVIII], studiōsus,-a,-um [XVIII]

eagerness, studium,-i n. [XXVIII]

earth, tellūs, tellūris f. [XXVII], terra, -ae f., *

easy, facilis, -e, *

eat, vescor, vescī, ---- (+abl.) [XIII]

edge, ōra, -ae f., *

effect (verb), efficiō, -ere, effēcī, effectum [XXV]

eight, octo, *

either…or, aut…aut, *

elect, creō (1) [X]

eloquence, ēloquentia,-ae f. [XIX]

embrace, sinus, -ūs m., *

empty, vacuus, -a, -um, *

enclose, inclūdō, -ere, inclūsī, inclūsum, *

encourage, confirmō (1) [I], hortor (1) [XXII]

end, finis, -is (-ium) m., *

endure, ferō, ferre, tulī, lātum, * patior, patī, passus sum, * perferō, perferre, pertulī, perlātum [II]

enemy, hostis, hostis (-ium) m., *

engage, committō, -ere, commīsī, commissum [IX]

enjoy, fruor, fruī, fructus sum (+abl.) [XIII], ūtor, ūtī, ūsus sum (+abl.) [XIII]

enjoyment, fructus, -ūs m., *

enlist, conscrībō, -ere, conscrīpsī, conscrīptum [XIII]

enmity, inimīcitia,-ae f. [XXVIII]

enough, satis [XIV]

enroll, conscrībō, -ere, conscrīpsī, conscrīptum [XIII]

enter, ineō, -īre, inīvī/iniī, initum [XX]

enthusiasm, studium,-i n. [XXVIII]

entire, tōtus, -a, -um, *

entirely, omnīnō, *

entrust, committō, -ere, commīsī, commissum [IX], crēdō, -ere, crēdidī, crēditum [XV]

envoy, lēgātus,-ī [VIII]

envy, invidia, -ae f., *

equal, pār, paris [XXV]

escape (noun), fuga, -ae f., *

escape (verb), sē ēripere [V], vītō (1), *

especially, praesertim, adv. [XIV]

establish, cōnstituō, -ere, cōnstituī, cōnstitūtum, *

esteem, honor, honōris m. [V]

Ethiopian, Aethiōps, Aethiopis m.,

even, aequus, aequa, aequum [XX]

even, etiam, adv.*

even as, velut/velutī, adv. [XXIV]

evening, vesper, vesperis m. [XVIII], vespera,-ae f. [XVIII]

ever, umquam, adv. [VII]

every, omnis, -e, *

everywhere, undique, adv [III]

evil (adj.), malus, -a, -um, *

evil (noun), nefãs (indecl.) n. [XXIV]

examine, perspiciō, -ere, perspexī, perspectum [XVIII]

excellence, virtūs, virtūtis f. [IX]

excess, nimium,-ī n. [XXIX]

exhaust, exanimō (1), *

exhausted, fessus, -a, -um, *

exhibit, praestō, -āre, praestitī, praestatum, *

experience, experior, experīrī, expertus sum [XXIX], patior, patī, passus sum, * ūtor, ūtī, ūsus sum (+abl.) [XIII]

experienced, perītus,-a,-um [XV]

explain, expōnō, -ere, exposuī, expositum [XIII]

expose, expōnō, -ere, exposuī, expositum [XIII]

extend, pertineō, -ēre, pertinuī, pertentum [II], tendō, -ere, tetendī, tentum, *

eye, oculus, -ī m., *

F

faction, factiō, factiōnis [IX]

fail, dēficiō, -ere, dēfēcī, dēfectum [XXV], dēsum, dēesse, dēfuī, dēfutūrus [XV]

fair, aequus, aequa, aequum [XX]

faith, fidēs, -eī f., *

faithful, fidēlis,-e [VIII]

fall, cāsus, -ūs m., *

fall away, dēficiō, dēficere, dēfēcī, dēfectum [XXV]

fame, gloria, gloriae f. [XVII]

family, familia, familiae f. [XVII]

famine, famēs, famis f.

far, longē, *

farmer, agricola, -ae m., *

fashion (verb), fingō, -ere,finxī, fictus [XXIV]

fate, fãtum, -ī n., *

father, pater, patris m., *

favor (noun), beneficium,-ī, n. [XXIII], gratia, -ae f., *

favor (verb), faveō, -ēre, fãvī, fautum (+dat.) [XV]

fear (noun), metus,-ūs, m. [I], terror, terrōris m., timor, timōris m.

fear (verb), timeō, timēre, timuī, -----, * vereor, verērī, veritus, * metuō, metuere, metuī, metitum [XXVII]

feed on, vescor, vescī, ---- (+abl.) [XIII]

feel, sentiō, -īre, sēnsī, sēnsum, *

fetter, vinculum,-ī n. [V]

few, paucī, -ae, -a, *

field, ager, agrī m., * *(plain)* campus, -ī m., *

fierce, ācer, ācris, ācre, *

fight, pugnō (1), *

finally, tandem, *

find, inveniō, -īre, invēnī, inventum [XII] *(by looking),* reperiō, -īre, repperī, repertum [XIX]

fine, bellus,-a,-um [XVIII]

finish, conficiō, -ere, confēcī, confectum [XIX], perficiō, -ere, perfēcī, perfectum [XXV], transīgō, -ere, transēgī, transactum, * *(a life),* exigō, -ere, exēgī, exactum [XIV]

fire, ignis, -is (ium) m., *

firm, firmus,-a,-um [IV]

first, prīmus, -a, -um, *

five, quinque, *

flame, flamma, -ae f., *

flat, aequus, aequa, aequum [XX]

flee, fugiō, -ere, fūgī, fugitūrus, *

flight, fuga, -ae f., *

flood, flūctus, -ūs m., *

fly, volō (1), *

follow, cōnsequor, cōnsequī, cōnsecūtus sum [XVII], sequor, sequī, secutus sum, *

food, cibus,-ī, m. [VIII]

foot, pēs, pedis m., *

for, enim, conj., * nam, adv. *

for a long time, diū, *

for a longer time, diūtius (compara. of diū), *

for a very long time, diūtissimē (superl. of diū), *

for the longest time, diūtissimē (superl. of diū), *

forbid, vetō, -āre, vetuī, vetitum, *

force (noun), vīs, vīs f. (pl. vīrēs, vīrium) [VII]

force (verb), cogō, -ere, coēgī, coactum [XIV]

foreign, aliēnus,-a,-um [XX]

forest, silva, -ae f., *

forget, oblīviscor, oblīviscī, oblītus sum [XXIX]

forgetful, immemor, immemoris [XXV]

forgive, ignoscō, -ere, ignōvī, ignōtum (+dat.) [XV]

form, forma, formae f. [XVII]

formerly, anteā, adv. [XXV], quondam, adv.*

fortify, mūniō, -īre, mūnīvī, mūnītum, *

fortune, fortūna, -ae f., *

forum, forum,-ī n. [V]

found (a city), condō, -ere, condidī, conditum [XIII]

four, quattuor, *

free, līber, lībera, līberum, *

free, līberō (1) [XIII]

freedom, lībertās,-tātis, f. [II]

freely, libenter, *

friend, amīcus, -ī m

friendly, amīcus, -a, -um, *

friendship, amīcitia,-ae, f. [III]

frighten, terreō, -ēre, terruī, territum, *

from, ā, ab (+ abl.), *, ē, ex (+ abl.), *

from above, dēsuper, *

from all sides, undique, adv [III]

from here, hinc, adv. [XX]

from there, deinde, adv. [XXV], inde, adv. [XXV]

from this place, hinc, adv. [XX]

from where, unde, adv. [VIII]

fruit, fructus, -ūs m., *

function, mūnus, mūneris n. [XXVII]

fury, furor, -ōris m., *

G

gain, cōnsequor, cōnsequī, cōnsecūtus sum [XVII]

gain possession of, potior, -īrī, potītum sum [XIII]

Gaius Julius Casear, Caesar, Caesaris m.,

Gallic, Gallus, -a, -um*

game, lūdus, -ī m., *
gate, porta, -ae f., *
gather, cogō, -ere, coēgī, coactum [XIV], comparō (1) [III]
Gaul, Gallus, -a, -um*
general, commūnis,-e [XIV]
get, nanciscor, nanciscī, nactus sum [VII]
ghost, umbra, -ae f., *
gift, donum, -ī n., * (of the gods), mūnus, mūneris n.
    [XXVII]
girl, puella, -ae f., *
give, do, dare, dedī, datum, *
give a speech, ōrātiōnem habēre [IX]
give back, reddō, -ere, reddidi, redditum, *
give out, ēdō, -ere, ēdidī, ēditum, *
give thanks, gratias agere (+dat), *
gladness, gaudium, ī n., *
glory, decus, decoris n. [XVII], fāma, -ae f., *gloria, gloriae f.
    [XVII]
go, conferō, conferre, contulī, collātum , * cēdō, -ere, cessī,
    cessum [IX], eō, īre, iī(īvī), itum, *
go away, abeō, abīre, abiī (-īvī), abitum, [XX]
go back, redeō, -īre, rediī (-īvī), reditum [XXIX]
go forward, prōgredior, prōgredī, prōgressus sum, *
go in, incēdō, -ere, incessī, incessum, *
go in, ineō, -īre, iniī (inīvī), initum, *
go out, ēgredior, ēgredī, ēgressus sum [V], excēdō, -ere,
    excessī, excessum, * exeō, -īre, exīvī/exiī, exītum [XX]
go past, praetereō, -īre, preaterivī/-iī, praeteritum [XX]
go to, adeō, adīre, adiī (-īvī), aditum [XX]
go toward, adeō, adīre, adiī (-īvī), aditum, * accēdō,
    -ere, accessī, accessum [IX]
god, deus, -ī m., *
goddess, dea, -ae f., *
gold, aurum, -ī n., *
good, bonus, -a, -um, *
Gorgon, Gorgo(n), Gorgonis f.,
graceful, gracilis, -e, *
grandfather, avus, -ī m., *
grant, concēdō, -ere, concessī, concessum [IX]
grasp, comprehendō, -ere, -hendī, -hensum, *
great, magnus, -a, -um, *
greater, māior, maius (comp. of magnus), *
greatly, magnopere, *
greed, cupiditās,-tātis, f. [II]
greedy, avidus,-a,-um [VII], cupidus,-a,-um [XVIII]
greet, excipio, -ere, excēpī, exceptum [IV]
grief, dolor, dolōris m., *
grieve, doleō, -ēre, doluī, dolitum [XXIII]
groan, fremitus, -ūs m., *
ground, tellūs, tellūris f. [XXVII]
guard (noun), custōs, custōdis, m. [XXVII]
guard (verb), servō (1), *
guardian, custōs, custōdis, m. [XXVII]

H

habit, mōs, mōris m. [V]
hand, manus, -ūs f., *

hand across, trādō, -ere, trādidī, trāditum, *
hand down , trādō, -ere, trādidī, trāditum, *
handsome, bellus,-a,-um [XVIII]
happen, fiō, fiērī, factus sum [X]
happy, beātus, -a, -um, * fēlīx, fēlīcis, * laetus, -a, -um, *
hardly, vix, *
hardness, gravitās, gravitātis f. [XXVIII]
hardship, labor, labōris m., *
hardy, patien, -entis,
harm, noceō, nocēre, nocuī, nocitum (+dat.) [XV]
hasten, currō, -ere, cucurrī, cursum, *
hatred, invidia, -ae f., *
have, habeō -ēre, habuī, habitum, *
have a reason, causam habēre,
have no knowledge of, ignōrō (1), *
he, she, it, is, ea, id, *
head, caput, capitis n., *
hear, audiō, -īre, audīvī, audītum, *
heart, pectus, pectoris n., *.
heaven, caelum, -ī n., *
heavenly, dīvīnus,-a,-um [XXVIII]
heavy, gravis, -e, *
helmet, galea, -ae f., *
help (noun), auxilium,-ī, n. [XXII], beneficium,-ī, n. [XXIII]
help (verb), iuvō, -āre, iūvī, iūtum [XIX]
here, hīc, adv. [XX]
high, altus, -a, -um, *
highest, summus,-a,-um [XV]
hindrance, impedīmentum,-ī, n. [V]
his, her, its, suus, -a, -um, *
hither, hūc, adv., *
hold, habeō -ēre, habuī, habitum, * obtineō, -ēre, obtinuī,
    obtentum [II], teneō, -ēre, tenuī, tentum, *
hold (up), sustineō, -ēre, sustinuī, sustentum [II]
hold back, retineō, -ēre, retinuī, retentum [II]
hold together, contineō, -ēre, continuī, contentum [II]
holy, sacer, sacra, sacrum, *
home, domus, -ūs, f., *
honor, decus, decoris n. [XVII], honor, honōris m.,
hope (noun), spēs, speī f., *
hope (verb), spērō (1) [III]
horn, cornū, -ūs n., *
horrible, horribilis, -e, *
horse, equus, ī m., *
horseman, eques, equitis m. [XIV]
hostile, inimīcus,-a,-um [VII]
hostility, inimīcitia,-ae f. [XXVIII]
hour, hōra, -ae f., *
household, domus, -ūs, f., *
household slaves, familia, familiae f. [XVII]
how?, quōmodo [VIII]
how great?, quantus,-a,-um [VIII]
how long?, quamdiū, adv. [VIII]
how many?, quot [VIII]
how much?, quantus,-a,-um [VIII]
how often?, quotiēns, adv. [VIII]
however, autem, *

huge, ingens, ingentis, *

human, homō, hominis m., *

humble, humilis, -e, *

hundred, centum, *

hunger, famēs, famis f.

hurl, conicio, -ere, coniēcī, coniectum, *

hurry, contendō, -ere, contendī, contentum, *

hurt, vulnerō (1), *

I

I, ego, *

idle, ignāvus, -a, -um, *

ignorant, imperītus,-a,-um [XXIX]

imagine, fingō, -ere,finxī, fictus [XXIV], reor, rērī, ratus sum [XXVII]

immediately, confestim, adv. [I], statim, *

imprison, inclūdō, -ere, inclūsī, inclūsum, *

improper, prāvus,-a,-um [XXIX]

in, in (+abl.), *

in a higher position, super (+acc), *

in front of, praeter (+acc.) [XII]

in front of, prō (+abl.), *

in order that, ut (+ subj.) [II]

in the presence of, apud (+ acc.) [X]

in vain, frustrā, adv. [XX]

increase, augeō, -ēre, auxī, auctum [X]

inevitable, necessārius,-a,-um [XXVIII]

inexperienced, imperītus,-a,-um [XXIX]

infant, infans, infantis (-ium) m./f., *

influence(noun), auctōritās,-tātis, f., [II]

influence(verb), addūcō, -ere, addūxī, adductum, [X], indūcō, -ere, indūxī, inductum [XII]

inform, certiorem facere

inhabit, incolō, -ere, incoluī, ---- [VIII]

inhabitant, incola, -ae m., *

innate quality, ingenium,-ī n. [XIX]

intention, mens, mentis (-ium) f., *

into, in (+acc.), *

iron, ferrum, -ī n., *

island, insula,-ae, f. [III]

it is fitting, oportet, oportere, oportuit [XXVII]

it is necessary, necesse esse [XXVII]

it is permitted, licet, licēre, licuit or licitum est [XXVII]

Italy, Ītalia, -ae f.,

J

javelin, tēlum, ī n., *

jealousy, invidia, -ae f., *

journey, iter, itineris n., *

joy, gaudium,-ī n. [XXIII]

joyful, laetus, -a, -um, *

Jupiter, Iuppiter, Iovis m., *

Juppiter, Iove (abl. sg. of Iuppiter)

just, modo, *

just as, velut/velutī, adv. [XXIV]

K

keen, ācer, ācris, ācre, *

keenness, studium,-i n. [XXVIII]

keep off, prohibeō, -ēre, prohibuī, prohibitum [XIII]

kill, interficio, -ere, -fēcī, -fectum, *

kind, genus, -eris n., *

kindness, beneficium,-ī, n. [XXIII]

king, rēx, rēgis m., *

kingdom, rēgnum, -ī n., *

know, sciō, -īre, scīvī (or sciī), scītum,

L

labor, labor, labōris m., *

lack, inopia, inopiae f. [XVII]

lament, dēplōrō (1), *

land, tellūs, tellūris f. [XXVII], terra, -ae f., *

large, magnus, -a, -um, *

Larisa, Larisa, -ae f.

last, nōvissimus,-a,-um

late, tardus,-a,-um [XVIII]

law, iūs, iūris n., * lēx, lēgis f., *

lazy, ignāvus, -a, -um, *

lead, dūcō, -ere, dūxī, ductum, *

lead a life, vītam agere, *

lead across, trādūcō, -ere, trāduxī, trāductum [XII]

lead away, dēdūcō, -ere, dēdūxī, dēductum [X]

lead in, indūcō, -ere, indūxī, inductum [XII]

lead out, ēdūcō, -ere, ēdūxī, ēductum, *

lead through, perdūcō, -ere, perdūxī, perductum, *

lead to, addūcō, -ere, addūxī, adductum, [X]

leader, dux, ducis m., * princeps, principis m. [XVII]

learn, discō, -ere, didicī,---- [XVIII]

learned, doctus,-a,-um [XXIX]

leave, discēdō, -ere, discessī, discessum, * ēgredior, ēgredī, ēgressus sum [V], relinquō, -ere, relīquī, relictum, *

leave behind, relinquō, -ere, relīquī, relictum, *

left, sinister, sinistra, sinistrum [XXVII]

left hand, sinister, sinistra, sinistrum [XXVII]

legate, lēgātus,-ī [VIII]

letter, epistula, -ae f., * littera,-ae, f. (pl.) [III] *(of the alphabet),* littera,-ae, f. [III]

level, aequus, aequa, aequum [XX]

liberate, līberō (1) [XIII]

life, vīta, -ae f., *

lift, tollō tollere, sustulī, sublātum [XVIII]

light, lūmen, lūminis n., * lūx, lūcis f., *

like (verb), amō (1), *

like (adj.), pār, paris [XXV], similis, -e, *

likewise, item, adv. [IV]

limit, finiō, -īre, finīvī/finiī, finitum [XXIII]

listen to, audiō, -īre, audīvī, audītum , *

literature, littera,-ae, f. (pl.) [III]

little (a), paulō, adv. [XXVII]

little, parvus, -a, -um, *

live (inhabit), habitō (1), *

live, vīvō, -ere, vīxī, vīctum, *

Livy, (Titus Livius), Livius, Liviī m.,

long, longus, -a, -um, *

long for, cupiō, -ere, cupīvī, cupītum [XXIII]

longing, cupidus,-a,-um [XVIII]

look down on, despiciō, -ere, despexī, despectum [XVIII]

look into or upon, inspiciō, -ere, inspexī, inspectum, *

look out, exspectō (1), *

loosen, solvō, -ere, solvī, solūtum [XIV]

lose, āmittō, -ere, āmīsī, āmissum [IX]

love (noun), amor, amōris, m. [XII]

love (verb), amō (1), *

low, humilis, -e, *

lowest, īmus,-a,-um [XVIII]

loyal, fidēlis,-e [VIII], pius, -a, -um, *

loyalty, fidēs, -eī f., *

luck, fortūna, -ae f., *

M

magical, magicus, -a, -um

magistracy, magistrātus,-ūs, m. [I]

magistrate, magistrātus,-ūs, m. [I]

maiden, virgō, virginis f., *

mainland, continens, continentis f., *

make, faciō, -ere, fēcī, factum, * fingō, -ere,finxī, fictus [XXIV]

make a journey, iter facere, *

make a mistake, errō (1), *

make effort, contendō, -ere, contendī, contentum, *

make ready, conficiō, -ere, confēvī, confectum [XIX]

make up, fingō, -ere,finxī, fictus [XXIV]

man, homō, hominis m, * vir, virī m., *

manner, modus, -ī m., *

many, multus, -a, -um, *

march, contendō, -ere, contendī, contentum, * iter facere, *

march forward, prōgredior, prōgredī, prōgressus sum, *

marketplace, forum,-ī n. [V]

marry, in mātrimōnium ducere, *

master, dominus, -ī m., *

matter, rēs, reī f., *

meanwhile, interim, adv. [XIV]

Medusa, Medusa, -ae f.

meet, conveniō, -īre, convēnī, conventum [XII]

memory, memoria, memoriae f. [XVII]

mention, memorō (1) [XXIV]

merely, modo, adv. [XXII]

messenger, nūntius, -ī m., *

mind, animus, -ī m., * mens, mentis (-ium) f., *

mindful, memor, memoris [XXV]

mine, meus, -a, -um, *

Minerva, Minerva, - ae f.

misfortune, cāsus, -ūs m., *

mistaken, falsus,-a,-um [XXIV]

moist, ūmidus, -a, -um [XXIV]

money, pecūnia, -ae, f. [III]

monster, monstrum, -ī n.

more (adv.), magis (comp. of magnopere), *

more (noun), plūs, plūris n. [XXIX]

moreover, autem, *

most, maximus, -a, -um, (superl. of magnus) *

most, plurimus, -a, -um (superl. of multus), *

most recent, nōvissimus,-a,-um, C

mother, māter, mātris f., *

Mount Olympus, Olympus, -ī m.,

mountain, mōns, montis (-ium) m., *

mourn, dēplōrō (1), *

mouth, ōs, oris n., *

move, adficiō, -ere, -fēcī, -fectum, * moveō, -ēre, mōvī, mōtum, *

much (adv.), multum, *

much (adj.), multus, -a, -um, *

multitude, multitūdō, multitūdinis f. [IX]

my, meus, -a, -um, *

N

name (noun), nōmen, nōminis n., *

name (verb), appellō, (1) [I]

narrow, angustus,-a,-um, [V]

nation, gēns, gentis (-ium) f., *

native land, patria, -ae, *

natural, nātūrālis,-e [XXVIII]

nature, nātūra,-ae, f. [XV]

near (prep.), prope (+acc.) [XXV]

near (adj.), propinquus, -a, -um [V]

nearly, ferē, adv. [II]

necessary, necessārius, -a, -um [XXVIII]

neck, collum, -ī n., *

neighboring, finitimus, -a, -um [VIII], propinquus, -a, -um [V]

neither, neuter, neutra, neutrum, *

neither…nor, neque…neque, *

Neptune, Neptūnus, -ī m.

never, numquam, adv. [XXV]

nevertheless, tamen, *

new, novus, -a, -um, *

next (adv.), deinde, adv. [XXV]

next (adj.), proximus, -a, -um, *

nice, bellus,-a,-um [XVIII]

night, nox, noctis (-ium) f., *

nine, novem, *

no, nullus, -a, -um, *

no one, nēmō, nēminis m., *

noble, nōbilis,-e [VIII]

nobody, nēmō, nēminis m., *

nod, nūmen, nūminis n. [XXVIII]

noise, clāmor, clāmōris, m. [IX]

none, nullus, -a, -um, *

nor, nec/neque, *

not, nōn, *

not any, nullus, -a, -um, *

not at all, haud, adv. [I]

not know, nesciō, nescīre, nescīvī/nesciī, nescītus [XII]

not only … but also, nōn modo … sed etiam, *

not to want, nōlō, nōlle, nōluī, -----, *

not to wish, nōlō, nōlle, nōluī, -----, *

not yet, nōndum [XXV]

nothing, nihil (indecl.) n., *

notice, animadvertō, -ere, animadvertī, animadversum, [III]

now, iam, adv., *nunc, adv., *

number, numerus,-ī, m. [IV]

O

obey, pāreō, -ēre, pāruī, pāritum (+dat) [XV]

observe, tueor, tuērī, tuitum [XXVII], conspiciō, -cere, conspexī, conspectum [XVIII], perspiciō, -ere, perspexī, perspectum [XVIII]

obtain, nanciscor, nanciscī, nactus sum [VII], obtineō, -ēre, obtinuī, obtentum [II]

obtain (by asking), impetrō (1) [X]

of one's own accord, spontē [X]

offend, offendō, -ere, offendī, offēnsum, *

office, honor, honōris m [V], officium,-ī n. [XIII]

often, saepe, *

old, vetus, veteris, [XXIII]

old man, senex, senis m. [XIX]

on, in (+abl.), *

on account of, ob (+acc), * propter (+acc.), *

on all sides, undique, adv [III]

on behalf of, prō (+abl.), *

once, quondam, *

one, ūnus, -a, -um, *

only (adv.), modo, adv. [XXII]

only (adj.), sōlus, -a, -um, *

onto, in (+acc.), *

open, aperiō, īre, aperuī, apertum [XXIII]

opinion, sententia,-ae, f. [III]

opportunity, facultās, facultātis f. [X]

opposite, contrā (+acc.) [XVII]

or, aut, *

oracle, ōrāculum, -ī n., *

order (noun), ordō, ordinis m. [XVII]

order (verb), imperō (1) [XXII], iubeō, iubēre, iussī, iussum, * praecipiō, -ere, praecēpī, praeceptum [IV]

order . . . not, vetō, -āre, vetuī, vetitum, *

other, alius, -a, -um, * (of 2), alter, altera, alterum, *

our, noster, nostra, nostrum, *

out of, ē, ex (+ abl.), *

outrage, incendō, -ere, incendī, incensum [III]

over, super (+acc), *

P

pain, dolor, dolōris m., *

painfully, aegrē, *

palace, rēgia, -ae f., *

panic, pavor, pavōris m., *

part, pars, partis (-ium), f., *

particularly, praesertim

past, praeter (+acc.) [XII]

patient, patien, -entis

pay a penalty, poenās dare, *

pay attention to, animadvertō, -ere, animadvertī, animadversum, [III]

peace, pax, pacis, f. [III]

people, populus,-ī, m. [IV]

perceive, cernō, -ere, crēvī, crētum, * sentiō, -īre, sēnsī, sēnsum, *

perfect, perficiō, -ere, perfēcī, perfectum [XXV]

perform, fungor, fungī, functus sum (+abl.) [XIII]

perhaps, fortasse, adv. [XXVIII]

peril, perīculum,-ī n. [V]

Perseus, Perseus, Perseī, m.

persuade, persuadeō, -ēre, persuasī, persuasum [XXII]

pertain, pertineō, -ēre, pertinuī, pertentum [II]

pick out, legō, ere, lēgī, lēctum, *

pierce, transīgō, -ere, transēgī, transactum, *

pirate, pīrāta, -ae m., *

place (noun), locus, -ī m (loca, -ōrum n. pl.), *

place (verb), pōnō, -ere, posuī, positum, *

plain, campus, -ī m., *

plan, cōnsilium, -ī n, *

playing field, campus, -ī m., *

pleasing, grātus, -a, -um, *

plebs, plebs, plebis f. [XVII]

plunge, mergō, -ere, mersī, mersum, *

poet, poēta, -ae m., *

Pompey , Pompeius Magnus, Pompeiī Magnī, m.

power, facultās, facultātis f. [X], imperium, -ī n., * ops, opis f. [XIII], potestās,-tātis, f. [II]

powerful, potens,-ntis [I]

practically, paene, *

practice, ūsus, -ūs m., *

praise (noun), laus, laudis f. [XVII]

praise (verb), laudō (1), *

prefer, mālō, mālle, māluī, -----, *

prepare, comparō (1) [III], parō (1), *

preserve, servō (1)

pretty, bellus,-a,-um [XVIII]

prevent, prohibeō, -ēre, prohibuī, prohibitum [XIII]

previously, anteā, adv. [XXV]

prize, praemium,-ī n. [XXIII]

proceed, tendō, -ere, tetendī, tentum, *

produce, efficiō, -ere, effēcī, effectum [XXV]

profit from, fruor, fruī, fructus sum (+abl.) [XIII]

prominent, insignis,-e [XIV]

prophet, vātēs, vātis m., *

protect, tueor, tuērī, tuitum [XXVII]

protection, praesidium,-ī n. [V]

protector, custōs, custōdis, m. [XXVII]

province, prōvincia,-ae, f. [III]

provisions, cōpia, cōpiae f. (pl.) [XVII]

prudent, prūdens,-ntis [I]

public, pūblicus, -a, -um, *

Punic, Poenus, -a, -um,

punish, puniō (4), *

punishment, poena, -ae f., *

pursue, cōnsequor, cōnsequī, cōnsecūtus sum [XVII]

put, pōnō, -ere, posuī, positum, *

put down, dēpōnō, -ere, dēposuī, dēpositum, *

put off, exuō, -ere, exuī, exūtum, *

put on, induō, -ere, induī, indūtum, *

Q

queen, rēgīna, -ae f., *

quick, celer, celeris, celere, *

quiet, quiēs, quiētis f., *

R

rage, furor, -ōris m., *

raise, tollō tollere, sustulī, sublātum [XVIII]

rank, ordō, ordinis m. [XVII]

read, legō, -ere, lēgī, lēctum, *

reason, ratiō, ratiōnis, f. [IX]

receive, accipiō, -ere, -cēpī, -ceptum, * excipio, -ere, excēpī, exceptum [IV], recipiō, -ere, recēpī, receptum [IV]

recently, nūper, adv. [XXV]

regard, existimō (1) [XXIII]

relate, narrō (1) [XII], referō, referre, rettulī, relātum [XIX]

release, solvō, -ere, solvī, solūtum, *

remain, maneō, -ēre, mānsī, mānsum, *

remaining, cēterī, -ae, -a, * reliquus,-a,-um [V]

remarkable, mīrābilis,-e [XXIV]

remember, meminī, meminisse [XXIX]

remove, dēdūcō, -ere, dēdūxī, dēductum [X]

repair, reficiō, -ere, refēcī, refectum [XXV]

report, nūntiō (1), * perferō, perferre, pertulī, perlātum [II]

reputation, fāma, -ae f., *

rescue, ēripiō, -ere, ēripuī, ēreptum [V]

resolute, firmus,-a,-um [IV]

resolve, cōnsulō, -ere, cōnsuluī, cōnsultum, *

resources, ops, opis f. [XIII]

respect, vereor, verērī, veritus, *

respond, respondeō, -ēre, respondī, responsum [XXIII]

rest (noun), quiēs, quiētis f., *

rest (adj.), reliquus,-a,-um [V] cēterī, -ae, -a, *

restore, reficiō, -ere, refēcī, refectum [XXV]

restrain, retineō, -ēre, retinuī, retentum [II]

retreat, sē recipere [IV]

return (noun), reditus, -ūs m., *

return (verb), redeō, -īre, rediī (-īvī), reditum [XXIX], revertō, -ere, revertī, ---- (usu, deponent in pres.) [XIV]

reveal, aperiō, īre, aperuī, apertum [XXIII]

reward, praemium,-ī n. [XXIII]

right (adj.), dexter, dextera, dexterum [XXVII]

right (noun), iūs, iūris n., *

right hand, dexter, dextera, dexterum [XXVII]

rim, ōra, -ae f., *

rise, orior, -īrī, ortus sum [XXVII], surgō, -ere, surrēxī, surrēctum, *

road, iter, itineris n., * via, -ae f., *

roar, fremitus, -ūs m., *

rock, saxum, -ī n., *

roll, volvō, -ere, volvī, volūtum, *

Roman, Rōmānus, -a, -um

Rome, Rōma, -ae f.

room, spatium,-ī n. [XXIII]

rouse, excitō (1), *

rule (noun), imperium, -ī n., *

rule (verb), regō, -ere, rēxī, rēctum, *

rumble, fremitus, -ūs m., *

rumor, fāma, -ae f., * rūmor, rūmōris m. [XII]

run, currō, -ere, cucurrī, cursum, *

run away, fugiō, -ere, fūgī, fugitūrus, *

run through, transīgō, -ere, transēgī, transactum, *

run to, accurrō, -ere, accursī, accursum, *

S

sad, trīstis, -e, *

safe, incolumis,-e [XIV], salvus,-a,-um [XXIX], tūtus, -a,-um [XVIII]

safe conduct, fidēs pūblica

safety(personal), salus, salūtis [XXII]

sailor, nauta, -ae m., *

same, īdem, eadem, idem, *

sand, harēna, -ae f., *

save, servō (1), *

say, dīcō, -ere, dīxī, dictum, *

scan, tueor, tuērī, tuitum [XXVII]

scarcely, vix, *

scatter, differō, differre, distulī, dīlātum [II]

sea, flūctus, -ūs m., * mare, maris (ium) n., *

seat, sēdēs, sēdis f., *

second, secundus, -a, -um, *

second time, rursus [XXVII]

secretary, scrība, -ae m., *

secretly, clam, adv. [I]

see, videō, -ēre, vīdī, vīsum, *

seek, petō, -ere, petivī, petītum, *

seek, quaerō, -ere, quaesīvī, quaesītum, *

seem (pass.), videō, -ēre, vīdī, vīsum, *

seer, vātēs, vātis m., *

seize, capiō, -ere, cēpī, captum, * *(understand)* comprehendō, -ere, -hendī, -hensum, *(military)* occupō (1), *

-self (intensive), ipse, ipsa, ipsum, *

-self (reflexive), suī (gen. sg.), *

senate, senātus, -ūs m., *

send, mittō, -ere, mīsī, missum, *

send away, āmittō, -ere, āmīsī, āmissum [IX], dīmittō, -ere, dīmīsī, dīmissum [IX]

send back, remittō, -ere, remīsī, remissum [IX]

Seneca, Seneca, -ae, m.

sensible, prūdens,-ntis [I]

serious, gravis, -e, *

seriously, graviter

seriousness, gravitās, gravitātis f. [XXVIII]

service, beneficium, -ī n., *

set, certus,-a,-um [VII]

set fire to, incendō, -ere, incendī, incensum [III]

set out, proficiscor, proficiscī, profectus sum [VII]

set up, pōnō, -ere, posuī, positum, *

seven, septem, *

severity, gravitās, gravitātis f. [XXVIII]

shadow, umbra, -ae f., *

shameful, turpis, -e [XIV]

shared, commūnis, -e [XIV]

sharp, ācer, ācris, ācre, *

shelter, tegō, -ere, tēxī, tēctum, *

ship, nāvis, nāvis (-ium) f., *

shore, lītus, lītoris n., * ōra, -ae f., *

short, brevis, -e, *

shoulder, umerus, -ī m., *

shout (noun), clāmor, clāmōris, m. [IX]

shout (verb), clāmō (1), *

show, monstrō (1), * ostendō, -ere, ostendī, ostentum [XV], praestō, -āre, praestitī, praestatum, *

shut off, interclūdō, -ere, interclūsī, interclūsum [XIII]

shut up, inclūdō, -ere, inclūsī, inclūsum, *

Sicily, Sicilia, -ae, f.

sick, aeger, aegra, aegrum, *

sickle, falx, falcis, f., *

sight, cōnspectus,-ūs, m. [I], speciēs, -ēī f., *

sign, signum,-ī [V]

signal, signum,-ī [V]

similar, similis, -e, *

sing, cantō (1), *

sink, mergō, -gere, mersī, mersum, *

sister, soror, sorōris f., *

sit, sedeō, -ēre, sēdī, sessum, *

situation, rēs, reī f., *

six, sex, *

skill, ars, artis f. [XXIX], facultās, facultātis f. [X], ūsus, -ūs m., *

skilled, perītus,-a,-um [XV]

skip, praetereō, -īre, preaterivī/-iī, praeteritum [XX]

sky, caelum, -ī n., *

slave, servus, -ī m., *

slavery, servitūs, servitūtis f. [IX]

sleep (noun), quiēs, quiētis f., * somnus, ī m., *

sleep (verb), dormiō, - īre, dormīvī, dormitum , *

slender, gracilis, -e, *

slip, lābor, lābī, lapsus sum, *

slow, tardus,-a,-um [XVIII]

small, parvus, -a, -um, *

smaller, minor, minus (comp. of parvus), *

smallest, minimus, -a, -um (superl. of parvus), *

snake, anguis, -is m./f., *

snatch, ēripiō, -ere, ēripuī, ēreptum [V]

so, adeō, adv. [IV], ita, adv. [IV], *(with verbs only)* sīc, adv. [IV], *(with adj. and adv. only)* tam [IV]

so great, tantus,-a,-um [IV]

so many, tot, adv [IV]

so much, tantum,-ī n.

so that, ut (+ subj.) [II]

soldier, mīles, mīlitis m., *

sole (only), sōlus, -a, -um, *

someone, aliquis, aliquid

sometime, aliquandō, adv. [XXIII]

somewhat, paulō, adv. [XXVII]

son, fīlius, -ī m., *

song, carmen, carminis, n., *

soon, mox, *

sort, genus, -eris n., *

space, spatium,-ī n. [XXIII]

spare, parcō, -cere, pepercī,---- [XV]

speak, dīcō, -ere, dīxī, dictum, * loquor, loquī, locūtus sum [VII]

speech, ōrātiō, ōrātiōnis, f. [IX]

speed, celeritās, celeritātis, f. [X]

spirit, animus, -ī m., *

sport, lūdus, -ī m., *

spot, conspiciō, -ere, conspexī, conspectum [XVIII]

spouse, coniunx, coniugis m./f., *

stain, inficiō, -ere, infēcī, infectum, *

stand, stō, -āre, stetī, statum, *

standard, signum,-ī [V]

star, sīdus, sīderis n., *

state, cīvitās,-tātis, f. [II], rēs pūblica, reī pūblicae f., *

stay, maneō, -ēre, mānsī, mānsum, *

step, gradus, -ūs m., *

still, adhūc, adv.* tamen, adv.*

stir up, turbō (1), *

stone, saxum, -ī n., *

stop, cōnsistō, -ere, cōnstitī, cōnstitum, * interclūdō, -ere, interclūsī, interclūsum [XIII]

storm (noun), tempestās, tempestātis f., *

storm (verb), expugnō (1) [XXIII]

strength, vīs, vīs f. (pl. vīrēs, vīrium) [VII], virtūs, virtūtis f. [IX]

strengthen, confirmō (1) [I]

stretch out, tendō, -ere, tetendī, tentum, *

stretch out before, ostendō, -ere, ostendī, ostentum, *

stretch upward, surgō, -ere, surrēxī, surrēctum, *

strike (noun), ictus, -ūs m., *

strive (verb), contendō, -ere, contendī, contentum, *·

strong, firmus,-a,-um [IV], fortis, -e, *

struggle, certāmen, certāminis n., *

student, discipulus, -ī m., *

such, tālis, -e [IV]

suddenly, subitō, *

suffer, patior, patī, passus sum, *

suitable, idōneus, -a, -um, *

sun, sōl, sōlis, m. [XIII]

supply, cōpia, cōpiae f. [XVII]

support (noun), beneficium,-ī, n. [XXIII]

support (verb), faveō, -ēre, fāvī, fautum (+dat.) [XV], suscipiō, -ere, suscēpī, susceptum [IV]

suppose, reor, rērī, ratus sum [XXVII]

surely, nōnne (introduces a question expecting "yes" answer) [VIII]

surely…not, num (introduces a question expecting "no"answer) [VIII]

surpass, superō (1) [XIII]

sustain, contineō, -ēre, continuī, contentum [II], sustineō, -ēre, sustinuī, sustentum [II]

swallow, dēvorō (1), *

sweet, dulcis, -e, *

swell, surgō, -ere, surrēxī, surrēctum, *

swift, celer, celeris, celere, *

swiftness, celeritās, celeritātis, f. [X]

sword, ferrum, -ī n., * gladius, -ī m., *

sword (curved), falx, falcis, f., *

T

take, capiō, -ere, cēpī, captum, *

take off, exuō, -ere, exuī, exūtum, *

take up, sūmō, -ere, sūmpsī, sūmpsum [XIV], suscipiō, -ere, suscēpī, susceptum [IV]

talk, loquor, loqui, locūtus sum [VII]

talk about, dē ... agere , *

tall, altus, -a, -um, *

task, mūnus, mūneris n. [XXVII]

task, opus, operis n., *

teach, doceō, -ēre, docuī, doctum, *

teacher, magister, magistrī m., *

tear, lacrima, -ae f., *

tell, dīcō, -ere, dīxī, dictum, * narrō (1) [XII]

tell a lie, mentior, mentīrī, mentītus sum, *

tempest, tempestās, tempestātis f., *

ten, decem, *

territory fīnis, -is (-ium) m. (pl.)., *

terror, pavor, pavōris m., * terror, terrōris m.,

test, experior, experīrī, expertus sum [XXIX], temptō (1) [I]

than, quam, *

thank, gratias agere (+dat), *

thanks, gratiae, -ārum f., (pl.) *

that, ille, illa, illud, * is, ea, id, *

that(relative), quī, quae, quod, *

that (of yours), iste, ista, istud, *

their own, suus, -a, -um, *

then, deinde, adv. [XXV], tum, * tunc, *

thence, inde, adv. [XXV]

theory, ratiō, ratiōnis [IX]

there, ibī, adv., *

therefore, igitur, *

these (pl.), hic, haec, hoc, *

thing, rēs, reī f., *

think, existimō (1) [XXIII], puto (1), * reor, rērī, ratus sum [XXVII]

third, tertius, -a, -um, *

this, hic, haec, hoc, * is, ea, id, *

those (pl.), ille, illa, illud, *

three, trēs, tria, *

three hundred, trecentī, -ae,-a [XXVII]

through, per (+ acc.), *

throw, coniciō, -ere, coniēcī, coniectum, *

throw together, coniciō, -ere, coniēcī, coniectum, *

thus, ita, adv. [IV], sīc (modifies verbs only)[IV]

tie, adligō (1), *

time, tempus, tempōris n., *

tired, fessus, -a, -um, *

to, ad (+ acc.), *

to such an extent, adeō, adv. [IV]

to that place, eō, *

to this place, hūc, adv. [XX]

to this point, adhūc, *

to where?, quō, adv. [VIII]

today, hodiē, adv., *

together, ūnā, adv [XIV]

tolerant, patien, -entis

tomorrow, crās, *

too, nimis, adv. [XXIX]

too little, parum, *

too much, plūs, plūris n. [XXIX]

top of, summus,-a,-um [XV]

toward, contrā (+acc.) [XVII], ad (+ acc.), *

town, oppidum, ī, n.

trade, ars, artis f. [XXIX]

tradition, mōs maiōrum [V]

train, exerceō, -ēre, exercuī, exercitum [XXIII]

tranquil, tranquillus, -a, -um, *

transform, mūtō (1), *

treat, afficiō, -ere, affēcī, affectum, [XXV], agō, -ere, ēgī, actum, *

treat well, utor bene

tree, arbor, arbōris, f. [XII]

tribe, gēns, gentis (-ium) f., *

tribune, tribūnus,-ī [VIII]

troops, cōpia, cōpiae f. (pl.) [XVII]

true, vērus,-a,-um [XII]

trust (noun) fidēs, fideī, f.

trust, confīdō, -ere, confīsus sum, (semi-deponent) [XVII]

try, cōnor (1), * experior, experīrī, expertus sum [XXIX], temptō (1) [I]

turn, vertō, -ere, vertī, versum, *

turn back, revertō, -ere, revertī, ---- (usu. deponent in pres.) [XIV]

two, duo, duae, duo, *

two hundred, ducentī, -ae, -a [XXVII]

U

unbind, solvō, -ere, solvī, solūtum, *

uncover, aperiō, īre, aperuī, apertum [XXIII]

under, sub (+abl.), *

undergo, subeō, -īre, subiī (subīvī), subitum, *

understand, intellegō, -ere, intellēgī, intellectum [III]

undertake, suscipiō, -ere, suscēpī, susceptum [IV]

uneven, inīquus,-a,-um [XX]

unfair, inīquus,-a,-um [XX]

unfriendliness, inimīcitia,-ae f. [XXVIII]

unfriendly, inimīcus,-a,-um [VII]

unhappy, miser, misera, miserum, *

unharmed, incolumis,-e [XIV], salvus,-a,-um [XXIX]

unlike, dissimilis, -e, *

unrelated, aliēnus,-a,-um [XX]

unsheath, ēdūcō, -ere, ēdūxī, ēductum, *

unskilled, imperītus,-a,-um [XXIX]

untie, solvō, -ere, solvī, solūtum [XIV]

untouched, integer, integra, integrum [XVIII]

untrue, falsus,-a,-um [XXIV]

unwilling, invītus,-a,-um [VII]

urge on, incitō (1) [V]

use (noun), ūsus, -ūs m., *

use (verb), ūtor, ūtī, ūsus sum (+abl.) [XIII]
useful, ūtilis, -e, *

V

Valerius Maximus, Valerius Maximus, Valeriī Maximī m.
vast, ingens, ingentis, *
Vergil (Publius Vergilius Maro), Vergilius, Vergiliī, m.
very greatly, maximē, *
very many, plurimus, -a, -um (superl. of multus), *
very much, nimis, adv. [XXIX]
village, vīcus,-ī, m. [IV]
violence, vīs, vīs f. (pl. vīrēs, vīrium) [VII]
virtue, virtūs, virtūtis f. [IX]
voice, vōx, vōcis f., *
voluntarily, spontē [X]

W

wage war, bellum gerere, *
wall, mūrus, -ī m., *
walls, moenia, -ium n. pl., *
wander, errō (1), *
want, volō, velle, voluī, -----, *
war, bellum, ī n., *
warn, moneō, -ēre, monuī, monitum, *
watch over, servō (1), *
water, aqua, -ae f., *
wave, flūctus, -ūs m., * unda, -ae f., *
way (route), iter, itineris n., * (road) via, -ae f., *
way, modus, -ī m., *
we, nōs, *
weapon, tēlum, ī n., *
weather, tempestās, tempestātis f., *
weep, fleō, flēre, flēvī, flētum [XXIII]
weight, gravitās, gravitātis f. [XXVIII]
well (adv.), bene, *
well (adj,), salvus, -a, -um [XXIX]
well-being, salus, salūtis [XXII]
what kind of?, quālis, -e [VIII]
what sort of?, quālis, -e [VIII]
what?, quis, quid [VIII]
when, ubi, *
when?, quandō, adv. [VIII]
whence, unde, adv. [VIII]
where, ubi, *
whether...or, utrum ... an [VIII]
whether...or not, utrum ... annōn [VIII]
which, quī, quae, quod, * (of two), uter, utra, utrum, *
while, dum, *
whither?, quō, adv. [VIII]
who (relative pron.), quī, quae, quod, *
who? (interrogative pron.), quis, quid [VIII]

whole, integer, integra, integrum [XVIII], tōtus, -a, -um, *
why?, cur, adv. [VIII]
wicked, malus, -a, -um, *
wife, uxor, uxōris f., *
will (divine), nūmen, nūminis n. [XXVIII]
willingly, libenter, *
wind, ventus, ī m., *
winged sandals, tālāria, -ium n. pl., *
winter, hiems, hiemis f. [XVIII]
wise, sapiēns, sapientis, *
wish, cupiō, -ere, cupīvī, cupītum [XXIII], volō, velle, voluī, -----, *
with, cum (+ abl.), *
with difficulty, aegrē, *
with the result that, ut (+subj) [II]
withdraw, discēdō, -ere, discessī, discessum [XVII], exeō, -īre, exīvī/exiī, exītum [XX]
without, sine (+abl.), *
woman, mulier, mulieris f. [XXVII]
wonder at, mīror (1) [XXVII]
wonderful, mīrābilis,-e [XXIV]
wooden, ligneus, -a, -um, *
woods, silva, -ae f., *
word, verbum, -ī n., *
work, labor, labōris m., * opus, operis n., *
worry, cūra, -ae f., * sollicitūdō, sollicitūdinis f. [IX]
worse, peior, peius (comp. of malus), *
worst, pessimus, -a, -um (superl. of malus), *
worthy, dignus,-a,-um (+ abl.) [V]
wound, vulnerō (1), *
wrath, īra, -ae, f., *
wretched, miser, misera, miserum, *
write, scrībō, -ere, scrīpsī, scrīptum, *
writer, scrība, -ae, m., *
wrong, nefās (indecl.), n. [XXIV]

Y

year, annus, -ī, m., *
yesterday, heri, *
yet , adhūc, * tamen, *
yield, cēdō, -ere, cessī, cessum [IX], concēdō, -ere, concessī, concessum [IX]
you (sg.), tū, * (pl.), vōs, *
young man, iuvenis,-is, m. [XVIII]
your (sg.), tuus, -a, -um, * (pl.), vester, vestra, vestrum, *
yours (sg.), tuus, -a, -um, * (pl.), vester, vestra, vestrum, *
youth, adulēscēns, adulēscentis m./f., * iuvenis,-is, m. [XVIII]

Z

zealous, studiōsus, -a, -um [XVIII]

INDEX